THE FORTUNATE PILGRIMS

THE
FORTUNATE
PILGRIMS

Americans in Italy
1800-1860

PAUL R. BAKER

HARVARD UNIVERSITY PRESS

CAMBRIDGE, MASSACHUSETTS

1964

For

ALMA AND LOREN BAKER

MY MOTHER AND FATHER

ACKNOWLEDGMENTS

THE EVIDENCE for this study has come from a variety of sources — primarily the published and unpublished travel accounts, letters, diaries, and journals written by Americans who visited Italy. For help in finding the evidence I am indebted to a great many scholars both in the United States and in Italy. Anyone working in this field must of course turn to the pioneering work of Professor Giuseppe Prezzolini, formerly director of Casa Italiana at Columbia University. Although my approach and my conclusions often differ considerably from his, Professor Prezzolini's investigations in *Come Gli Americani Scoprirono l'Italia, 1750–1850* provided a valuable starting point for my researches.

My debts are many to the personnel of several libraries for assistance in locating often heretofore unused materials. I feel grateful to the staffs of the Archivi di Stato, the Biblioteca Nazionale Centrale, the Biblioteca Marucelliana, the Kunsthistorisches Institut (Professor Ulrich Middledorf), and the United States Information Service Library, all in Florence; the Centro Italiano di Studî Americani (Dr. Umberto Fongoli), the Istituto della Storia del Risorgimento (Professor Alberto Maria Ghisalberti), the Vatican Library, and the library of the American Academy (Mrs. Inez Longobardi), all in Rome; and, in the United States, the

Library of Congress, the New-York Historical Society, the Boston Public Library, the library of the Boston Museum of Fine Arts, the Massachusetts Historical Society, the Boston Athenaeum, the New York Public Library, the Huntington Library, and, most particularly, the Harvard College Library and the Houghton Library.

To the late Bernard Berenson and to Miss Nicky Mariano, I am indebted for their hospitality and their generosity in allowing me free use of the magnificent library resources of I Tatti. To Laurance P. Roberts, former director of the American Academy in Rome, I feel a special obligation for his providing me with a home at the Academy, the use of its excellent resources, and helpful contacts in the world of Italian scholarship. Mr. and Mrs. Roberts set the tone for a gracious and creative atmosphere at the Academy, and many are those in the world of arts and letters who share my debts to them. To Professor Herbert Bloch of Harvard University and the School of Classical Studies and to Princess Margherita Rospigliosi of the Academy staff I am also indebted. Signora Vera Cacciatore of the Keats-Shelley Library in Rome was most kind in providing me with relevant letters and pointing out possible sources of additional information.

To various other Italian friends who assisted me with my researches and helped me to know Italy better I must express my thanks: Countess Bona Gigliucci, Marchesa Nannina Fossi, Dr. Anna Martelloni, Mrs. Nelda Cassuto, Signora Giuliana Artom Treves, Professor Giorgio Spini, and Dr. Mario Casalini. In Rome, Marchesa Iris Origo and Professor Mario Praz, who have both worked on the subject of Americans in Italy, were most kind. And in Florence, I am indebted to Miss Clara Louise Dentler for insights on Hiram Powers, and to Mr. Henry C. Brewster for the opportunity to look at family letters in his possession. To the family of Avvocato Mario Feri in Florence I am grateful for a comfortable home during the chilly Florentine autumn.

I should also like to express my appreciation to Harvard University and the donors of the Kennedy Traveling Fellowship, which enabled me to spend the better part of a year in Italy seeking out unpublished source materials and following in the footsteps of the nineteenth-century Americans. I should further like to thank for their assistance several members of the faculty, including Professors Myron C. Gilmore, Benjamin Rowland, H. Stuart Hughes, John Coolidge, Mason Hammond, and John Conway. I am indebted as well to the late John P. Marquand, who provided me with some materials on Margaret Fuller.

Various friends have read the manuscript of this study at some stage in its preparation, and to the following I am appreciative for their critical observations: Professors Gardner Taplin, Rodman Paul, Cushing Strout, George D. Langdon, Robert Conhaim, and Ruth McIntyre. To Professor Edgar Rosenberg I am especially indebted: his keen editorial eye was responsible for saving me from countless blunders, and his suggestions greatly helped to sharpen the presentation. Finally, to Professor Howard Mumford Jones and to Professor Oscar Handlin, I feel a particular obligation and indebtedness. Advising me on the research and formulation of this study, they gave me both needed encouragement and a free hand to pursue my own interests, and offered many suggestions that helped to bring focus, structure, and movement to the essay; in their own scholarly energy, in their wide-ranging interests and knowledge, and in their deeply human sympathy, they have been a constant inspiration.

My obligations for help on this study are thus considerable. For whatever merit there is in the work, these other scholars, these friends and acquaintances, must share the credit; for the basic interpretations, for any shortcomings of penetration, insight, and exposition, I alone am responsible.

PAUL R. BAKER

Pasadena, California
July 1963

CONTENTS

ILLUSTRATIONS

THE FORTUNATE PILGRIMS

Americans in Italy, 1800–1860

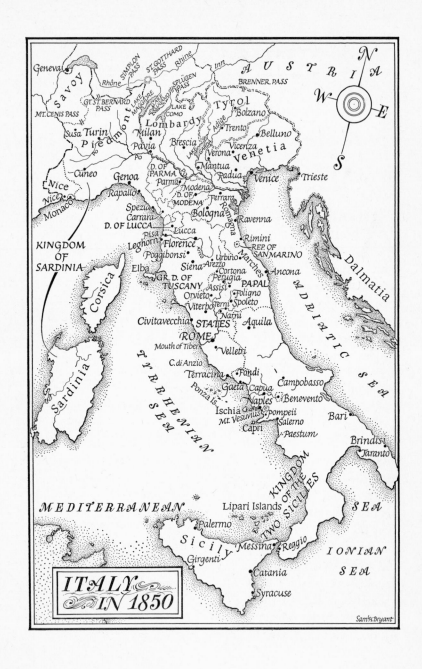

ITALY IN 1850

INTRODUCTION

A MERICANS have always had a special place in their
hearts for Italy. To one Italian they owe the discovery of the Western Hemisphere, to another the
name "America" itself, and they are indebted as well to Ver-
razano and the Cabots, Italians sailing under foreign flags,
who pursued important explorations of the newly discovered
land. Through their inherited European literature, Americans came to feel the attraction that Italy held for northern
peoples. During the nineteenth century, American maga-
zines and newspapers both followed and further stimulated
the public interest with countless articles on Italian literature, art, society, and customs. Volumes of Italian travel
were read and reread, handed on from those fortunate
enough to make the journey to those who could only dream
about it at home. Italian Renaissance paintings came to
form the heart of several major art collections in the United
States, while Italian opera has consistently maintained its
popularity among American music lovers. Since World
War II — as in the mid-nineteenth century — Italy has been
the favorite goal of American travelers on the Continent,
and a visit there has generally been a high point of modern-
day discoveries of Europe.

Partly because of the restrictions of the English naviga-
tion laws little interchange took place between North
America and Italy prior to the American Revolution. Only

a few Americans reached Italy in the years before the war, and we have, for the most part, scanty records of their visits. With national independence, however, contacts grew in importance. The first American consuls were named during the last decade of the eighteenth century, though regular diplomatic relations with the various Italian states did not commence for several years.[1] Toward the end of the eighteenth century teachers of Italian appeared in the major communities of the United States, and an ability to read the language came to be considered a desirable accomplishment for the well-educated young person.[2] Thomas Jefferson studied the violin with an Italian master, and both Benjamin Franklin and Jefferson knew the language well. Few Italian books were translated and published in the United States before 1800, but American booksellers sold volumes brought from Italy as well as Italian grammars and travel books published in England.

In the early decades of the nineteenth century, a minimal acquaintance with Italian literature became increasingly common, and the major poets — Dante, Petrarch, Ariosto, Tasso, Metastasio, and Alfieri — were widely studied. As the century advanced, enthusiasm for Italian literature reached its height in the cult of Dante. Longfellow, Lowell, Charles Eliot Norton, Thomas William Parsons, and Richard Henry Wilde all made scholarly translations, and the Cambridge enthusiasts met regularly as the informal Dante Club (1865), which later became the Dante Society (1881), taking special delight in interpreting the difficult passages.

As the Continent was reopened after the Napoleonic Wars, Americans visited Italy in rapidly expanding numbers, and many of them published accounts of their travels. American visits periodically decreased during difficult recession years, and they decidedly fell off during the Civil War, but a general increase took place during the century as a whole. By 1858 nearly two thousand Americans were visiting Florence annually, and by the last decade of the nineteenth century Rome had a permanent colony of some two hundred American residents and about thirty thousand annual American visitors.[3]

Both in travel books written for the public eye and in letters meant for private communication, in the straight-forward personal records of daily journals and in the often cryptic comments of secret diaries, nineteenth-century Americans revealed time and time again that Italy was the most interesting, the most meaningful place they had ever visited. George Bancroft, who had recently studied in Germany, asserted in 1822 that "everything conspires to make a journey in Italy the most interesting in the world."[4] And James Fenimore Cooper said, "If there is any country out of my own in which I would wish to live, it is Italy. There is no place where mere living is such a luxury."[5] To young Henry Adams, a visit to Italy in July 1859 was the realization of one of the ends of life: "Further, on these lines, one could not go. It had but one defect — that of attainment. Life had no richer impression to give; it offers barely half-a-dozen such, and the intervals seem long."[6] Italy, it seemed, had a particular significance for Americans.

The responses of Americans coming into direct contact with Italy reveal certain changes in emphasis through the nineteenth century. After the eighteenth-century "dis-coverers," who blazed the trails, came the "explorers," who set the tone for the period through the third and fourth decades of the nineteenth century. The explorers came to Italy for a variety of reasons, but above all, in Italy, they wanted to learn, to bring back information about social life and social institutions that might be of value to their own country. Many of them had not read extensively about the country, and, unencumbered with the stock responses prevalent later on, they often brought a fresh and original quality to their experiences. They viewed much of what they found in moral terms, and their impressions reveal a characteristic moral intensity.

Well before the middle of the century, however, a large number of American travelers began to embody another approach. By the time of the American Civil War the "romanticizer" had come into his own. As travel books and diaries multiplied, as photography advanced, as Italy moved along the road to the modern world, any sensations of surprise were increasingly blunted. Innocence, freshness, and spontaneity of response became more and more difficult to maintain. By this time the traveler was bringing with him any number of inherited stock impressions; the curtain of memory itself often obscured a clear view of contemporary life.

For this new group of visitors, impressions of Italy had been fixed by the English and American travel literature of the previous years. American institutional life had gradually settled into established ways, and travelers no longer felt as strong a need to learn about foreign society in order to report home their findings. As they became more confident of their own cultural patterns, Italy became for them more exclusively a land of the past, a graveyard of ruined monuments and ancient tombs. Interest in contemporary life declined, and significant personal contacts with individual Italians became fewer. Instead, Americans looked for the quaint and pleasantly picturesque, quoted Byron, and wanted to be entertained.[7]

By midcentury one finds among the romanticizers an increasing sense of disillusion. Since much of the picturesque the traveler had heard about was fast disappearing, his sense of discovery was muted. Only rarely did he face for the first time a novelty that astounded, delighted, or puzzled him. By the close of the American Civil War, when Italian national unification was well advanced, the American often expressed a yearning for the "old Italy," which had not yet undergone modernization, which, in retrospect, seemed somehow more genuine, more true to the past. Henry James a few years later particularly evoked this nostalgia for a past he himself had not known but that two of the subjects of his biographies, William Wetmore Story and Nathaniel Hawthorne, had experienced; he lamented that all the discoveries had been made, that the intensities of feeling had already been enjoyed by these fortunate precursors.

Finally, toward the end of the century, came the "exotics," who had become bored with the old three-star sights. Italy, it seemed, had been written about so much that Americans knew the cathedrals of Tuscany and the stones of the Roman Forum better than they knew their own home-town churches and civic centers. Italy had become a commonplace. Often professional travel writers, the exotics emphasized the oddly picturesque or the bizarre. They avoided the customary tourist routes, and in striking out on their own across the countryside they came into a fresh and intimate relationship with unusual elements of Italian life. They took special delight in the Middle Ages and enjoyed lingering in such medieval towns as Cortona and Orvieto. These travelers were even more detached from contemporary life than the romanticizers had been. They did not seek to learn in response to utilitarian motives as the explorers had; instead, they sought the fleeting impression, the backward glance. Introspective, they sometimes were more interested in their own responses to a particular place or object than in the place or object itself. A few other writers in the latter part of the century did take, however, a more realistic view of Italy, emphasizing the common details of everyday life and trying to present a more accurate, balanced picture of the country.

Throughout the nineteenth century those American visitors who wrote about Italy, like all travel authors, revealed in their work a great deal about themselves. What a visitor derives from his journeys, of course, is largely determined by the nature of the man himself — by the quality of his intellect and emotions — and an analysis of his responses can usually show what some of these personal elements are. Nevertheless the mental baggage he packs to carry with him does not contain solely his own possessions. Frequently the visitor shapes his comments with an eye to a particular audience of readers. Sometimes, as well, he is unable himself to see new things except through the eyes of earlier visitors whose comments and attitudes he has absorbed. Then, too, his views are often changed in the course of his journey, so that he eventually comes to accept as a matter of course many aspects of the life and culture that first struck him as worthy of record.

Beyond personal attitudes, however, remarks about a foreign scene also reveal many of the assumptions of the commentator's own culture. In observing the foreign scene, a traveler quickly discovers that many customs and ideas he has unreservedly accepted as the natural ways of doing and thinking are not accepted abroad. He finds that values common in his own society — which, in fact, serve as a kind of cementing force, holding the social structure together like mortar binding bricks — are not a part of the social structure he is now encountering. What he responds to most frequently and with the highest degree of emotional intensity are those elements of society and thought that seem strange or "wrong." What particularly strikes the American in a foreign situation is quite naturally often just the reverse side of that which makes a strong impression on the foreigner visiting the United States.

This book will attempt to show exactly why Americans went to Italy in the first place, what they saw and did when they got there, what personal contacts they had, what aspects of Italian life and culture particularly impressed them, what evaluations they made of their experiences, and what meaning the country ultimately had for them. Along with many comments of specific individuals, the attitudes, responses, and judgments of great numbers of travelers are frequently summarized and presented in this study as those of an anonymous "American traveler." Since such summary comments, in a sense, present the lowest common denominator, they must sometimes seem commonplace, their obviousness a partial reflection of the visitors' often superficial acquaintance with the country and its people or their reliance on handed-down stereotypes. The perspective of the travelers was often limited, and though their comments did not always describe the "true" Italy, they do reveal how an important group of Americans responded to an unfamiliar situation.

This analysis of the American response to Italy, together with its substratum of assumptions and attitudes common to American thought in this period, aims to give a better understanding of the American mind and American culture during the early and middle years of the nineteenth century.

The first six decades of the century form an appropriate unit for analysis, since by 1860, with the expansion of railroads and with national political unification largely completed, conditions of Italian travel had considerably changed from the first part of the century. American travelers themselves were changing, too, for by the Civil War the typical tourist was the romanticizing spectator. The morally earnest explorers and the earliest romanticizers, therefore, provide the focus of this study, with particular emphasis on the fresh responses of the newcomer. We shall follow these early travelers, the fortunate pilgrims, on their journeys through Italy, and their self-revelations will be our special concern.

CHAPTER I

THE DISCOVERY OF ITALY

As ENGLISH colonists, Americans of the seventeenth and eighteenth centuries looked primarily to the mother country for their cultural heritage. Therefore the English exploration of Italy provided the background for their own. Accordingly, the writings of English travelers (and, to a lesser extent, those of other northern Europeans) were bound to influence the American response to the Italian scene, helping to form their impressions and in part setting the tone of their remarks. Until well into the nineteenth century English works dominated the travel literature about Italy that Americans consumed.

Italy had begun to play an important role for the English during the Middle Ages, as pilgrims made the long and difficult journey to the heart of Western Christianity, many of them bound still farther as crusaders to the Holy Land. For about three and a half centuries after 850 an English church and hospice were located near St. Peter's in Rome. Bishops were expected to visit Rome every two or three years, and, before 1300, archbishops were obliged to come to Rome to receive the pallium of office.[1] The first extended account of a visit to Rome by an Englishman was that of Master Gregory, who, late in the twelfth century, enthusiastically de-

scribed the marvels of the city.[2] After 1300 the periodic
holy years particularly attracted pilgrims, and church
councils, such as the one at Pisa in 1409, drew large English
delegations.

But churchmen and pilgrims were not the only visitors to
come to Italy for serious purposes. English students began
to study law and medicine in Italian universities in the
twelfth and thirteenth centuries. English mercenaries, such
as the famous Sir John Hawkwood, found employment in
the incessant wars among the Italian city-states. By the fifteenth century English merchants were established in the
peninsula, and in 1485 an English consul was appointed to
Pisa. Finally, there were the diplomatic representatives of
the crown; after 1413 envoys of the English king regularly
resided at the Papal Curia.[3] Chaucer, it will be remembered,
had twice visited Italy on diplomatic missions: to Genoa
and Florence in 1372–1373, and to Milan and Pavia in 1378.
He thus discovered Dante, Petrarch, and Boccaccio on their
own soil.

The sixteenth century brought a new type of traveler,
the scholar eager to know the world and to make himself
into the ideal, well-rounded man. As Italian universities
gained in reputation, more Northerners came for humanist
studies. William Grocyn, William Lily, John Colet, and
Thomas Linacre all visited Italy, bringing home to England
the new Greek scholarship along with the tastes and attitudes of the Renaissance. Travel was primarily regarded as
a means of self-improvement, though it was also realized that
journeys abroad could develop skills needed for diplomacy.
In view of England's increasing commercial and political
contacts with Italy, knowledge of the country, her language, and her customs had become a national asset.

A change in the English attitude became apparent by the
end of the sixteenth century. English moralists inveighed

against the corruption of the Italians, and fear of the Inquisition and the Jesuits frightened away many possible visitors. But some still came, including Inigo Jones, John Evelyn, and John Milton in the seventeenth century. Another Englishman, George Sandys, must be considered the first person both to live in America and to visit Italy, although his Italian visit preceded by ten years his residence in Virginia. Setting out from France, Sandys passed through northern Italy on his way to Greece, Turkey, the Levant, and Egypt in 1610, and returned through Italy, visiting Sicily, Naples, Rome, Siena, Florence, Bologna, Ferrara, and Venice the following year.[4] Even though France remained the chief goal of the English traveler in the seventeenth century, the fashion of the Grand Tour became increasingly popular after the Restoration, and Italy provided the usual high point of this excursion.

The term 'Grand Tour' was first used by Richard Lassels in *The Voyage of Italy* (1670). The author had made five tours through Italy, and he offered practical advice for the young gentleman traveler. As a rule, the Grand Tour included France, Germany, and the Low Countries, as well as Italy, and it aimed less at serious instruction than at the pleasures of satisfied curiosity. Some travelers carefully planned the trip, studying tourist manuals, reading history, and learning languages; but most, no doubt, went relatively unprepared. A young gentleman undertaking the tour frequently spent two or three years journeying in a fashionable carriage, accompanied by one or more servants, and loosely supervised by a tutor-companion often no older than he. As more comfortable coaches were built, as the roads were improved, and as better maps and roadbooks were printed, it became easier to make the journey, and by the late eighteenth century the Grand Tour had lost much of its aristocratic exclusiveness.

A spate of books made Italy increasingly familiar to the English. Generally, the presentation was favorable to the Southern land. Joseph Addison's *Remarks on Several Parts of Italy* (1705) was perhaps the book on Italy most quoted during the eighteenth century. Samuel Sharp's *Letters from Italy* (1766) and Tobias Smollett's *Travels Through France and Italy* (1766) attacked the Italians as dirty, indolent, and superstitious, but Joseph Baretti's *Account of the Manners and Customs of Italy* (1768), Mrs. Piozzi's *Observations and Reflections* (1789), and Dr. John Moore's *View of Society and Manners in Italy* (1792) defended and diffused knowledge about the Italian people. *The Grand Tour* (1749) by Thomas Nugent and *The Gentleman's Guide in his Tour Through Italy* (1787) by Thomas Martyn were offered as guidebooks to be taken on the trip, and included practical information on money values, routes, prices, hotels, and picture galleries. Sir Joshua Reynolds' *Discourses* (1769–1790) praised the energy of Michelangelo and helped restore Italian art to favor.[5]

Among the Italians, the English had a reputation for eccentricity and extravagance, a reputation encouraged alike by their introduction of hunting with hounds on the Roman Campagna and by their clannish aloofness. The average English traveler remained "insular" even in Italy, whose society he had no wish to penetrate, and, as a result, in the eighteenth century he usually responded in stereotyped ways to the ruins and to the people. Sometimes he expressed and undoubtedly often felt a genuine love for the country, but he also considered himself superior to the Italians. He brought back to England collections of paintings, statuary, and furniture, redesigned his houses and public buildings, and planned his gardens under the influence of what he had seen.

The fashion of the Grand Tour had become a compelling

one. So many English, in fact, came to Rome in the eighteenth century that the area around the Piazza del Popolo
became known as the *Ghetto degli Inglesi.* The Old Pre-
tender arrived in Rome in 1717; his sons, Charles Edward
and Henry, Cardinal of York, spent most of their lives in
Italy. Sir Henry Raeburn, George Romney, John Flaxman,
and other English artists flocked to Rome for study, as did
wealthy collectors like Lord Burlington. Edward Gibbon,
visiting Rome in 1764, found inspiration for the study of the
decline and fall of ancient Rome in the Capitoline ruins
and the singing of the friars at the church of Aracoeli. It
remained, though, for Dr. Johnson, who never got to Italy,
to summarize the feelings of the age when he said: "A
man who has not been in Italy, is always conscious of an
inferiority, from his not having seen what it is expected a
man should see." [6]

Information about Americans in Italy during the seventeenth and eighteenth centuries is very limited. More often
England and France were the goals of the few colonial
visitors to Europe. Benjamin West is customarily reported
as the first American to have visited Italy, but undoubtedly
a few others born in the colonies preceded him there on
merchant vessels stopping at Leghorn or Genoa. Like those
who came later these "discoverers" made the journey for a
variety of reasons.

A few colonials at one time studied medicine in Italian
universities. After residence at Cambridge University, Robert Child studied at Leyden and then transferred to Padua,
which awarded him a doctorate in medicine in 1638. He
later traveled extensively in Italy, Spain, and France, before
coming to New England in 1639 for the first time, and returning there again six years later to attempt to develop iron
and silk industries. When Child joined with others to un-
dermine the Puritan oligarchy, he was suspected of working

with the Jesuits, arrested, fined, and, in 1647, sent back to England. Another Englishman, John Winthrop, Jr., who became a good friend of Child in Europe and again in Massachusetts and worked with him in the development of the infant iron industry and in various agricultural enterprises, had in his youth traveled through Italy and the Near East. Winthrop later became governor of Connecticut. When Nathaniel Eaton was dismissed as the first master of Harvard College, "being accused for cruell and barbaros beating of Mr Naza: Briscoe, and for other neglecting and misvseing of his schollers," he fled New England and eventually went to Padua to study medicine, obtaining there doctorates in medicine and philosophy in 1647.[7] Finally, there was Henry Saltonstall, a member of the first class of Harvard College, who also went to Padua for medical studies, obtaining the doctorate in 1649 and going on to Oxford to teach.

Some Americans visited Italy in the eighteenth century to study art. Certainly the most important of these was Benjamin West, who arrived in Rome in July 1760, having journeyed to the Old World on a Philadelphia vessel carrying wheat and flour to Leghorn. The merchants Rutherford and Jackson entertained him in Leghorn and gave him a letter of introduction to the great Cardinal Albani, owner of the largest private collection of antique sculpture in Rome. The Quaker artist was an immediate sensation in the drawing rooms of Rome, and a torchlight party was quickly arranged to take the young visitor to the sculpture galleries of the Vatican Museum, so that his fresh and direct responses to the works of art could be observed. His comparison of the Apollo Belvedere to a Mohawk warrior at first shocked the Romans, but their dismay turned to delight when West explained how much he admired the poise, dignity, and bodily perfection of the best specimens of American Indians. He remained in Italy for about three years, visiting several cities to study and sometimes copy the paintings. He was elected to the academies of Parma, Florence, and Bologna, and was presented to the court of Parma. Leaving Italy in 1763, West moved directly to London, where he soon achieved fame and became the most influential American painter of his time.[8]

Other American artists also made the journey to Italy. Henry Benbridge, who was born in Philadelphia, made such good progress in studies in Rome under Pompeo Battoni and Raphael Mengs that in 1768 he was sent to Corsica to paint for James Boswell a full-length portrait of General Pasquale de Paoli, the Corsican patriot.[9] Charles Bulfinch, the famous Boston architect, made a tour of Italy in 1786, spending only three weeks in Rome.[10] Edward Savage, painter and engraver, apparently visited the peninsula sometime before his return to the United States from a European trip in 1794, and another painter named Steele was reported to have visited the country long before Charles Willson Peale met him in 1762.[11] Two sources mention "old Mr. Smith," an American said to have been 116 years old in 1834, who had been living in Italy since 1764; unsuccessful as a painter, he had become a picture dealer, thus setting an example for some future expatriates.[12] There was John Smibert at the beginning of the century; before coming to America with Dean Berkeley in 1728, Smibert had worked in Italy from 1717 to 1720, and was even employed for a time as a painter for the grand duke of Tuscany.[13]

Our information about the tour of Italy that the painter John Singleton Copley made in 1774–1775 is more complete. Arriving at Genoa, he bought elegant new clothing, fitting himself out like a dandy. Then he went on through Leghorn, Pisa, and Florence to Rome, where he found himself much at home in the English colony. In Naples he met Mr. and Mrs. Ralph Izard of Charleston, South Carolina, who had been pleased to find many Italian well-wishers for the Revolutionary cause.[14] Copley and Izard visited Paestum together and were probably the first Americans to have seen a genuine Greek temple.[15] Back in Rome, Copley painted the Izards seated at a table and surrounded by antique objects. At Parma he copied on commission from Lord Grosvenor "St. Jerome" by Correggio, a picture that West had also copied.[16]

Religion attracted an occasional visitor in the eighteenth century. Probably the first American Roman Catholic to visit Italy was a young priest from Maryland, John Carroll, later the first American bishop and archbishop. After study at the Collège de St. Omer in French Flanders and at Liége, he traveled to Rome in 1772 as companion to the son of Lord Stourton, spent a few months in Naples, and returned to Rome for the winter. Carroll vigorously defended Church practices in his journal, and objected to foreigners blaming conditions in the Papal States on Church rule, though he admitted that there was indolence in the Church government.[17]

Just ten years after Carroll's visit, John Thayer, a Protestant minister from Boston, came to Rome. Though Thayer intensely disliked Catholicism, he wanted to learn more about it. His studies and discussion of the Catholic system soon led to his own conversion, and he quickly rushed into print to defend his action. His case received widespread attention, and the *Account of the Conversion* (1787) was reprinted in several languages.[18]

A journal dated 1736–1737 probably provides the earliest extant account of an Italian pleasure tour by an American visitor.[19] It is said to have been written by Benjamin Pollard, who from 1743 to his death in 1756 was sheriff of Suffolk County, Massachusetts. At Naples, where the fragmentary diary begins, Pollard saw Virgil's tomb, climbed

Mount Vesuvius, attended the opera, and had his picture taken in miniature. He also visited a Carthusian convent, "show'd it by a Gentleman of the Convent who was uncommonly civil, & of a goodly behaviour," and found it so agreeable that he was "allmost tempted to live therein." But he resisted the temptation, went on to Rome, and after a few days traveled by way of Loretto to Venice, where he "had the hon^r of a Bow from the Doge." Subsequently Pollard stopped at Bologna, Florence, and Leghorn, where he again enjoyed the opera, before taking a vessel to England and returning shortly to Boston.

One of the more important American visitors in the eighteenth century was Dr. John Morgan of Philadelphia, a founder of the first medical school in America and later head physician of the Revolutionary Army, who toured the peninsula in 1764 with his fellow townsman, Samuel Powel. A fragment of Dr. Morgan's journal has survived and shows not only many of his responses to the Italian scene but also gives evidence of Morgan's interest in painting, especially in the pictures of Guido Reni. The account is noteworthy for Morgan's visits to the medical schools at Bologna and Padua. In Bologna he called on Laura Bassi, a celebrated female professor of physics, and in Padua he visited Giovanni Morgagni, a professor of anatomy, who showed him his pathological and anatomical specimens and to whom Morgan presented a copy of his doctoral thesis. At Rome, Parma, and Turin, he met other scholars, including perhaps Giambatista Beccaria, the economist. Morgan was presented to the king of Sardinia and to the pope, and in Rome he was made a member of the Accademia degli Arcadi.[20]

Thomas Jefferson's visit to Italy in 1787 — the same time that Goethe was fulfilling his lifelong dream of seeing the Southland — falls squarely in the prevailing tradition of the next half century. He made his trip for a specific utilitarian purpose — in this case, to help agriculture in his own country. Traveling by land from Marseilles and Nice, the minister to France visited the countryside around Turin and Milan, observing the cultivation of rice and the type of machines used for cleaning it, in order to discover why grain from this region was less broken than grain from America. Discovering that the rice-cleaning machines in Italy were similar to those used in the United States, he concluded that the strain planted was responsible. Although the Sardinian government forbade export of rice in the rough state, Jefferson took measures to have some clandestinely shipped to him and he also carried a small sample in his luggage back to France. His fact-filled journal of the three weeks' tour notes the crops grown and techniques of cultivation, the nature of the soils and rocks, the types of land leases, the building materials and forms of the dwellings, and the food, dress, and appearance of the inhabitants.[21]

The following year two young Americans, John Rutledge, Jr., and Thomas Lee Shippen, armed with letters of introduction and travel advice from Jefferson, visited northern Italy on a general tour of Europe. At Milan, William Short, Jefferson's secretary in Paris, joined Rutledge, and the two went on together to Bergamo and eventually to Venice, Bologna, and Rome, which Rutledge found "of all places in this world . . . the most agreeable and charming." [22] After several weeks in Rome, where the young visitors engaged a tutor to help them study architecture, they traveled to Naples, seeing Vesuvius, Herculaneum, and Pompeii, and then passed northward to France by way of Rome and Florence.[23]

These and a few others were the Americans who discovered Italy. From the scanty records we can see at least that they were intensely interested in what they found. Like those who followed, they generally came to learn what they could from a country that in many ways seemed far more advanced than their own. They found famous cities and historic buildings, a display of the greatest works of art, scholarly acquaintances, instruction in painting and architecture, the learning of medical science, and the traditional practices of the Church. Here they discovered ties to the past that they had not known at home. Like those who came later, they could for a time throw off the restraints and responsibilities of life at home and live the life of the student or the observer, sometimes of the dandy. They might unearth values they had not known before. These discoverers, themselves taking their cues from earlier English visitors, blazed the trails for their countrymen who were to make the tour of Italy in subsequent years. By the early part of the nineteenth century a European tour and a visit to Italy had become a significant American cultural phenomenon.

CHAPTER II

THE BUSINESS OF TRAVEL

WITH TRAVEL to the Continent cut off almost completely during the Napoleonic Wars, only a few Americans visited Italy during the earliest years of the nineteenth century. The number of American tourists, however, gradually increased by the third and fourth decades. In 1835 a traveler reported that between two and three hundred Americans had passed through Rome that year and about fifty American ladies had visited the city during Holy Week; and by the mid-1840's it was estimated that about one thousand Americans came to Italy each year.[1] In Rome one spring day in 1833, Ralph Waldo Emerson was delighted to count fifteen persons from Boston alone.[2] Roman newspaper lists of American arrivals and departures from 1848 to 1850 included nine hundred names, apart from residents and family members.[3]

An outpouring of travel volumes written by Americans in the 1850's both reflected the American influx and at the same time stimulated more visitors to come. Late in the decade, in 1858, Nathaniel Hawthorne found more American names on the register at a hotel in Terni than names from any other country.[4] The number of Americans in Rome in the winter of 1859–1860 was reported to be somewhat under four hundred.[5] The Civil War cut off the flow of tourists, but following Appomattox Americans deluged Europe. By March 1868, Bayard Taylor was able to report the presence of some twelve hundred Americans in Rome, most of whom left the city immediately after Easter Week.[6] And a freshet of new Italian travel volumes appeared.

Though by far the largest group of American visitors came from New England, other parts of the country were also represented. A declaration of local allegiance along with an attempt to attract the attention of certain readers are evident in some of the titles of volumes published during the 1840's and 1850's: *Rome: as Seen by a New Yorker; Tales and Souvenirs . . . By a Lady of Virginia; A Tennessean Abroad; A Buckeye Abroad.*[7]

Buckeye or Brahmin, Virginian or New Yorker, the American in Italy cut across not only a good many geographical divisions, but professional ones as well. Among the 1848–1850 group of visitors to Rome listed in the *Dictionary of American Biography*, clergymen, businessmen, painters, and sculptors predominate.[8] If many of the travel books were written by Protestant clergymen, the explanation is simple: frequently a minister was given an expense-paid trip by his congregation, and his letters to the stay-at-homes were later published. It was the least he could do for his benefactors. Physician, scientist, politician, diplomat, lawyer, merchant, journalist, social reformer, and educator are similarly represented among those who published accounts of their Italian experiences.

A variety of motives brought Americans to Italy. Sometimes they simply passed through the country on a general European tour. Charles and Martha Babcock Amory, for example, visited Italy in 1833–1834 on their wedding journey. Others, such as Charles Sumner on his first trip in 1839, came to learn the language and acquaint themselves with the art and literature of the land. Richard Henry Wilde, poet and constitutional lawyer, spent the years 1835 to 1841 working in the Medicean archives on a study of Dante. Others had more specialized interests. Dr. Pliny Earle and Dorothea Dix, for example, traveled to inspect insane asylums, and Benjamin Silliman, the geologist, made a point of studying fossil fish *in situ*. Some visitors, such as Margaret Fuller, held newspaper assignments, and sent home detailed letters (afterwards often collected in published volumes) of their impressions.

Many Americans came to Italy intent upon broadening themselves and gaining instruction from the sights of the ancient world. Some hoped to satisfy childhood dreams and longings; they were eager to see the places associated with those ancient poets, statesmen, and historians whom they had come to know as young students and whose writings many of them still remembered well and quoted freely. When Rembrandt Peale, the painter, returned to America from a trip to northern Europe only, he was gravely troubled that his youthful hopes of seeing the homeland of Raphael and Guido Reni might never be realized. "Italy," he wrote, " which was my reverie by day, became the torment of my dreams at night." [9] Visitors early in the nineteenth century seemed to be much better grounded in the classics and made far more allusions to classical sites, authors, and political figures than did travelers of the middle and latter years of the century.

Almost every American who traveled abroad had at least a little interest in art, and the rich historical content of artistic treasures was an important attracting force. Those working in one of the plastic or visual arts were drawn by the unsurpassed opportunities for study of the treasures of painting, sculpture, and architecture. For the architect, survivals from antiquity provided a standard of artistic value and an inspiration for contemporary forms. The sculptor found a dependable supply of the finest Carrara marble, considered the most appropriate medium for statuary. For the painter, antique ruins, picturesque villages, colorfully costumed peasants, a well-domesticated countryside, the "wild" Campagna and Apennine wastes all offered fit subjects for the brush. Live models were readily available for both the sculptor and the painter at a fraction of the cost in America. For the connoisseur and the collector, Italy provided a tantalizing feast of contemporary works and the excitement of the hunt for precious objects surviving from the past.

Others were attracted for religious reasons. Few American Catholic laymen visited the land during the first part of the nineteenth century; nevertheless, Rome, as the center of Western Catholicism, naturally drew many American Catholic clergy for study and administrative work.

For still others the voice of fashion was all important. As with the English in the eighteenth century, socially fashionable Americans now had to see Italy. By the latter part of the century, a European tour with a winter in Rome and Naples had become a mark of achieved status, especially for the newly successful merchant or industrialist.

Finally, some came in search of health. Francis Parkman, for example, during his senior year at Harvard College, was nearly incapacitated by severe illness; he sailed on a small vessel to the Mediterranean, and, happily, after extensive travel through Sicily and the Italian mainland, at least temporarily regained his health. Others were less fortunate. When in 1861 Richard Hildreth, the historian, was appointed American consul in Trieste, he was already very ill. His worsened condition soon forced him to give up his position, and he died in Florence in 1865, just five years after the death in the same city of the Unitarian clergyman

Theodore Parker, who also had come to Italy in the hope of somehow staying the disease which was destroying his lungs.

Although the Mediterranean area generally enjoyed a popular reputation abroad as a good refuge for invalids, most writers who touched on this subject expressed the opinion that the cold, damp, and drafty buildings of Italy not only failed to benefit tubercular patients, but were decidedly harmful. Even so, medical writers sometimes suggested that travel through the peninsula could be salutary to patients suffering from nervous disorders. They emphasized, too, that foreigners would gain the greatest well-being by following the usages of the Italians themselves rather than their own in such matters as rest, food, and drink.

Travelers were warned of the *mal'aria* in Rome, in the surrounding Campagna, and in the Pontine Marshes to the south. The "Roman fever" had given that city a bad reputation for the summer months, though it was felt that by taking necessary precautions, a visitor could safely reside there even during the hot spell. Since malaria was attributed to noxious gases issuing from the earth, an upper story of a building was strongly recommended. The foreigner was advised never to venture out after sunset and always to keep his bedroom window closed at night. Areas near the ruins and the farms and gardens within the walls were considered especially dangerous. Even more unsafe was the Campagna — the silent tombs and broken aqueducts told their own story. The tourist was far better off in the hill towns, where he remained relatively safe from the deadly vapors. Despite the frequent warnings and advice, some Americans did fall ill with the disease.

The climate was a general topic of concern. Most American travelers were surprised to find just how cold and dismal Italy actually could be during the winter. On arriving in Rome in midwinter 1858, Nathaniel Hawthorne caught a bad cold and was miserable for weeks. In his discomfort he inveighed against Rome and everything it seemed to represent, but his spirits improved with the weather, and eventually he and his wife came to feel sincere affection for the city. Newcomers were almost invariably delighted with the clear warm days of spring, and relatively few suffered from the reputedly scorching summers. Although the visitors enjoyed the sun, they did not seek it out. Except for an occasional mention of horseback riding on the Campagna and sight-seeing walks, almost no evidence exists of outdoor physical activity on their part. They praised the limpid, clear air for its effect on the view, not for its effect on the human body.

Before setting out from America, extensive preparations were always necessary. First of all, the traveler had to arrange to obtain funds for his travel needs. The usual procedure was to procure bills of exchange or a letter of credit, purchased either in the United States or in England, which Italian representatives of the issuing bank would then honor. Few Americans apparently fell into financial difficulties.

Next the traveler had to decide just what he should take with him on the journey. Usually he was burdened by one or more small trunks as well as the more easily handled carpetbags; managing the luggage invariably took considerable time, entailed much fuss and worry, and always proved expensive. Even so, Americans traveled more lightly than some Englishmen, who followed guidebook advice to bring their own sheets, well-stocked medicine chests, food supplies, and even grease for their carriages.

Then it was important for the prospective visitor to familiarize himself with the itinerary he expected to follow. Before leaving home some tourists studied histories, travel books, and guidebooks, prepared themselves with a background of factual information, and made a slightly self-conscious effort to maintain an open mind and heart. Books on Italy, its literature, and its culture, were found in many American homes. One writer in 1847 even complained in the *American Whig Review*: "There is glut in the market. People have their houses full of Italian views, and their libraries full of Italian travels, and boardingschool misses are twaddling nelle parole Tuscane." [10] Other visitors, not surprisingly, came poorly prepared, and as a consequence looked only at what their guidebooks told them to.

Guides were plentiful in Italy — often too plentiful. Especially in the area around Naples, crowds of men, women, and children descended on strangers, refused to go away when assured their services were not wanted, and loudly demanded a gratuity at the end of the excursion, whether they had been of use or not. Guides could be helpful, of course, in finding a monument or a ruin in an out-of-the-way place. But their astounding glibness and limitless faith in their own omniscience annoyed the visitor, who, as often as not, found himself reconciled, nonetheless, once he recognized how small their fees were. The guides of Rome generally were better qualified than those elsewhere, perhaps because the visitor here usually employed a guide only for a specific site.

Sometimes the traveler made use of English travel works of the eighteenth century, though he usually brought with him as well other volumes somewhat more up to date. Four works in particular, two of them certainly not conventional guides, were his principal guidebooks during the first decades of the nineteenth century.

The Reverend John Chetwode Eustace made "a classical tour through Italy" in 1802, and his description of this journey, although presented in four awkward volumes, remained one of the standard accounts through the early part of the century. Eustace recommended a long period of intensive preparation before setting out: the tourist should study the classics, the language, history, architecture, painting, sculpture, medals, and music of the country. Just as important was the need for developing "an unprejudiced mind," and he urged "some indulgence to the errors, and some compassion for the sufferings of less favoured nations." The chief goal of the tour was moral improvement. At the very least, Eustace believed, the visitor needed one and one-half years to see Italy, which might be spent as follows: crossing the Alps into Italy in September and proceeding to Rome by the end of November; on to Naples for January, February, and March; then back to Rome for April, May, and June; to the Alban Hills for July and August; to Florence in September, with the second winter in Tuscany. Eustace's book, in fact, was more appropriate to the wealthy, leisured gentleman on the Grand Tour fifty years earlier, than to the new post-Napoleonic traveler, who often lacked the time and money available to his grandfather.[11]

Both Eustace and another Englishman, Joseph Forsyth, hurried to Italy during the lull in the Napoleonic Wars following the Peace of Amiens. But when war was resumed, Forsyth was arrested at Turin while attempting to flee to Switzerland. He was not released from prison until 1814; the hardship of prison life had undermined his health, and he died the following year. Forsyth's book was a more compact guide than Eustace's and contained much practical information on modern Italian customs and institutions. It was probably the volume most often referred to by the Americans visiting Italy in the first half of the nineteenth century.[12]

It was through the eyes of Madame de Staël and Lord Byron, however, that Italian scenes made the greatest impression on New World visitors. *Corinne* (1807) celebrated Madame de Staël's discovery of the charms of the South, and provided, as additional stimulus, a thinly disguised record of her own love affairs.[13] The mysterious poet and *improvvisatrice* Corinne guides the melancholic Lord Nelvil to the principal sights of Italy and helps to acquaint him with Italian culture and character. As the reader joined them in their tour, he found a convenient guide not only to his own journey but also to appropriate emotional responses in such chapters as "Pictures and Statuary," "Manners and Character of the Italians," "Popular Festivals and Music," and "Holy Week." Hawthorne's *Marble Faun* would serve the same function in the latter part of the century.

The emotional impact of Italian scenes and situations on the hero of *Childe Harold* likewise gave the visitor a clue as to how he might respond.[14] The quotations from the fourth canto of this poem are legion in both the public and the private writings of Americans. Certain Italian sites especially drew forth Byronic utterances. Those who visited the falls at Terni invariably quoted what Byron had written — adding petulantly that he had exaggerated the falls and, in a way, spoiled the pleasure of subsequent visitors. At Ferrara the Americans examined Tasso's cell, found Byron's name on the wall, and parroted everything the English poet had said. Mount Soracte, the Colosseum, and the Tomb of Cecilia Metella could be counted on to provoke the appropriate lines. Byron, it was suggested, had revealed Italy to his generation as no one else had been able to do. "He came, saw, and became master or conqueror of the land, by reproducing it in words. The truth of his portraiture is marvellous." [15]

A few other guidebooks found their way into the visitors' hands: Mrs. Starke's *Travels in Europe*, Lady Morgan's *Italy*, William Beckford's *Italy, with Sketches of Spain and Portugal*, and Samuel Rogers' poem *Italy*. When Silas P. Holbrook, a Boston merchant, visited Italy, he revealed acquaintance not only with the books of Forsyth, de Staël, and Morgan, but also with *The Political State of Italy* (1820) by Theodore Lyman, Jr., *Letters from Europe* (1827) by Nathaniel Hazeltine Carter, and the *Diary of an Ennuyée* (1826) by Mrs. Anna Jameson.[16]

During his visit to Italy in 1844, the Reverend William Ingraham Kip, later the first Protestant Episcopal bishop in California, used several of these volumes, and Kip was also one of the first to mention the guidebooks of John Murray, the English publisher. Murray's guidebooks, which were very widely used during the middle years of the century, furnished useful, convenient, and abundant information not only on such matters as routes, cities, buildings, and galleries, but on clothing, luggage, and money rates as well; they advised the reader what to see, what to do, and even what to pay for various services. Little wonder that the Murray guidebook soon came to be regarded as the Bible of the European traveler!

What Murray did for the whole of Italy, Mariano Vasi did for Rome in particular. Vasi's *New Guide of Rome, Naples and Their Environs* offered as a special attraction an eight-day plan for seeing the sights of Rome, which the young architect Russell Sturgis, for one, resolved to follow. Apparently it could not be done, however, unless one shared Vasi's own mercurial mobility. As for Sturgis, he soon gave up the project in disgust. "The fifth day of Vasi," he lamented, "requires two or three of anyone else." [17]

George Stillman Hillard's *Six Months in Italy* (1853) went through twenty-one editions during the century and, everything considered, it was probably the most popular book about Italy written by an American. John Lothrop Motley, the historian, thought it the best book on Italy he had ever read — so good that, with it as competition, he felt disinclined to write home his own Italian descriptions.[18]

Countless others carried the volume along with them, following Hillard's trail through the peninsula.

After he had selected his itinerary, the traveler next had to decide on his means of transportation. The tourist had his choice of several forms of carriage travel. He could use his own private coach with his own team of horses, as did some wealthy Englishmen. When Byron came to Italy, he brought several carriages full of furniture and books, seven servants, and five coachmen. The Blessington family moved so splendidly through the country that the caravan was christened a circus. But few Americans could afford such luxuries.

There were also public coaches. Posting coaches varied in size from the mail coach, which accommodated no more than three passengers inside, to the diligence, with a large central inside compartment, a small forward section, and a rear compartment or a high outside seat. At the back and on the top of the coach were receptacles for luggage and underneath a tray or net in which pet dogs could ride. Along the most frequented routes there were regular posting stations, where horses were available to take the carriages on to the next station. Usually both a driver and a conductor operated the coaches, and a postilion, who was a boy in livery, managed each pair of horses — too many men doing the work one good man should be able to do, thought the Americans. Small coaches could be hired at the posting houses, and a group of travelers could rent a carriage and could post together. Rates for posting were fixed by law, although with the demands of the postilions for a *buonamano* and new postilions coming on at each station, and with the bargaining necessary for each meal and each night's lodging, the cost of this form of travel could mount rapidly.[19] The use of a stronger team than the carriage required according to the rates fixed by law, with the addition of several mules or oxen for the long hills on the road, increased the cost for the passengers. The particular advantage of posting was the speed: from Florence to Rome by post usually took three days, as compared with five or six days by *vettura*. The fast diligences could cover as much as eighty miles a day, but the schedules were often poorly arranged, leading to long and tedious delays, and the coaches usually traveled by night. Foreign visitors wanting to see something of the countryside generally preferred a more leisurely pace.

The *vettura* system was the most common type of travel arrangement. For a fixed sum, a coachman, or *vetturino*, agreed to provide transportation, lodgings, and meals. Occasionally the traveler's own coach was used, the *vetturino* providing only the horses, but more often the coachman furnished both carriage and horses. Family parties without coaches of their own usually journeyed this way. Along the more frequented routes those traveling alone were usually able to find a *vetturino* willing to take to the road as soon as three or four more passengers could be located. Sometimes passengers were exchanged along the route like articles of merchandise, and a new coachman took over the obligations of the original driver — much to the annoyance of the Americans, who were hardly used to such highhanded treatment.

The *vettura* covered thirty-five to forty miles a day, at the rate of little more than three miles an hour. Since at midday the coachman stopped for two or three hours to rest his horses, the hours on the road were tediously long, and generally the vehicle had to start out before sunrise. Because of the limited accommodations at the roadside inns, carriages would frequently race each other by late afternoon, trying to pass one another in order to arrive first and have a choice of what was available. Experienced travelers sometimes sent couriers ahead to arrange for rooms. The trip from Florence to Rome by *vettura* cost about twelve dollars per person, meals and lodgings included.

Before starting on the journey the traveler and the *vet-turino* signed a contract, usually on a printed blank and drawn up according to a standard formula, which specified just what the coachman would provide for such and such an amount. The details of the trip were explicitly set forth, including the exact route, the stops to be made, the places of lodging, the meals and even the number of dishes to be provided, whether or not there was to be a fire in the traveler's chamber, and how much was to be paid for unscheduled additional stops. Usually the traveler paid half the fee at the beginning and the other half at the end of the trip. On signing the contract, the driver sometimes gave the traveler a small sum, which the latter could keep if the coachman failed to fulfill his obligation — a unique form of deposit-in-reverse. A gratuity not only was expected but was demanded at the end of the journey, and, though supposedly given according to the services rendered, was almost invariably a specific proportion of the fare.

Americans complained how slow the *vettura* was; the long stop at midday, which was made wherever the coach happened to be, was especially irritating. One annoyed traveler asserted that "a good pedestrian would travel through Italy on foot much faster than with a Vetturino who always uses his [own] horses." [20] The visitors also voiced fears about the safety of the equipment, for the horses were often decrepit nags and the coach and harness dangerously worn-out. Breakdowns, in fact, sometimes occurred. A further source of complaint was the *vetturino's* occasional attempt to economize at the expense of the tourist by paying less to the innkeepers for meals than he had agreed, so that the travelers were sometimes obliged to reach into their own pockets to pay for enough extra food to appease their hunger. In that case they were sure to revenge themselves by deducting the amount from the *buonamano*.

But by and large this system had advantages that seemed to outweigh the disadvantages. It was decidedly cheaper than travel in a posting coach. It gave the visitor the opportunity to stop when he wished and to see what he wanted. In moving slowly, it increased the delights of anticipation. It placed the traveler in a personal relation with the coachman. Above all, it removed the worry of bargaining for every room and every meal on the road.

Although the *vetturini* enjoyed a questionable reputation, the Americans generally found them honest and amusing, and certainly no worse than men doing such a job in other countries. The Hawthornes were especially enthusiastic about their Gaetano, who took them from Rome to Florence, and about "the Emperor," who drove their carriage southward again to Rome. James Fenimore Cooper, too, approved of the system, even though he discovered that his *vetturino* enjoyed far better cooking in the kitchen than Cooper himself was served upstairs.[21]

Visitors spending more than a few days in one place found lodgings in private apartments or villas, but while moving through the countryside and on first arriving in a city they had to rely on inns and hotels. In their letters and in their travel writings, the Americans had much to say about their accommodations and their meals. Not surprisingly, the quality of the food and the comfort of the lodgings often determined how they responded to a particular place. Probably only a few Americans came to realize that travel was, in fact, an art, and that the experienced traveler could increase his pleasures by his own attitude of mind. Irving, for one, cheerfully tried to take things as they came, and when he could not get a dinner to suit his taste, he endeavored, he revealed, to get a taste to suit his dinner.[22]

Lodgings in the cities contrasted sharply with accommodations along the road. In the leading urban hotels, guests were well-housed, well-served, and well-fed; in private lodgings in the cities, though the chambers were often unexpectedly grand and correspondingly cold and drafty, tourists could usually find adequate comfort. But outside the principal cities, the inns were almost always poor and frequently were wretched; the rooms were dirty, the beds damp, and travelers often discovered they were obliged to share their quarters with fleas or lice. In the past there had been no tradition of comfort along the road for the middle-class traveler. Wealthy foreigners and Italians themselves had usually stopped at convents or monasteries or had been handed along from one acquaintance or contact to another, and the less fortunate had been left to shift for themselves as best they could.

In Rome the hotels patronized by the English and Americans were all located near the Piazza di Spagna, centrally situated for excursions to the sights of the city. Here visitors found clean rooms, good service, excellent food, French-speaking servants, and the companionship of their fellow countrymen. In Florence most of the hotels at which the English and Americans stayed were close to the Arno, in Naples along the edge of the bay, and in Venice beside the lagoon or along the Grand Canal — the same places where the big cosmopolitan hotels are located today. The larger inns had a reputation for honesty, though the traveler was cautioned, nonetheless, always to establish the price of the room, meals, and a fire before moving in.

Some of the practices of the Italian hotels astonished the Americans. Men, not women and girls, customarily cleaned

the chambers and made the beds. Meals were often served
not at a general table, but in the bedchambers. Along the
road, men and women, strangers to one another, occasionally were obliged to share a room. Double beds were seldom
encountered; "the idea of putting two people in the same
bed, even if married, scarcely ever comes into the heads of
the Europeans of the Continent." [23] The occasional double
bed, though, was usually an enormous affair. At Nemi, in
the Alban Hills, the only inn had only one bed, but one
night it was big enough for Worthington Whittredge,
Sanford R. Gifford, William Beard, William Stanley Haseltine, and Thomas Buchanan Read, "and there was room
for one more." [24]

Those staying in lodgings seldom had meals prepared
there. It was customary either to take meals at a public
house or have food sent from a neighboring *trattoria*, a
small restaurant or eating house. In this way the traveler
was not forced to pay fixed charges as was the custom in
America. In Florence, it was reported, dinner for five
brought from a *trattoria*, consisting of soup, three courses
of meat, vegetables, wine, pastry, and fruit, cost only a
dollar and a quarter a day. Herman Melville recorded in
his Roman journal in 1857 that he had "dined on 19 cents
at Lepri's." [25]

The visitors found the low cost of living attractive, and
their letters are full of praise for Italian prices. "The celestial cheapness of the early times," seemed indeed to Henry
James, looking back fifty years later, "the last cloying sweet
in the rich feast of Italy." [26] Prices were higher in Rome
than in Florence, Naples, or the other cities. At that, Wilbur Fisk, president of Wesleyan University, who stayed in
Rome in 1836, discovered that his entire expense for coach
hire, guides, entrance fees, lodgings, and meals came to only
two dollars per person a day.[27] Large palaces rented for

three or four hundred dollars a year. An artist had to pay only about two hundred dollars annually for a good studio, and around sixty dollars a month to his journeymen carvers and a dollar or less a day to his models.

Americans accepted the fact that as foreigners they had to pay higher prices than did the Italians themselves, but they were sometimes vexed with English travelers for the lavish way they threw money about. "The English," reported Fisk, "have ruined the foreign market for all that use their language." [28] To Hawthorne the Italian shop-keeper's policy of asking different prices from different customers, based on his estimate of what each could pay, was a just system, even though it probably led those dealing with foreigners to try to get all they could.[29] But American travelers resented bargaining, which they considered debasing; the arguing and the noise necessary for such transactions appeared inappropriate to the situation. Fenimore Cooper's experience was typical, though: as soon as he condescended to discuss prices, the charges for room and meals fell to nearly half of what he had previously been paying.[30]

The complicated passport procedures of the different states provided occasional headaches for the traveler. Americans, nevertheless, found themselves as a group more favorably treated than were the citizens of other countries, perhaps, as one observer believed, "because they never interfere in the affairs of the country." [31] Before entering a state, the traveler had to obtain the signature of a representative of that government, in addition to the signature of his own consul. When leaving the state, as well, official signatures were needed. Fortunately, only the American consul among the officials customarily charged for the signature itself; however, a courier was usually sent to obtain the necessary names, and he, of course, had to be paid.

Often an American complained that this consular charge was petty and unbecoming, but he realized that the practice was necessary as long as the consuls received no other remuneration.

The tourist may be forgiven for regarding the bureaucratic processes as needlessly cumbersome. Take the enlightened grand duchy of Tuscany. On his arrival in Florence, the visitor had first to surrender his passport, in exchange for which he was given a sojourn card guaranteeing him the protection and benefit of the laws of Tuscany. When he wanted to leave, he had to surrender the sojourn card in its turn and obtain a passport requisition form. Then, at another office, turning in the completed form he retrieved his passport along with permission to leave within three days. If he planned to proceed to Rome, he next had to apply for a visa to enter the States of the Church. The more impressive looking the passport, the shorter the delay at the borders; a bright array of stamps and signatures and formidable titles accelerated the inspection. On returning to Italy in 1851 after an extended trip to the United States, the sculptor William Wetmore Story presented to the guards at the gates of Rome his passport in which he figured as "Esquire." " 'Ah, Esqui-*re*! Re degli Esqui — sua Maestà!' " The guard bowed low, and the carriage was promptly allowed to pass.[32]

At each border crossing and along the principal roads, tedious customs' inspections lay in ambush for the tourist, procedures that became increasingly bothersome the farther south he went. The practice of tipping the customs' agents to avoid baggage inspection was long established. Although many Americans considered this open acceptance of bribes by public officials as a telling example of dishonesty in the Italian character and of the low level of morality, most of them believed the expense was worth the time and the trouble saved. Characteristically, they apparently didn't ask themselves if offering a bribe was not as immoral as accepting one: the criminal was always the other fellow. Baggage could be sealed through a particular territory, a procedure calculated to remove the need for inspections, but a fee was charged for putting on the seals, and along the road the seals themselves were invariably inspected — for a fee.

Although these fees and tips were never large, the total rapidly mounted in proportion to the number of customs' stations encountered. The relentless demand for petty sums proved a constant source of annoyance. One visitor recorded those persons to whom he had been forced to make payments on arriving at an Italian port: the boatman, the carrier who took the trunks on shore, the porter who ran off with them, a police officer, the guide to the customhouse, the official at the customhouse who opened the trunks, the certifying officer, the man who sealed the trunks, and the two porters who handed the luggage up and strapped the pieces on the carriage.[33] Next in line were the clerk who had the passports stamped, the American consul, the stable boys, the driver of the carriage, the postilions, and the beggars who saw the carriage off. Later came the hotel employees, and the doorkeepers and guides at the museums, churches, and palaces. When finally the tourist sighed with relief in the conviction that he had at last discharged all obligations and gratified all monetary demands, he merely discovered that the latest recipient was by no means satisfied but asked to be paid all over again. The American, with a sinking feeling that this could only end with his instant return to the United States, wearily paid up a second time. "These are the things which wear away the gold of a traveller, as a stone is worn by the continual dropping of water." [34]

Horace Greeley, who visited Europe in 1851, suggested that the papal government might be able to attract far more visitors and considerably improve its financial position by abolishing the passport vexations along the road, encouraging the building of railroads and better stagecoach lines, forbidding private demands for services rendered, and then charging each stranger in Rome a flat sum for entrance and guidance through all the sights of the city. The visitor's money could thus be used for improvement of the country and maintenance of the archeological excavations, instead of being frittered away in endless petty extortion by government officials and private persons.[35]

Quarantines occasionally made for further inconvenience. They were sometimes imposed on tourists coming to Italy from foreign ports, and even within the country on those passing from one state to another. Elizabeth Seton and her dying husband, arriving in Leghorn in 1803, were forced to spend four weeks in the *lazzaretto*, because of an outbreak of yellow fever in New York. Though their rooms were somewhat improved by beds and curtains sent to them by friends, the prison was so cold that Mrs. Seton and her small daughter had to skip rope to keep warm.[36] A year following, Washington Irving spent nearly three weeks in quarantine at Messina. Though time hung heavily on his hands, he managed to pass the days reading and rowing about the harbor, listening to the sounds of the chanting of ships' crews coming across the water. The practice of quarantine, Irving felt, was a heavy tax on commerce and would cause American trade in the Mediterranean to decrease.[37] As another example, George Ticknor, together with some twenty compatriots, was confined for a fortnight in 1836 at the borders of the Papal States. Those in quarantine had to avoid all physical contact with new arrivals on pain of remaining for the full term of the newcomers. Their passports were handled with tongs and fumigated, and their money was dipped in vinegar. Sometimes the traveler had to show a recent bill of health before he was allowed to cross a frontier.[38]

Reports of highwaymen, too, aroused anxiety. There were alarming stories of robberies, especially along the road between Rome and Naples, through the Pontine Marshes, near Terracina, Fondi, and Gaeta, and on the road from Salerno to Paestum. After a certain point, every suspicious-looking individual on the road began to look unmistakably like a highwayman; and to the American a great many of the men along the road appeared suspicious.

Only a handful of Americans, however, encountered trouble with highwaymen. Joseph Green Cogswell, passing from Florence to Rome at the end of the first decade of the century, was stopped by a gang of brigands who ordered him out of his carriage, made him lie down in a woods, and took all his belongings except the clothes he was wearing. They failed to take his life only when he convinced them that he was an American and not a Frenchman. The criminals were later captured and executed.[39] Charles Butler, a founder of the Union Theological Seminary, who made a fortune in Chicago real estate, was stopped by bandits near Viterbo, but rescuers arrived just in time, and the outlaws fled.[40] Another American was said to have been kidnaped, along with the small orchestra of which he was a member, while returning to Rome from a visit to Monte Cassino. The group were taken by their captors to play at the wedding of the chief brigand's oldest daughter, and during a week's confinement, the American and a younger daughter fell in love and were married. He brought the girl back to Rome, where she died of typhoid fever shortly afterwards.[41] But one must imagine this story in technicolor! Earlier, in 1804, the American vessel on which Washington Irving was sailing from Genoa to Messina had been fired on and stopped by a privateer near the island of Elba. The ship was searched, but no money was found and only a few provisions, ship's supplies, clothing, and a watch were taken. Irving lost nothing whatsoever.[42]

A few travelers became involved with the Italian police, but by and large the Americans were a law-abiding group. Some complained about the close watch apparently kept on their activities by border guards, city police, and secret spies. The painter Thomas Cole, taking a walk in the Cascine at Florence one day, was almost run down by a mounted dragoon; in his anger, Cole broke his cane across the flank of the horse, and the following morning he was ordered to leave Tuscany. The intervention of friends, however, enabled him to remain.[43] When George Bancroft and some companions sailed down the coast to Amalfi and forgot to take along their passports, they were forced to spend two nights in a filthy prison until the matter could be straightened out.[44] In Rome, Dr. Samuel Gridley Howe, the educator and social reformer, got into a scuffle with a bullying soldier and was held under arrest in a military barracks for several hours until George Washington Greene, the American consul in Rome, could gain his release.[45] And a young law student, William C. Preston, later a senator from South Carolina and an opponent of Andrew Jackson, became involved in a fight with an officer at Portici near Naples after their carriage wheels had locked. Preston and his friends were obliged to stand for an inquiry, but they were borne off by the American consul before their trial began.[46] The happy issue of all these disputes seems to be almost as much a part of the pattern as the disputes themselves are.

Other hazards of travel were perhaps less important but more widespread. The emotions with which the traveler

approached the tangible relics of the past were sometimes
shattered by the shocking contrasts to the no less tangible
surroundings. He discovered that his imagination "glowing
with blue skies, and spring breezes, and ambrosial sweets,"
had played him false. "One cannot but laugh at his own
misconceptions, when the sober reality dissipates the delu-
sions with which poesy and romance have invested Italy." [47]
Long before his first Italian tour Ralph Waldo Emerson
had dreamed that he would "come suddenly in the midst
of an open country upon broken columns and fallen friezes,
and their solitude would be solemn and eloquent," but to
his dismay he discovered instead that the ruins were "carefully fenced round like orchards," and filled with "this
vermin of ciceroni and padroni." [48] Many things, reported
young Henry Wadsworth Longfellow, who was also disillusioned, "are not altogether so delightful in reality as
we sometimes fancy." [49]

On occasion, the American condemned contemporary
Italian life wholesale just because it intruded on the colorful
remnants of the past. "The Rome that *is* seemed but an
intruder," wrote one traveler, "as impertinent a thing within
these precincts as a street of work-shops would be among
the cypresses and yews of an ancient cemetery. I wished
it away." [50]

Not surprisingly, though, Italians did not like being
wished away. They objected to being considered mere
custodians of a national museum or actors in a vast theatrical spectacle, and they felt that foreign visitors who came
solely to enjoy the "picturesque" and look at the show were
missing the real Italy. They found somewhat ridiculous
those foreigners whose pictorial ideal seemed to be summed
up in the view of a country boy with a girl from Trastevere dancing on a gondola to the music of a shepherd
piper.

Finally, weariness with walking and viewing, with constant adjusting to new quarters, and with frequent change of scene was a common complaint. Even George Hillard, whose steps were followed by many an American visitor, noted in his journal: "I always breathe a sigh of relief when I have done the sights of a city." [51] Erastus Benedict, a New York admiralty lawyer and educator, who had gone to Italy for reasons of health, tiredly noted: "The view from [the Campanile at Venice] . . . is said to be — it must be — of great interest. I did not go up, I was always too weary." [52]

The business of travel thus involved many dimensions. In the process of moving about the country, the American travelers often complained about their food and lodgings, the tiresome bureaucratic procedures, and the countless demands for gratuities. Yet, all things considered, they commonly responded positively to their treatment and finally affirmed that the pleasures of coming to know the land far outweighed the petty annoyances of travel conditions.

⟦Some American writers reflected on the general significance of foreign travel; usually they concluded that the experience could be of value both to the individual and to his country. Travel abroad, it was suggested, could foster an increase in intelligence and a lessening of prejudices and could thus lead to greater personal maturity. An American's sensitivity to new impressions and his capacity for absorbing them could be sharpened through the impact of new experiences, and his understanding of his native culture and institutions could, in consequence, be counted on to deepen. Highly self-confident, these nineteenth-century Americans were sure that a trip abroad was bound to strengthen the mature American in his own "Republican virtues." Such a tour, moreover, could be a strong nationalizing force by engendering in the American affection for his country as a whole rather than just for his own locality.⟧

Even so, the traveler was warned of the hazards of visit-

ing the Old World. A young man, whose habits and principles had not yet been securely established, it was often
stressed, might not be able to withstand the impact of the
"enervating influences" of European life. There was fear,
as well, that corrupt morality might be brought back to
the United States, and that American delicacy in taste might
be blunted. An American must be thoroughly schooled in
his own system of government and the ways of his country before being allowed to venture abroad.

The value of an American staying away for a long period
of time from his native land was also questioned. Nathaniel
Hawthorne, for example, felt that the exile of Hiram
Powers, the sculptor, was particularly unfortunate because
he seemed so essentially "American" and was only living
in Italy for the convenience of finding workmen. (Powers
himself felt that he did not want to remain, but still he
stayed on.) [53] To Hawthorne, who himself had already been
abroad nearly five years, a life spent in exile did not make
for a satisfying existence. The expatriate, who did not com-
mit himself to one country or another, always deferred the
reality of life to a future moment, and eventually there were
no future moments; returning to his native land, the expatriate found that life had shifted its reality to the other "temporary" country. "So between two stools we come to the
ground, and make ourselves a part of one or the other country only by laying our bones in its soil." [54]

By midcentury travel conditions were changing mark-
edly. Railroad construction began on a substantial scale in
Italy during the decade of the 1850's. The liberal govern-
ment of the Kingdom of Sardinia first encouraged railroads;
the Papal States and the Kingdom of Naples and the Two
Sicilies trailed behind. By 1851, Venice was connected to
Verona, and a portion of a line running eastward from
Milan was completed. Florence had been joined to Leghorn

shortly before, and a line from Turin to Genoa was soon begun. A line connecting Rome with its port, Civitavecchia, was finished in 1859, but Rome was not joined to Florence until the middle of the next decade.

The introduction of railways within the peninsula and the joining of Italy by rail to the countries of western and northern Europe had a significant influence on the nature of Italian travel, as well as on the meaning of Italy to the foreign visitor. Instead of a continuous unfolding of the Italian scene, a gradual transition from the peculiarities of one section to those of another, travel in Italy revealed itself increasingly as a series of stops — visits, for example, to Florence, Rome, Naples, and Venice, and nothing more. As travel became easier, acquaintance with the country, paradoxically, became less complete. American visitors who had been fortunate enough to make the pilgrimage to Italy relatively as pioneers, before the coming of the railroads, had spent considerable time in each place before moving on, and they had come to know each locale with something of an insider's knowledge. With the changes in transportation the old leisurely pace began to disappear. A visitor who had limited time and money could now afford to make the "complete" tour of Italy without entering half so completely into the life of her inhabitants as the traveler had done earlier; usually he had time only for what he already knew about. No longer did he experience the same sense of excitement or of personal discovery that was common to the earlier visitors.

CHAPTER III

THE ITALIAN SCENE

T HE GRAND TOUR of the eighteenth century had included certain customary patterns of movement, determined by the location of long-established routes and the principal cities as well as by current fashions. The eighteenth-century visitor generally felt little or no interest in natural scenery and largely confined his observations to a few cities. He went to the localities that men had long been going to, places with the art and society that appealed to him. The eighteenth-century routes set the fashion for visitors in the following century.

The serious traveler of the first part of the nineteenth century commonly came into Italy for the winter months, spending the late autumn in Florence and the Christmas season in Rome, going on to Naples for the late winter, and returning to Rome for the Holy Week observances in the spring. Later, perhaps, he would go on to Venice and the north. Not until the second half of the century did the tourist deviate significantly from the old travel patterns.

A person entering Italy over the Alpine barrier from France usually crossed the pass at Mount Cenis. If he chose this route, or if he came by way of Switzerland or Austria, to some extent he had already been prepared for Italy by what he had encountered in the countries to the north. He had already seen his share of picturesque scenery, quaint buildings, and colorful costumes; he had become acquainted with Roman Catholic ceremonies; he had been initiated into unfamiliar customs and had come to know strange foods and drinks; and he had been able to inspect some of the old masters. For an American so "initiated," Italy was bound to lose some of her spectacular impact.

The Mount Cenis road was the most direct route from Paris to Italy, leading through Lyons and Chambery, then across the pass, and down to Susa and Turin. In the previous century it had been necessary to dismantle carriages and transport them piecemeal on mules across the mountains. But the road had been sufficiently improved by Napoleon during the first decade of the nineteenth century so that horses, aided by an extra team of mules, could draw coaches up the steep road. To negotiate the pass in winter, the wheels might be removed from the coach, and runners put on like a sleigh. The sculptor Horatio Greenough, going into France from Italy on this route in 1831, was overwhelmed by the savage cruelty of the craggy landscape, so different from anything he had known in New England.[1] For Charles Brooks, a Bostonian who crossed the pass in 1842, "the sublimity of these scenes surpasse[d] all description." [2]

The visitor could also enter Italy over the Simplon Pass, leading from Geneva to Milan by way of Domodossola and Lake Maggiore. In that case he would travel along another new road that Napoleon had constructed. Young George Ticknor, journeying southward from Germany in 1817, used this route, first climbing to the summit of the St. Bernard Pass to visit the famous monastery, and then crossing on the new Simplon Road. Like many others he was struck by the immediate change in the natural scene, the crops, and the architecture, as soon as he began to descend into Italy.[3]

Leaving the peninsula on his way to northern Europe, the American was most likely to cross the Alps by way of the relatively low Brenner Pass into Austria and Germany. Venice, Verona, Trento, and Bolzano lay directly on this route, and past the Brenner, the traveler could proceed easily to Innsbruck and Munich. The Great St. Bernard, the Splügen, and the St. Gotthard passes were less often used.

If he came by sea, the visitor might disembark at one of a dozen ports — Genoa, Leghorn, Civitavecchia, Naples, Palermo, Messina, Syracuse, Brindisi, Bari, or Venice. Especially during the early years of the century a large number of Americans journeyed directly from the United States by ship. Small trading vessels, sailing from New England harbors, often carried a few passengers; after putting in at Gibraltar, these freighters went to Malta, or to one of the ports of Sicily or the Italian mainland to pick up a cargo of fruit or wine. By the mid-1850's it was said that more than three hundred American vessels were landing in the Kingdom of the Two Sicilies each year.[4] Americans coming directly this way were thus plunged at once into the life of the country without the preparation of first seeing other less exotic lands. After midcentury, the American visitor to the Continent customarily landed in northern Europe and moved southward, then journeyed back again to a northern European port to embark for the United States.

One of the most common routes of entry was by ship from Marseilles or Nice to Genoa. Small *feluccas*, or coasting vessels, moved close along the shore, putting into land at night. The accommodations in the small coastal inns were wretched, though usually the discomforts of bed and board were minor compared with the inevitable seasickness. It took Washington Irving four days to go this way from

Nice to Genoa in 1804. One day strong winds forced his *felucca* to turn back, and on another the vessel was fired on by a privateer.[5]

Frequently the traveler concentrated on coastal transport within Italy, making side trips inland to important cities. This was often faster and easier than carriage travel along the principal roads; some preferred this means of transport because it seemed safer. Since the road between Genoa and Florence along the coast was especially bad, the tourist commonly sailed from Genoa to Leghorn and then moved by carriage through Pisa, and sometimes Lucca, to the Tuscan capital. From Florence he could go to Rome by way of the ports of Leghorn and Civitavecchia. The latter town was particularly unpleasant because of the gross extortions levied on those passing through. Usually the tourist went from Rome to Naples by land. Beyond Paestum, south of Naples, he almost never ventured; the route to Sicily was by sea. The American did not visit the island of Sardinia.

Genoa, the principal seaport of the Kingdom of Sardinia, always made a strong impression, especially since for one coming from France by ship this was his first Italian city, and it was important to the American emotionally because of its associations with Columbus. The first view of the city, rising abruptly behind the waters of the harbor, seemed to justify the epithet by which the city was widely known — "the Superb."

During the few days he spent in Genoa, the newcomer established a formidable sight-seeing schedule, far more intensive than the itinerary he followed later when the novelty of things Italian had begun to wear off. The steep, dark, twisted alleys bewildered him; the buildings were so high and the streets so narrow that even in the middle of the day the visitor almost needed a lantern to find his way. The noise, too, amazed him, as did the colorful crowd of priests, soldiers, beggars, and women in their distinctive local dress. The inhabitants, he quickly discovered, were noted for their sharp dealings, and if this was his first experience with the country these "Yankees of Italy" probably helped form his responses to the Italian people as a whole. Sometimes the dialect of the Genoese unexpectedly jarred, for the American had anticipated that his book-Italian would carry him along. Horatio Greenough arriving in Genoa thought the local speech the worst jargon he had ever heard; he was thankful that some of the servants spoke bad Tuscan — "otherwise one might have to starve." [6]

In Genoa, American visitors often called on the Marchese di Negro, who, though a member of an old and noble family, was noted for his marked republican feelings and his love for the United States. His house was open to callers one day each week, and in his garden stood a bust familiar to the Americans, with the inscription "Alla Memoria di Washington." Many Americans carried away pleasant memories of the Italian's hospitality.

The Genoese houses and palaces occupied much of the sight-seer's time. Though impressed, the American felt that the elaborately frescoed walls, the tessellated marble floors, and the lush gardens failed to outweigh the obvious discomforts of the dwellings. It was hard to imagine how people could actually live in such museums. He also visited the great churches, the university, Byron's house, and the reputed birthplace of Columbus, and as elsewhere he spent much of his time inspecting hospitals, orphanages, poorhouses, and insane asylums. Sometimes he lingered beside the harbor. James Fenimore Cooper so enjoyed the sounds and smells and the hum of commerce in the harbor, reminding him of his early seagoing days, that he was tempted to remain in Genoa for a full summer.[7] Most Americans quickly moved on, however, for their goals were elsewhere.

To the northwest of Genoa, a short distance from the foot of the Alps, was Turin, the first Italian city to greet travelers on the land route from France. Turin hardly ever failed to delight the American, whether it was his first or his last stop in Italy. The city's regular plan, different from that of most Italian communities, gave it a surprising charm and reminded him of Philadelphia and other cities at home. The streets and buildings were remarkably clean, the city itself unusually livable, the people fashionable and prosperous, and relatively few priests and beggars were to be seen. But since he found little of historic or artistic interest in Turin, the visitor remained but a short time.

Milan detained him longer, though his goals, it must be remembered, were almost always to the south. John Griscom, a professor of chemistry and natural philosophy in the New York Institution, pronounced Milan the handsomest city he had yet seen in Europe; he was especially struck by the clean, white appearance of the houses, the wide, elegant avenues, and the careful method of paving the streets with small pebbles and two rows of flat stones in the center for carriage wheels.[8] Milan was a city of architecture, and her buildings, probably more than anything else, impressed the American. Although tourists did not always go to the hospitals, the prison, and the mint as Griscom did, they did visit the Ambrosian Library, La Scala Theater, the Brera Gallery, the Certosa at neighboring Pavia, the Napoleonic Arch, Santa Maria delle Grazie (with the badly damaged "Last Supper"), and, above all, the cathedral.

Second in size only to St. Peter's among Italian churches, the Gothic cathedral of Milan, with its thousands of statues, its delicate tracery, and its magnificent view, seemed to the American one of the memorable attractions of all Italy. The lavishly decorated glass tomb in the crypt, in which the body of St. Carlo Borromeo was exhibited, elicited astonished praises from a few visitors but deprecating condemnation from most, who were revolted by the waste of money and the macabre display. The sacred character of the cathedral, too, was occasionally tarnished for a traveler when he discovered a pickpocket trying to make off with his handkerchief.

In Milan, also, a few visitors sought out Alexander Manzoni, Italy's most popular novelist of the first half of the century. When George Ticknor called on Manzoni in 1836 and 1837, he was struck by the Italian's simple and retiring habits, his frank opinions, sensitive disposition, and liberal political views, and his sincere Catholicism. To Ticknor, Manzoni expressed fears that attempts to introduce new liberal institutions might terminate in an even heavier despotism and that the turning from religion might end in the clergy gaining new and dangerous power. He spoke ardently of the need for abolition in the United States, and felt that America must work to ensure emancipation.[9] Catharine Maria Sedgwick, the novelist, called on Manzoni in 1839, and, like Ticknor, she was cordially received into the bosom of the family; Manzoni expressed gratitude to her for the treatment that Italian exiles had been given in the United States.[10] After Margaret Fuller had had a long conversation with Manzoni in 1847, she thought she would return for another visit, for the Italian had seemed so much to enjoy talking with her.[11]

On his way to Florence, the tourist usually stopped at Leghorn, but the town, bustling and modern, had little of interest beyond the Jewish synagogue and the Protestant cemetery, where Tobias Smollett was buried. The hotels were bad, and a delay here always proved tedious. Leghorn, in fact, had a poor tourist reputation. Not far away was Pisa, already well known to the American but also "a dull town," which had lost most of its former grandeur, its buildings and monuments merely recalling its "bygone importance, and its present insignificance." [12] The broad streets of Pisa were noble but silent and deserted, and the town appeared wholly lifeless. The cathedral, baptistry, leaning tower, and cemetery detained the visitor only a few hours. Occasionally he also stopped for a short time in Lucca, not far away, and Bagni di Lucca, in the mountains to the north, was a favorite resort for the American residents of Rome and Florence during the hot summer months.

Along with Rome and Naples, Florence was one of the most important Italian cities for the American traveler, and for the American expatriate it stood next to Rome in popularity. Above all, the city meant the great painting, sculpture, and architecture of the Renaissance. Here the visitor found not only masterpieces of art, but also abundant facilities for work in painting and sculpture. More than any other place Florence signified art.

Although the climate of Florence was severe — hot and humid during the summer, and cold and damp during the winter — and its society aloof, the many attractions of the city far overshadowed these drawbacks and drew enthusiastic visitors. The world-famous Uffizi, Academy, and Pitti Palace galleries, the many historic churches, the great public buildings, the pleasant drives and excursions in the environs, the atmosphere of art, and the colony of resident Americans all served to draw foreign visitors for long stays.

Florence was enjoyable, too, for other reasons. Some of the aspects of Italian life that disturbed tourists elsewhere, such as the desperate poverty and the consequent importunities of beggars, or the presence of great numbers of priests, were less evident here. Busy and intellectual, the city often reminded Americans of Boston. The Florentines themselves were physically attractive and unusually agreeable. The medieval quality of Florence was appealing also:

James Russell Lowell, for example, felt himself strongly drawn by the remnants of the Christian Middle Ages with which the city was filled.[13] All in all, it was a stimulating place both to visit and to live in. Nathaniel Hawthorne, who spent his days in Florence writing at his desk and then sight-seeing in the neighborhood, expressed a common response when he wrote: "I hardly think there can be a place in the world where life is more delicious for its own simple sake than here." [14]

Florence had another important advantage: it was cheap. The Coopers in 1829 found it the least expensive place they had yet lived in while in Europe.[15] Though the prices of food, clothing, and services were far below those in the United States, there were other expenses, for it was considered essential that the fashionable visitor keep a box at the opera and a private carriage.

Then there was the court of Tuscany, which added considerably to the brilliance of this cosmopolitan city. James Fenimore Cooper twice saw the Tuscan ruler, Grand Duke Leopold II (1824–1859), during his visit in Florence. At a reception the monarch singled Cooper out to ask him about the number and size of American towns, the habits of the people, and the general conditions of the country, and also reported that he had heard Cooper's books well spoken of. Cooper was struck by the ruler's integrity and solid geographical knowledge and felt that he had been treated with unusual distinction principally on account of his country. Before he left Florence, the novelist enjoyed a private audience with the monarch, and they again spoke of the United States, the grand duke expressing his great esteem for George Washington and his awareness of the difficulties that Americans had faced during the Revolution.[16] To Edward Everett, who was given an audience in 1840, the grand duke offered the use of the public archives, ordinarily closed.[17]

George Ticknor, who probably met more important people on his tours of Italy than did any other American of his period, visited the hospitable Leopold II both in 1836 and in 1856. On his first visit, bearing a letter of introduction from Prince John of Saxony, a Dante scholar, Ticknor found the sovereign shy and lacking in firmness, but well-meaning, eagerly curious, and "greedy of matter-of-fact knowledge." Indeed, during their discussions of the manners, way of life, and income of the Americans, the grand duke took notes "and wrote as diligently as a German student at a lecture." The monarch expressed pain at the corruption of domestic relations in Italy and regret at the decline of the great fortunes of the Italian nobility. On Ticknor's visit twenty years later, when he was again well received, he reported that the ruler continued to maintain a spotless personal life, as well as a lively interest in the United States.[18]

Seeing the sights naturally occupied much of the stranger's time in the city of flowers. He wandered each day through the vast rooms and echoing halls of the great private palaces and public galleries and libraries. Occasionally he was disappointed with the art works, but more often he was not, and he returned again and again, frequently spending hours contemplating one or two pictures or statues. One particular institution, the Museum of Natural History, exerted a curious fascination; the visitor invariably commented on the exhibits of wax sections of the human body and the frighteningly graphic models showing the ravages of the plague. He studied the paintings, frescoes, and statuary of the Florentine churches. Sometimes these edifices were disappointing, for they lacked the unity of style that the American had found in the Gothic structures of northern Europe, and they often appeared cluttered with too many pieces of brightly colored marble and tin-crowned, fully-clothed Virgins. Like the Borromeo tomb in the cathedral of Milan, the Medici tombs in the Florentine church of San Lorenzo favorably impressed some Americans by their richness and disgusted others by their ostentatiousness. Then there were the gardens and the parks. Along with the British residents and the local nobility, the American paraded around the Cascine in a rented carriage, and he made excursions to the monastery at Vallombrosa, the shrine of St. Francis at La Verna, the house of Boccaccio at Certaldo, the great Medici country villas, and, most frequently, the hillside village of Fiesole.

The nucleus around which American society revolved in Florence was the sculptor Hiram Powers, who had come in 1837 to study his craft and have several busts carved into marble. He remained for the rest of his life. Practically every important American visitor who came to the Tuscan city during the middle years of the century visited Powers' studio, "a curious, rambling old place, with lofty, spacious rooms succeeding each other, and dark passages leading to remote portions of the structure." [19] Gregarious by temperament, Powers moved easily in society, though not necessarily in the most fashionable circles. He welcomed visiting Americans to his home each Wednesday evening, where they were entertained by "conversation interspersed with music or an occasional recitation, and refreshed by tea and cakes." [20] Hawthorne and other visitors found Powers' conversation highly interesting, though his manner tended to be ponderous and his thought provincial. Many Americans apparently considered Powers a sort of national representative in Florence, and he was often requested to take care of duties that an American official ordinarily would have attended to — shipping to the United States the bodies of Americans who had died in Florence, arranging for burials, finding living quarters and servants for newcomers, storing in his own house the goods and personal possessions of others. Although he spent the greater part of his creative life in Florence, he and his family participated little in Italian affairs, and they lost none of their feelings of attachment to the United States. To Hawthorne, they somehow seemed "hermetically sealed in a foreign substance" with which they could not even begin to become assimilated.[21]

The sculptor Horatio Greenough and his family provided Americans with another gathering place in Florence. Greenough had settled in Florence in 1828, and spent most of his life there until 1850, the year before his death. The artists Joseph Mozier and John Gadsby Chapman also regularly entertained American visitors. Since the group from the United States was relatively small, new arrivals soon became widely acquainted and caught up in the local entertainment of gossip.

Then, of course, there was Casa Guidi, the residence of Robert and Elizabeth Browning, whose acquaintances included the famous from two continents. The Brownings had arrived in Florence in 1847, and the city remained their permanent home until Mrs. Browning's death in 1861. George William Curtis, George Hillard, William Ware, Caroline Kirkland, the Storys, Christopher Cranch, Margaret Fuller, Harriet Beecher Stowe, William Cullen Bryant, the Hawthornes, the Greenoughs, Kate Field, James Jackson Jarves, Charles Eliot Norton — sooner or later, they all came to pay their respects. Other Americans found the Brownings in London or in Rome, where they occasionally lived during the winter months. In Rome, they were visited by William Page, Harriet Hosmer, Charlotte Cushman, John Lothrop Motley, Charles C. Perkins, Benjamin Paul Akers, and Theodore Parker.[22]

Americans who called on them in Casa Guidi, close to the Pitti Palace, were invariably impressed by Browning's warmth and his apparently uncomplicated, outgoing person-

ality, so markedly in contrast with his delicate wife's reserved and inward ways. The Brownings entertained simply
and quietly, but occasionally the visitor would be treated
to a performance of Mrs. Browning's hobbyhorse, a séance.
Hiram Powers, James Jackson Jarves, William Page, and
the Storys were all fascinated by the possibility of com-
municating with the dead, though Browning himself
thought spiritualism distasteful and absurd, and Hawthorne, who of all people might be expected to display every
symptom of interest, found the subject merely disagreeable.
Mrs. Powers had experienced several remarkable ectoplas-
mic manifestations: once she had felt in her lap the head of
one of her dead children, whom she had recognized by
touching the hair and features.[23]

Grouped around the Brownings in Florence were other
English expatriates and visitors: the novel-producing Trol-
lope family; Isa Blagden, a center of the Anglo-Florentine
group, and the Brownings' confidante; Seymour Kirkup,
settled in the midst of old furniture, pictures, and dusty volumes on magic and occult lore, engaged in his researches,
like something out of a medieval romance; and Walter Savage Landor, elderly and crotchety, but possessed of great
courtly charm.[24]

Landor left a particularly sharp impression on those who
met him. When Emerson visited Florence in 1833, he was
introduced to Landor by Horatio Greenough. Emerson
found the English writer happily established with his family in a large villa filled with pictures.[25] Landor had come
to Italy in 1815, and in 1829 he had settled at Fiesole, close
to Florence, but in 1835 he left his wife and children and returned to England, where he remained for more than
twenty years. A lawsuit forced him out of England, and he
returned to his family, who soon found life with the eccentric paterfamilias unbearable. In the meantime, Landor had

transferred all his property to his eldest son, so that when in 1859 his family turned him out, like "King Lear," he was left penniless. The Storys, vacationing at Siena that summer, took him in and found him delightful and amusing. Later the Brownings took care of him. To young and vivacious Kate Field, who had come to Florence to study singing but turned to journalism and wrote a lively series of articles on Florentine society, Landor was unreservedly attentive.[26]

The Florentine whom more Americans knew better than any other was Marchese Gino Capponi, historian of Florence, prime minister of Tuscany for a brief period under the constitution of 1848, and, after 1860, senator of Italy. Edward Everett, following his defeat for a fifth term as governor of Massachusetts, visited Capponi in Florence during the winter of 1840–1841, and, for a time served as an intermediary between Capponi and William Hickling Prescott, the American historian, who like Capponi was working under the handicap of blindness and who was interested in having Capponi translate one of his works. Several years before as professor at Harvard and editor of the *North American Review*, Everett had initiated an exchange of his magazine with the *Antologia*, which Capponi had founded.[27] George Ticknor became acquainted with Capponi on his visit in 1836, and saw the Italian often when he returned to Florence twenty years later; although totally blind, Capponi impressed Ticknor in 1856 as still possessing the spirit, courage, and vast knowledge that he had when Ticknor first knew him.[28] Horatio Greenough, in a gesture of respect, modeled a bust of the Italian statesman in 1840, and the following year received a commission from Capponi for a miniature copy of a bust of Washington as a gift for his daughter.[29]

Moving south from Florence, the traveler had the choice

of two land routes to Rome. He could journey along the more direct western road by way of Poggibonsi, Siena, Acquapendente, and Viterbo, taking about five days, or, spending a day or two longer, he could move southward through Arezzo, Perugia, Spoleto, and Terni. The shorter of these two routes was considered the less interesting, and the traveler generally selected the other, to the east, which passed through more attractive countryside, brought him to more historic places, and increased the pleasure of anticipation.

South of Siena — whose cathedral, one American felt, had "a whimsical, linsey-woolsey appearance" [30] — the western highway passed through an almost deserted countryside. The inns were notoriously bad, especially the one at the wretched village of Radicofani, which stood high on a dominating hill and looked like a great ruin itself, but, unfortunately, everyone had to stop there for a night. The limbs of executed criminals suspended along the roadside added to the excitement of this route.

The eastern road led through the richly cultivated valley of the Arno to Arezzo, where the tourist visited Petrarch's birthplace. To the south, the highway passed beside Lake Trasimeno, and each visitor with the help of his guidebook recalled schoolday memories of Hannibal's defeat of the Roman forces. Then, soon after, up the long, steep hill to medieval Perugia, with its dark twisted streets and magnificent prospect over the plains below. Sometimes the tourist made a side trip to Assisi and a visit to the Basilica of St. Francis; usually there was not enough time. Hawthorne did stop at Assisi on his way north from Rome to Florence, and the place seemed to him like a "fossilized city, — so old and singular it is, without enough life and juiciness in it to be susceptible of decay." [31] Foligno had a few churches of historic interest, and was customarily chosen as a stop for the night. Then on through the classic Valley of Clitumnus to Spoleto and Terni, where a visit was made to the celebrated falls, which looked puny, the traveler thought, compared to Niagara. The rest of the road lay through Narni and Civita Castellana, with Mount Soracte dominating the horizon, and finally across the Campagna on the Flaminian Way, entering Rome at the Porta del Popolo.

A few miles from Rome the traveler caught his first glimpse of the dome of St. Peter's, and this sight generally aroused an emotional outpouring, not unlike the expressions of some visitors as they caught their first view of Italy herself. The American had been emotionally and intellectually prepared for Italy long before, and the land meant much to him even before he visited it. Now, with the first sight of the heart of Italy and the capital of the ancient Roman Empire, he could scarcely restrain himself. Approaching Rome at the end of the 1820's, a young army lieutenant, John Farley, for one, "could not help feeling a flow of supernatural enthusiasm." His soul, he recalled, "was on the wing," and he felt already as if he were "imbued with the spirit of past ages." [32]

Other Americans, coming from the port of Civitavecchia, caught their first view of Rome from the west. From this direction the approach was especially tantalizing, for the dome of St. Peter's was in view hours before the traveler actually reached the city gates. Others arrived from the south, coming by carriage from Naples. Fenimore Cooper believed that the southern approach was the finest, since from this direction the visitor came immediately upon the heart of the ancient city. "My head became confused," he wrote of his arrival in Rome, "and I sat stupid as a country-man who first visits town, perplexed with the whirl of sensations and the multiplicity of the objects." [33]

Accommodations were not always easy to find. Especially during Holy Week, the city was crowded with foreigners, and the newcomer was often turned away from several of the major hotels before he found a bed for the night. During the first few days, the traveler who planned to remain some time looked for permanent lodgings, a tedious process that involved climbing hundreds of steps in the search for apartments that were clean, comfortably furnished, and not too cold. As soon as he was settled, he began to explore the city.

||Although Rome did not always live up to the American's expectations, it had much to offer, and with almost no exceptions he found it highly interesting and emotionally meaningful. Rome was the goal of his travels in Italy. Here were the classical sites he already knew and the many associations with antiquity. Here he found best displayed the Church ceremonies that fascinated him. Here, as in Florence, he became involved in the world of art, and here he found an established society of his countrymen to ease his way and share his pleasures.||

As today, Rome in the first half of the nineteenth century swarmed with English-speaking people, including many Americans. At certain tearooms, cafés, bookshops, and banks, near the Piazza di Spagna, the American was sure to meet some of his fellow countrymen. The English, nonetheless, so dominated the foreign society of the city that all foreigners regardless of nationality were known to the Italians as *Inglesi*.

The contrasts of Rome amazed the stranger. Many features of Italian life seemed intensified, and the resulting mixture not only astonished but often annoyed him. Wealth and poverty everywhere rubbed shoulders. Ragged beggars plied their trade directly before the great portals of princely palaces, and peasants from the countryside, emaciated and apparently starving, rushed to open the doors of a cardinal's coach. A stable or a carpenter's shop frequently occupied the street level of an aristocratic mansion. A fishmonger's stall lay in the shadow of a splendid church, while nearby a tall obelisk, already old when Rome was young, still stood among collapsed arches and broken columns. The narrow streets were often dreary and ugly, and the smells, impossible. Above all, the city made an impression of dirtiness, so unexpected and seemingly unbecoming for the capital of the ancient world. Particularly among the ruins ladies had to hold up their skirts and carefully watch their step because of the human excrement on the ground.

Enough palaces were open to the public to fill many days of sight-seeing. The Borghese Palace and Villa and the Doria Pamphili and Corsini palaces housed some of the major art collections of Rome, although the Vatican contained the greatest. The Vatican galleries were immense, and most visitors found themselves, like Herman Melville on his initial visit, "fagged out completely" after just a cursory inspection. Often the tourist went to the sculpture galleries at night to see the statuary take on new life under torchlight. The Colonna Palace had the most ornate hall of the city, while the Quirinale, then the papal residence, had the most attractive gardens. At the home of the Rospigliosi family the visitor saw Guido Reni's "Aurora," and at the Ludovisi, the "Aurora" of Guercino. He marveled at the ancient statue of Pompey in the Spada Palace, but never noticed the seventeenth-century Borromini perspective there. The gloomy Cenci Palace appealed to him because of the family's bloody history, and the Barberini Palace because the supposed portrait of Beatrice Cenci hung there. Sometimes he visited the Farnesina, the Farnese, and the Sciarra palaces. He was astonished at the size and lavish decorations of the rooms, at the lack of domestic comforts in the midst of this often shabby splendor, and at the practice of letting out some of the floors for studios, shops, or apartments, all of which had access to the frequently filthy grand staircase.

St. Peter's was like a magnet, drawing the newcomer again and again, impressing him more than any other place in the city. He was often disappointed by the façade and by his first view of the interior; the façade appeared cluttered, prevented the dome from being seen in the square below, and looked more appropriate for a private palace than for a great Christian church, while the interior was so perfectly proportioned that on first entering one had no real conception of the immense size. The response to St. Peter's was, of course, an example of the common attitude, handed down through guidebook and travel writings; even those few who were not disappointed with their first sight of the church usually apologized for differing from what was apparently expected of them. Almost invariably the American expressed disgust at the bronze statue of St. Peter, with the toe worn away by countless kissings and rubbings. He commented on the atmosphere inside the building and the way sounds were deadened. He was delighted with the great baldachin over the main altar and with the view from the lantern, and, without fail, he squeezed up into the copper ball at the very top. Sometimes he likened the church to Niagara Falls, as something to defy description.

Other churches drew the American, too, but usually only for a single visit on the rounds of the customary itinerary. At the church of San Pietro in Vincoli, he marveled at Michelangelo's "Moses." At Santa Maria della Pace and in Sant'Agostino, he sought out and expressed a stock admiration for the Raphael frescoes. At Santo Stefano Rotondo, he was shocked by the frescoes detailing the martyrdom of the saints. He considered himself daring and adventurous to cross the Tiber to the proletarian section of Trastevere in order to visit Santa Maria in Trastevere and Santa Cecilia. When he looked into the ornate baroque interiors of Il Gesù and Sant'Ignazio, he came away confused or disgusted.

The ruins of the antique structures in the city by and large disappointed him. Surrounded by commonplace modern buildings, often dirtied with human filth, and draped by sheets and clothing hung to dry, the ruins did not look at all as imagination and prints and engravings had led him to expect. Many were not happily placed for effect upon the eye or mind. They did not stand apart in solitary grandeur, "a shrine for memory." On the contrary, they were often in unfavorable positions, in "the shadow of disenchanting proximities," and inadequately detached from "the debasing associations of actual life." Cattle brought to the city for slaughter grazed in the Forum, the "pert villa of an English gentleman" intruded itself into the palace of the Caesars, and the temple of Antoninus Pius had been turned into a customhouse.[34]

The ruins were vast and often difficult to reconstruct imaginatively, for most were not well preserved. Even to begin to understand the remains, the stranger had to study them carefully, as did George Ticknor, who hired an archaeologist to accompany him and explain them. The Roman Forum was particularly confusing. Systematic excavations begun early in the nineteenth century, had not been continued, and the Forum was still used as a cow pasture and cattle market. The half-excavated ruins looked even less picturesque than those fallen buildings that had remained untouched by modern investigators and restorers. For the moralist, the glorious architectural triumphs of the past only accentuated all the more the feebleness and decay of the present.

A few of the ancient structures were in better condition. The Pantheon had been made into a Christian church, and here the sight-seer could linger at the tomb of his favorite painter, Raphael. The Colosseum, too, had retained its ancient outlines, so that despite the ravages of time and the plunders of the noble families of Rome, the visitor from the New World could still get a good idea of its former appearance. Customarily, the American made an excursion to the Colosseum by moonlight, which, because of the dangers of the night air and the possible presence of footpads, was considered a daring expedition. The adventurers echoed Byron's raptures, peopled the arena with shouting Romans glorying in bloodshed, and repeated the classic witticism that the place would certainly be a fine building when it was finished.

Society in Rome had a decidedly international tone and was more accessible than that of Florence or the other leading cities. When the stranger joined Italian families or foreign diplomats for a social occasion, he discovered that dinner was seldom served and that he had been invited instead for an evening of "conversation," with card games and music as additional diversions. The short-term visitor, as well as the expatriate, nevertheless, generally sought his diversion with his own countrymen. Resident artists formed the core of the social groups the Americans came to know well.

The leading American in Rome during much of the nineteenth century was the versatile William Wetmore Story. On the death of his father, Judge Joseph Story, Supreme Court justice and founder of the Harvard Law School, prominent Bostonians commissioned a monument for his grave, and it was decided that Justice Story's son, then a promising young lawyer with artistic inclinations, should undertake the work. So William Story went to Italy in 1847 to study sculpture, and he soon completed the monument.

Returning to New England, he decided that life there did not offer him the fulfillment that Italy could give. As a consequence, despite the objections of his friends and his family, he severed his New England roots, cut off his promising legal career, and in 1856 on his third return settled permanently in Rome. Story continued to devote himself to sculpture, and some of his works, such as the "Cleopatra" and the "Libyan Sibyl," were widely praised by his countrymen. He also engaged in many other activities: he painted, composed poetry, and made scholarly investigations into the history of ancient Rome and the modern city, compiling the best English-language work on modern Roman folklore and customs, *Roba di Roma*. His apartment in the Palazzo Barberini, like Powers' house in Florence, was a center for visiting Americans, though unlike Powers, he participated as much in Italian as in American society. Story's home, in fact, became a neutral ground after 1870, where Romans of differing political persuasions and where Protestants as well as Catholics could meet for friendly intercourse. His manifold talents were widely admired, and with adequate wealth and a large happy family he seemed to have all that a man could want, but he spread these accomplishments thin and — now almost forgotten — failed to achieve much that was lasting.

Other American homes in Rome also drew visitors. In her apartment near the top of the Spanish Steps, Charlotte Cushman, the dynamic actress, regularly entertained, though she complained of the rapid turnover of the American colony and the consequent dangers of becoming involved with adventurers. Later, at the end of the 1860's, the home of the painter William Stanley Haseltine became another nucleus of social life: here G. P. A. Healy, Longfellow, Bancroft, Charles Francis Adams, and Frederick Crowninshield, later director of the new American Academy in Rome, might sometimes be seen. Even Margaret Fuller, living frugally in Rome, received her friends each Monday evening.

Most visiting Americans found this cosmopolitan society in the midst of the evocative remains of antiquity exceptionally stimulating, and the talk largely centered on art. The long-time residents, however, felt a need for greater permanence in their contacts. Story despaired when Browning left Italy after his wife's death, for with Browning gone he felt that he did not have a single intimate friend with whom he could speak freely and sympathize fully.[35]

Many Americans became acquainted with the several members of the Bonaparte family who resided in Rome and Florence. George Ticknor, for one, was so well received at the Roman household of Lucien Bonaparte, a brother of Napoleon, that he felt he knew this family better than any other in Europe.[36] Lucien revealed to Edward Everett that he himself wanted to emigrate to the United States and that in honor of the country he had even composed an ode about America.[37] The most interesting member of the Bonaparte family, though, was Pauline, the Princess Borghese, sister of Napoleon and considered one of the most beautiful women of her day. Antonio Canova had portrayed her life-size in marble as a nude reclining Venus, a fact that lowered her reputation for some and apparently raised it for others. George Ticknor, Edward Everett, Joseph Green Cogswell, and Edward Brooks, visiting Rome in 1818, came to see Pauline, who impressed Ticknor as a "most consummate coquette." [38] When young George Bancroft first called on her in 1821, she received him in her private room, showed him her jewel collection, and expressed a desire to see him often. Needless to say, he returned.[39] Her husband, Prince Borghese, maintained a separate establishment in Florence, regularly receiving any stranger who chose to call.

The visitor from the United States realized that his emotional responses to the city of Rome had been experienced and described countless times before, yet the place usually meant more to him than any other he had ever visited. He believed that, compared to Rome, most American cities were dry and meager and that civic life in such places did not have the fullness possible in the Italian city. Emerson, on his first trip in 1833, looking without success (as usual) for the modern man worthy to walk the streets of Rome, was greatly impressed: "It is a grand town, & works mightily upon the senses & upon the soul. It fashions my dreams even, & all night I visit Vaticans." [40] Hawthorne, who at first had hated Rome, eventually felt that "no place ever took so strong a hold of [his] being as Rome, nor ever seemed so close . . . and so strangely familiar." [41] Mrs. Hawthorne, too, was moved by the city: "I can now understand the irresistible attraction it has to those who return a second time, and how it must become a sort of necessity of the soul to live here — either to remain or constantly to return." [42] The picturesque character of the city was a perpetual stimulus to the senses, though some people felt that the atmosphere was too exciting and could be too diverting, that there was something almost poisonous in the air capable of stifling individual effort and creativity.

From Rome the American traveler commonly moved south to Naples by carriage, taking four or five days for the trip, and passing through Terracina, Fondi, Mola, Gaeta, and Capua, along a road dotted with associations from antiquity. Because of the malarial air in the Pontine Marshes and occasional robberies in the region of Terracina, this route was considered dangerous; sometimes the carriages went in caravans or with a military escort.

The tourist customarily spent several weeks in Naples during the heart of winter. The surrounding area teemed with classical associations, and the contrasts and variety of the city — the largest in Italy — offered constant entertainment as well as the opportunity for moral instruction. The situation of Naples was most attractive: the sparkling waters of the bay provided a beautiful foreground to the stage setting of elegant palaces, ornate theaters, and monumental churches, with castellated hills and Mount Vesuvius as a backdrop. The mild climate invigorated the tired traveler, and he gloried in the midwinter flowers and the orange and lemon trees weighed down with ripe fruit.

Within the city precincts, the conscientious sight-seer inspected the Royal Palace, the San Carlo Opera House and the smaller San Carlino Theater, and the great Borbonico Museum, which housed most of the objects exhumed at Pompeii and Herculaneum. At the cathedral he might attend the ceremony at which the dried blood of St. Januarius miraculously liquified. But the noisy, bustling, crowded streets of Naples — such a contrast to the monastic quietude of Rome — made an even greater impression. All occupations, all life, seemed to be pursued under the open sky: cobblers and tailors, carpenters and blacksmiths, cooks and laundresses, doctors and dentists all worked in the open air, while nursemaids and deliverymen, soldiers and sailors, priests and police went about their business. Streetcorner orators, public letter writers, groups of card players, and the artificers of Punch and Judy shows attracted crowds of spectators and made passage through the narrow lanes even more difficult. Above all, there were the poverty-stricken, half-naked beggars and loafers, the *lazzaroni*, who lived their lives in the streets, eating, sleeping, and performing all their natural functions in full public view. Little wonder that an occasional visitor felt Naples "would have been a Paradise were it not for the Neapolitans." [43]

In spite of the bustling street activity and the appearance

of incessant industry, many of the Neapolitans besides the *lazzaroni* seemed to be constitutionally idle. The city had a bad moral reputation. Though he seldom felt the need to present evidence from his personal dossier, the American visitor usually condemned Naples as the most corrupt place in all Italy. The filth, the indolence, the superstition of the natives, the presence of the beggars and pickpockets were proof enough of Neapolitan degeneracy and Neapolitan depravity. Perhaps the near nakedness of the *lazzaroni* shocked the American more than anything else.

The environs of the city included much of interest. First, the traveler went on to see the current excavations at Herculaneum and Pompeii. Little beyond a part of the theater had been dug out at Herculaneum, but much of Pompeii had been uncovered, and the visit to Pompeii was always a highlight of the whole Italian journey. Here the American could vividly reconstruct the life of the ancient past. Sometimes the visitor suggested impractically that the Neapolitan government should speed up the excavations, for so much yet remained to be uncovered. Fenimore Cooper, however, approved of the slow and deliberate way in which the work was being conducted, and realized that only the most careful exploration could preserve what was being brought to light.[44]

To the north of Pompeii stood Vesuvius, which was next on the agenda. The expedition involved noisy haggling with donkey drivers, guides, and the dispensers of food and drink. Inevitably at the end of the journey a great many local inhabitants gathered round to demand money for obscure services. Donkeys were used for a part of the ascent, but the last steep climb had to be made either on foot, usually with the aid of guides pushing and pulling, or in a kind of sedan chair in which the visitor was precariously borne up the mountainside. In either case, it was an exhausting experience, and before it ended the traveler often regretted that he had ever come. Frequently the volcano was in mild eruption, so that on top of all his other vexations he had to dodge falling stones. An American naval lieutenant who approached too near the active volcano in 1850 had his arm so badly shattered by a falling rock that he died a few days later. Sometimes, ignoring the risk of life, the tourist climbed down on the floor of the volcano and up the sides of the small active cone within. Usually he brought away as a souvenir a coin that he had thrust into the molten lava. The descent from Vesuvius was rapid and exhilarating, and it took him only a few minutes, moving with giant steps down through the soft ash. At the base of the mountain, the traveler refreshed himself with a bottle of *Lacrima Christi* before starting back to Naples.

The area just to the north and northwest of the city was particularly associated with the events of antiquity. One passed through the grotto of Posillipo to visit Baia and Pozzuoli, where the ruins of ancient Roman villas could still be seen at the water's edge, and then went on to Lake Agnano, the Grotto del Cane, Lake Avernus, the Cumean sibyl's cave, the crater of Solfatara, and Lake Fusaro, famed for its oysters. But one's detached enjoyment of these antique views was forever being undermined by beggars. At the so-called tomb of Virgil, James Jackson Jarves was met by four volunteers who led him to the gate of the garden, which was directly before his eyes. Another insisted on guiding him along a path that led to the tomb as plainly "as Broadway does to Union Square." As a climax, the guardian opened this tomb to show him just how dark and empty it was within. The upshot was that all these guides "clamored for *bucksheesh* with an eagerness worthy of Bedouins." [45]

Only a few Americans ventured south of Naples and Salerno to the Greek temple ruins at Paestum, but those who did felt they were well rewarded for their trouble. John Singleton Copley, who had visited the site with Ralph Izard in 1775 considered Paestum "a place of as much curiosity as any I have seen, except Pompeii and Herculaneum." [46] The three temples at Paestum, wrote Joseph Green Cogswell in 1818, "are the sublimest monument anywhere to be found of the destruction of time. . . . Nothing has left such impression upon me as Paestum." [47] And Fenimore Cooper found the well-preserved temple of Neptune, built in the fifth century B.C., "the most impressive . . . edifice I know." [48]

Beyond Paestum the countryside was virtually unknown. John Lothrop Motley, the historian of the Dutch Republic, was perhaps unique during this period in traveling by land south through Calabria all the way to Reggio, crossing from there to Sicily. Edward Everett on his way to Greece in 1818 blazed a trail seldom followed for half a century by going overland from Naples to Bari, Taranto, Lecce, and Otranto in southeastern Puglia.

A surprising number of Americans, however, visited Sicily and even traveled extensively around the island. For the American who got this far, Sicily meant a look — usually his only look — at the remains of ancient Greek civilization, as well as an exploration of one of the most primitive parts of Europe. Usually he stopped off in Sicily either at the beginning or at the end of his tour, often directly bound to or from the United States or the eastern Mediterranean. A good many sailors and naval officers visited the island, since some Sicilian ports were used as bases by American vessels.

Syracuse was the Sicilian city the traveler most often saw. Here he inspected catacombs, convents, rock quarries, the Greek theater, and the famous Ear (or Cave) of Dionysius, remarkable for its acoustics. He might also stop for a short time at Messina and Taormina. Generally he passed directly through Catania, going on to Mount Etna to climb overnight the steep sides of the volcano for the rewarding view, at sunrise, over much of Sicily, the Lipari Islands to the north, and southern Italy to the northeast.

Occasionally the American crossed the island by land, a rigorous journey, "but worth doing at any cost and discomfort . . . such inns as it never entered into the heart of man to conceive — so nasty, so fleay, & all that." [49] The roads were bad — in fact, often nonexistent — and during rainy weather travel became practically impossible. Muleback or a *lettiga*, a kind of sedan chair borne by two mules, were the only transport on the rocky footpaths. The inhabitants, dark-complexioned, strangely dressed, and dirty, inspired in the traveler the fear of robbery, at the very least, but if he dreaded bandits, he seems to have dreaded firearms even more, for he never carried any. And indeed he did not need them.

Palermo, a city of lovely semitropical gardens, united comfort and excitement. The tourist visited the grim Capuchin cemetery, where mummified bodies were formidably displayed against the walls of an underground chapel. He noted with satisfaction the luxurious coaches driven each evening by the rich, and if he continued to be annoyed by the importunities of beggardom, he admired the patient methods used to care for the inmates of the local insane asylum.

The Lipari Islands remained all but virgin soil to Americans for the time being, though a very few assaults upon them took place even then. The author of the sketches in *Records of Travel* ascended the active volcano on Stromboli, and from vessels that passed nearby others saw these forbidding volcanic outcroppings. [50]

In traveling northward through the peninsula, the

American visitor often moved along a route across the Apennines from Florence to Bologna, and then over the rich Po Valley through Ferrara and Padua to Venice. Bologna suggests little in retrospect except a friendly and agreeable city with magnificent ranges of arcades, embedded in a countryside rather less prosperous than the Tuscan. Ferrara, accessible by a direct canal route, seemed to be under a ban of silence. Its streets were empty, grass-covered, and hushed, but the architecture was rich: a cathedral was there, the house of Ariosto, the castle of the d'Este family, and, above all, the prison of Tasso. Byron was thought to have spent several days living in Tasso's cell, and his name was prominently written on a brick arch within. *That* signature unfailingly tempted the American to add his own name. The house and the tomb of Petrarch were within easy distance at Arquà. In Padua, the American stopped to see the huge church dedicated to St. Anthony, the cathedral, and the university. On the other hand, he usually failed to visit the Giotto frescoes in the Scrovegni chapel and generally commented at greater length on the most richly decorated café he had ever seen than on anything else in the city. For one traveling by post, this café often was all of Padua that he saw. Occasionally the American got to Mantua or Parma, more frequently to Vicenza, where he visited Palladio's Olympian Theater, and to Verona, where the Roman arena was the outstanding tourist attraction.

The traveler could move from Rome to Venice, as well, by another, more easterly route. On this road he passed through Terni and Foligno, then crossed the Apennines, and stopped at the famous shrine of the Virgin's house at Loreto. He continued northward along the Adriatic coast by way of Ancona and Rimini, and possibly made a visit to San Marino, the oldest republic in the world, whose inhabitants appeared to hold the United States in great esteem.[51]

"Dream-like" was the comment with which the tourist invariably saluted Venice. As he approached the city over the placid waters of the lagoon and as he began to move down the Grand Canal, the place seemed to be little less than a phantasm, a dream-city. But there it sat, and the American found it delightful — for a few days. Then the charm began to fade, and the visitor began to feel as though he had been locked up in prison. Venice, reputed to be all gaiety and all vice, teeming with carnivals, masks, and intrigues, looked sad and deserted, a feeble relic of its former self. Particularly in the early decades of the century, the traveler, disillusioned and cheated, revenged himself by drawing morals from the plight of Venice, pointing out how a people might sink into decrepitude as a just punishment for profligacy, luxury, and submission to political tyranny.

Venetian society was tightly barred to the foreigner, but there were other entertainments available to him. The visitor lingered at the cafés on the Piazza San Marco, carefully selecting one patronized by the Venetians, who would not mingle with the Austrians. He explored the huge ducal palace, where he looked at acres of Tintoretto canvas, and he visited the damp, gloomy prisons, recalling the vivid stories he had heard of the city's past. He made the rounds of churches, galleries, and private palaces, and on the Lido he saw where Byron had taken his exercise on horseback along the water's edge. At the Armenian convent he talked with the monk with whom Byron had studied this language, and he took great delight in the somber, black gondolas that carried him about the labyrinthine waterways of the city.

In his tour of Italy, the American never forgot what he had left behind, and what he saw in Italy constantly reminded him of places and scenes he knew in the United States. Sometimes it was the bay of Naples compared with

Boston harbor, or the bustling Toledo in Naples compared with Broadway. And New Englanders coming to the seashore were constantly fancying themselves at Nahant. Comments on nature in Italy usually evoked comparisons with the American scene.

By common acknowledgment one of Italy's attractions was the picturesque quality of much of the landscape. Rocks and pinnacles decorated with a ruined tower or a castle were just as romantic as an imaginative traveler would have them. Grey villages, "stuck like wasps' nests against the acclivities," monasteries and churches, villages and castles dotted the landscape. Art and nature had been blended to aesthetic perfection. The countryside in most places had a lived-in look, and the smallest plot of ground was carefully tended to gain the greatest production. There was considerable variety in the natural scene, too, from the rugged mountains and the flat river plains of the North to the low rolling hills of much of the rest of the peninsula. The atmosphere of the country seemed to possess a peculiar property of softness — "the magic of moonlight is somehow mixed up with it," wrote Hawthorne — setting off objects to the best advantage.[52] Part of the charm of the natural scene in Italy, it was realized, arose also because poets of antiquity had visited these places and had described them.

The American's admiration was often qualified, however, as he compared the Italian scene to the attractions of his homeland. William Cullen Bryant, himself a poet of American nature, wondered why American landscape painters went to Italy except to study the masterpieces, since nature had as much to offer at home, and it was "a fresh and new nature." [53] The mellow, golden light that Claude Lorrain imitated so well in his pictures and that was said to be characteristic of Italian skies was not unique, declared the geologist Benjamin Silliman, for it was certainly found in

New England during Indian summer.[54] And the painter
Thomas Cole was of the opinion that though there was "a
peculiar softness and beauty in Italian skies, ours are far
more gorgeous." [55]

Occasionally the visitor took a different stand. Cooper
objected to the penchant of his countrymen to blow up
everything at home, and reported that he had never known
such glorious scenery as he had seen in lower Italy. American mountains were "insipid" compared with those of Italy,
and American lakes scarcely bore comparisons at all with
the finer lakes of northern Italy. "If it be patriotism to deem
all our geese swans," Cooper stoutly asserted, "I am no
patriot, nor ever was." [56] Margaret Fuller also spoke out,
finding that nothing in the United States compared with
the Italian lakes.[57] Samuel F. B. Morse was much struck by
Lake Como, the shores of which he thought resembled the
scenery of Lake George, though the Italian lake was superior in everything except the transparency of its waters
and the islands on the surface; the villages and villas beside
the lake and the well-cultivated fields extending up the
mountainsides combined to provide a charm not known in
the United States.[58]

The Italian scene thus presented considerable diversity.
Far more so than their twentieth-century descendants, these
early travelers were avid sight-seers, visiting all the historical
buildings in the towns where they stopped, looking at all the
works of art starred in their guidebooks. Sometimes one has
the impression that a curious sense of duty rather than real
interest kept pushing them on from one thing to the next.
Usually remaining some time in the more important cities,
they came to know these places well — at least the outward
aspects. Some of the visitors exhibited a profound feeling
for the past. Others merely parroted the comments of those
who had gone before, and did not respond deeply to what

they experienced, but even for them this personal encounter with the physical remnants of the Italian past undoubtedly had some significance.

Beyond the cities, the buildings, and all the traditional sights, the Americans also wanted to come to know the people. The Italian way of life differed markedly from what they were used to at home, and the visitors observed and recorded a great deal about the inhabitants, the social structure, and the national character. Many things about the Italian people surprised them, and some things shocked them.

CHAPTER IV

THE ITALIAN PEOPLE

THE AMERICAN'S personal contact with Italians was limited. He naturally saw much of carriage drivers, café waiters, hotelkeepers, and servants, but these were people whose language he in no sense spoke. Sometimes the tourist carried letters of introduction to those with whom he had something in common — a shared interest in literature or art, or a mutual friend who thought they ought to meet. In this way he came to know a few important aristocrats, some artists, scientists, and intellectuals, and occasionally some of the leading political figures. Such contacts, however, were necessarily short-lived, for the traveler soon moved on and seldom returned. Even the expatriates, usually artists, who remained for years in Rome or Florence, did not as a rule enter extensively into Italian social life and had few Italian friends. The American found his closest ties of companionship with those whom he had known in the past and with those who shared his experiences.

Until 1840 no diplomats officially represented the United States in the Kingdom of Sardinia, none in the States of the Church until 1848. During the better part of the first half-century, then, no official hierarchy of resident diplomatic officials in these important states could help the stranger bridge the gap and enter Italian society. The American was largely left to make his own way as best he could.

Language was, naturally, a further barrier to effective and extended friendships. Some of the visitors had prepared themselves to the extent of dabbling in copybook Italian, or they had learned a little French, the approved international tongue of the period, but few Americans had really mastered either language, and few Italians spoke English. To many travelers, therefore, life in Italy was "like lovely scenery to a blind man." [1]

Italian society was relatively closed — another obstacle to social mobility and social intercourse. To the aristocracy of Italy, looking back upon a long lineage of distinguished ancestors, the man coming from across the sea lacked the credentials conferred by high birth and an impressive family tree. Some of the American's heroes, men like Washington and Franklin, were known and praised throughout Europe, but theirs was an individual fame, independent of family roots. Moreover, the American was often handicapped by being indistinguishable from the Englishman, whom Italians disliked as an arrogant and demanding sort. An American was apt to be more welcome if he made it plain that he was positively not a Britisher.

Finally, Americans did not visit Italy primarily to meet people but to see things. To establish social contacts took time and energy, and when both were limited they were conserved for what the visitor felt was most important. Even when both were unlimited, probably a good many travelers did not even care to get involved in social life.

On the other hand, the American often discovered that many Italians were eager to meet him as a representative of a new land and curious to learn about conditions in the

United States. Though "the name of American was a passport to their attentions and civilities," the Italians usually
knew little of the New World.[2] They sometimes confused
North and South America, thought all Americans had dark
skins, and looked upon them as unfortunately backward in
civilization. In 1800, when John Cogdell, a young South
Carolina lawyer who later became prominent in state politics, stopped at a convent in Siena, the nuns were so anxious
to see a man from the New World that they opened the
main door of the establishment, customarily reserved only
for the bishop, and crowded around to ask questions. One
nun, whom Cogdell took to be a daughter of Montesquieu,
seemed especially surprised at Cogdell's nationality. When
he explained to "Miss Montesquieu" that he was an American, "she appeared all amasement & I drew up my coat
sleeve — and exhibited to her Eye my arm and assured her
my Countrymen, were as fair and many more so than my-
self. . . . Her countenance exhibited pleasure and relief by
my statements." [3]

Italians generally held a favorable idea of the United
States, little as they knew about it, and many contrasted the
situation of the American people with their own. Arriving
in Alessandria south of Milan in 1821, Theodore Dwight
and a companion found that some of the local inhabitants
stared at them in their carriage as if they were wild beasts.
A few, however, who knew something of America, came
up "with more suppressed curiosity, and much respect, as
towards the representatives of a country they considered
the happiest on earth, and to men born and educated among
political privileges and blessings far very far, superior to
those at which they were aspiring." The two travelers began to wish themselves "old and wise enough for sages, and
tall enough for giants," so that when descending from the
diligence they might produce an impression corresponding

to the ideas the Italians had formed of the wisdom and power of the United States.[4]

Despite the positive sympathy for his country he found in Italy, the American's over-all impression of the Italian people, based as much on accepted stereotypes as on his own experience, was to a considerable extent negative. Handed down from the past and often reinforced by contemporary travel literature, the most common picture was colored by the widespread poverty, by the contrasts between the modern country and ancient Rome and Renaissance Italy, and, above all, by the impositions on travelers at the hands of the few people with whom they ordinarily came in close contact. The most condemnatory reports on the national character were elicited when the traveler visited the South — Rome and especially Naples — where poverty was most intense and the social contrasts greatest. Shortly after his arrival in Naples in 1822, George Bancroft expressed elements of this view in a letter to his father. He found that the people were "so corrupt, the nation so cowardly, dishonest and degenerate," that the attractions of the climate were counterbalanced by the ignorance and vice. Men, he reported, did not even affect honesty; they lied as often as they spoke, and attempted to cheat as often as they dealt. Their word was "of less weight than straw," and their honesty "only a system of defrauding." [5]

The American, then, wore a pair of refracting spectacles, and ordinarily came prepared to view the Italian people in a particular way. Some visitors merely elaborated on the traditional view. Others, however, discovered that the people were much different from what they had anticipated. Estimates of the national character usually became more favorable the longer the time the visitor spent in the country, and the more personal contacts he actually experienced. A psychologically revealing conflict sometimes appeared when the traveler's experiences did not agree with what he had been led to expect. The novelist Catharine Maria Sedgwick, for example, repeatedly discovered that the natives were not so bad as they had been represented to her. "If the only Romans we chance to know would be valuable members of society anywhere, is it not a hint to us to take the denunciation of travellers with some allowance?" [6] The evaluations of Americans long resident in Italy had both positive and negative elements, nonetheless, and the conclusions of an expatriate like William Story were by no means exclusively favorable. This wavering between the traditional judgment, which so many things confirmed, and a far more positive view remains a dominant theme in the American response to the Italian people.

On the negative side first, dishonesty as a trait was often attributed to the national character — a not uncommon reaction, it must be admitted, of one people to another. In Sicily and in Naples, petty thievery was widespread. Elsewhere, along the road, the traveler was cautioned to have his luggage securely fastened to the carriage, or it might mysteriously disappear during the journey. William Berrian believed that even among Italians whom the visitors ordinarily did not meet "there seemed to be a settled design among all to impose on the ignorant, and to circumvent the cunning and informed. Perpetual vigilance and the nicest precautions, are the only security against perpetual plunder." [7]

From time to time an American made a particular point of an instance of honesty, since it was so out of keeping with what he had been led to expect. For example, Nathaniel Hazeltine Carter, who wrote one of the better travel volumes on Italy, was pleased to have returned to him a watch he had left in a lonely Apennine inn; he rejoiced that he had not experienced dishonesty and could cite only one instance of incivility in Italy.[8] Nathaniel Hawthorne care-lessly left behind in a Tuscan railway carriage a leather bag containing a manuscript book with the beginnings of *The Marble Faun*. The bag was promptly returned and Haw-thorne, unlike many others, expressed pleasure in his con-tacts with Italian public officials. In contrast, several months before, soon after his arrival in Rome, he had thought that no reliance whatsoever could be placed on the integrity of those with whom he was dealing.[9]

Allied to this, mendacity was set forth as a further ele-ment in the national character. Tourists reported that men lied when they were afraid and they lied to please, and that since the vice was so universal it led to distrust in all social relationships. On the other hand, lies could make men happy and could, as well, add interest to their lives. If guides, for example, had to tell the strict truth about what they were showing, the number of objects of interest would decline and the guides would starve. Since much lying was done in order to please, this vice, some critics recognized, was close-ly tied to the positive virtue of sympathy.

Next to dishonesty and mendacity, the most frequent charge was indolence. Again, the American came prepared to find this characteristic, and much of what he saw seemed to confirm it — the groups of *lazzaroni*, the beggers and the loungers, and those idling about on the frequent Church festival days. On the other hand, the observer sometimes warned that the customary view of Italian laziness was not at all what he had experienced. The lower classes, he had discovered, were often idle but not indolent, and they were idle only because they could not find any work to do. Some aristocrats, indeed, had the means to enjoy a do-nothing existence, but the vast majority were compelled to labor hard in order to provide for themselves. "Taken as a whole, they are a laborious, frugal, and patient people. Their nature leads to activity." [10] To one American, they were "the most industrious people in the world." [11]

Related to indolence was the charge that Italians lacked enterprise. They were considered inflexible in their habits and customs, unwilling to make desirable changes, and were said to be deficient in adapting means to ends, in contriving laborsaving devices, or in preparing themselves for the future. Most of the country's institutions, it was suggested, had been designed for past conditions and would have to be changed markedly to fit Italy into the modern world. The question was whether or not the people had the energy and adaptability to make such changes.

Paradoxically Italians were charged with a deficiency of intellect and yet credited with remarkable wit. The ignorance and credulity of the lower classes, characteristics that struck many visitors, were still tempered by elegance of expression and politeness of manner. Italian wit, unlike American humor, tended neither to the vulgar nor to the profane, expressing itself instead in burlesque, often sarcastic and pungent. The graceful turn of expression of even the most badly educated peasant reminded some visitors, those who could understand the language, of the age and experience of this people, the heirs of so many generations.

The Italian's reputation for a volatile and passionate temperament seemed justified. Beneath the Latin's polished manner, there was a turbulence that frequently burst forth into violence. He was addicted to sensual pleasures, and he tended to be intensely jealous. Though often moody, he quickly recovered from depression and anger. His quarrels took the form of loud shouts and furious gestures, but seldom developed into physical conflict. Italians also gave evidence of being unusually imaginative and enthusiastic. "They are, in truth, the children of feeling." [12]

The country had a bad moral reputation. Naples, as we

have seen, appeared to the traveler a modern Sybaris, a center of corruption, and brought forth the severest comments on Italian morality. Elsewhere, too, the reports of crime, the dishonesty of merchants, the shameless begging, the open display of affection (even grown men kissing one another in public!), and the public satisfaction of physiological needs were all taken as evidence of gross immorality. And were not Sunday gaming, cardplaying, and theatergoing further proofs of a low moral state? Nor, in the view of the visitors, was chastity what it should be. While most professional men probably led respectable lives, the sexual standard of the lower classes was all too obviously low and that of the upper classes was thought to be outrageously degraded.

Public morality, in contrast, was in some ways more elevated than in the United States. The traveler encountered far fewer prostitutes on the avenues, in the parks, or in the theaters, than he was used to in England or at home. It was sometimes said that Italian women were as virtuous as those in other countries but that freer manners had injured their reputations. But some Americans — perhaps guilty of wishful thinking — nonetheless believed that even though the streets were comparatively free from such annoyances, each woman had her price. Drunkards were seldom seen in public, and there were no reports of wild sprees. Gambling parlors were unknown, though gambling on a large scale in form of the lottery was not.

The Americans dwelt on the negative aspects of the Italian character far more at the beginning than toward the middle of the century. Warnings that Americans themselves might be corrupted by contacts with degenerate Europeans decreased during these years, and distrust of the dubious moral value of such entertainments as the opera, the carnival, and the ballet declined. Correspondingly, the

visitor made a greater effort to understand why the morality
of the Italian people was as it was, and he came to accept
social and political conditions as the determinants of individual morality. Individuals turned to vice and idle amusement because the rigid social hierarchy cut off paths of
personal development. If a man could make use of his talents and improve his station, morality would improve.
Criminal activity rose directly out of the prevalent poverty.
Ultimately, government and religion were considered responsible for the social conditions that formed character.
Once they were ameliorated, the national character itself
would improve.

The national character had its positive aspects as well.
The inhabitants were credited with courtesy, friendliness,
sociability, and temperance. They were thought free of the
intense self-consciousness that particularly characterized the
English and that had affected Americans. Their behavior
was lively and animated, and they had a whole language of
gestures and body movements. Good nature, though occasionally marred by passionate outbursts, was universal.
Seldom vain, they were endowed with a refinement and
sensitivity that made even the poorest peasant a civilized
individual.

The visitors agreed that Italians were born with an eye
for beauty and an instinct for taste that Americans had
hardly begun to acquire. Somehow, the experience of centuries of living had given these people a remarkable sensitivity to the refinements of decoration and ornament, of
form and style. Even the simple peasant knew how to wear
a flower or carve the wood of his cart so as to make his lot
more agreeable. The countryside itself displayed an in-
comparable union of the work of men and the beauties of
nature, and the "sublimity" and the "picturesqueness" of

the natural scene, two favorite qualities, were apparent in much Italian art.

Curiously, the American discovered that the Italian seemed happier than he himself was. This note of envy of the Italian's enjoyment of life seeps into the letters and journals again and again. The beauties of the land, the often easy satisfaction of basic needs, and the Italian's inability to change his condition had led him to squeeze the most from each moment of existence, and had brought him an enviable contentment. While the American felt that time had to be "spent" in certain ways, the Italian kept his time and savored it.

Mark Twain remarked on this different pace of life soon after his arrival in Italy. He saw an infectious change come over his own party of tourists: "Day by day we lose some of our restlessness and absorb some of the spirit of quietude and ease that is in the tranquil atmosphere about us and in the demeanor of the people. We grow wise apace. We begin to comprehend what life is for." [13] To Henry James this mood of enjoyment of common things was the fruit of the experience of ages, "the philosophy of people who have lived long and much, who have discovered no short cuts to happiness and no effective circumvention of effort, and so have come to regard the average lot as a ponderous fact that absolutely calls for a certain amount of sitting on the lighter tray of the scales." [14]

As with estimates of the national character, the American's responses to the various classes of Italian society were dependent both on the stereotyped view he brought along and on the nature of his contacts, most of which, as we have seen, were with those who served him. In the main he dealt with men in a superficial way; only rarely did he become well acquainted with an individual.

In viewing Italian society, the American was struck at once by the marked division between the few of the upper classes and the rest of the people — the peasantry and poor townspeople. Churchmen, distinguished by dress and occupation, clearly belonged either to the upper or to the lower class. University professors, doctors, and some governmental officials might have been considered a middle class, but acquaintance with this small group, found only in the more important cities, was limited. The rigidity of social status annoyed the visitor. That a man must always be what his father had been and continue in the same role throughout his life seemed both wasteful and wrong. Wilbur Fisk, a Methodist clergyman, thought it remarkable when a man in a hotel told him that he had been a waiter in that same place for forty years, something Fisk felt was unheard of in the United States.[15]

Despite the fact that the American usually thought highly of the few aristocrats whom he met, he had some harsh words for the upper classes. He frequently charged the nobility with ignorance. Irving, for one instance, early in the century, considered the Genoese nobility "a stupid set of beings without much talent or information." [16] Others found the aristocracy indolent and lethargic as well. According to George Ticknor, not all those of high rank and distinction who lived in a comfortless manner, without fires, carpets, or comfortable furniture, did so because of straitened circumstances. They lived this way merely because they just could not make the effort necessary to produce a change. Intellectual culture in this class, especially among women, Ticknor believed, was at a decidedly low level.[17] Cooper, on the other hand, thought better of the upper classes, who, he felt, displayed a graciousness, simplicity, and sincerity that made the cultivated Italian "the nearest a true standard of any gentleman of Europe." [18] Others echoed his opinion as to the courtesy and integrity of the aristocracy.

Perhaps the main defect of the nobility, in the eyes of the American, was the monotony of its existence, the fact that most people of this class had nothing to do. Tradition forbade them from entering commercial pursuits, there were only limited positions in the army, the church attracted a few (but sometimes not for religious reasons), and outlets in political and literary life were restricted. Prevented from exerting themselves in the world, and usually poorly educated, they turned to pleasure and amusement to occupy their days. Though often charming and sociable, they led idle and useless lives.

The American was occasionally surprised that the appearance of upper-class persons did not accord with their actual social positions. He did not feel it was wrong that society granted respect to some of its members, the upper class, but those people in turn, he felt, ought to have accoutrements that clearly made their identity known. When an aristocrat lived in a great mansion, had a large number of servants and followers, and made a lavish display on the streets, one could tell at once that this was a man of importance, but when the trappings of nobility were missing, when family fortunes had so declined that form and style could not be maintained even within the home, the impression given was somehow not appropriate. Then, too, the American discovered that some distinguished statesmen, artists, and writers, who were accorded the highest public respect, lived in depressed conditions, without the material goods and services their positions warranted.

Many of the upper classes, and sometimes those of the lower orders as well, the visitor further found, made a grand display in public (*fare la bella figura*) that they could ill afford. The Italian delighted in dressing smartly for the street and driving a grand equipage up and down the corso, seeing his friends and making sure that he was seen. But he often scraped and saved at home in order to spend abroad, and frequently he lived on a scale not at all commensurate with what he showed on the streets. Facing this discrepancy between appearance and reality, the American responded with marked disapproval.

Meaningful personal contacts with people on the lower ranges of the social scale were even fewer than those with the upper classes. The barrier of language kept the two nationalities separated; and the barrier of class position was added, since to lower-class Italians those who could afford to travel must be of the upper order of society.

The usual response of the American visitor to members of the lower classes, as such, was negative. Their strange dress, their often swarthy countenances, their suspicious curiosity gave them a forbidding aspect; and the traveler, passing through the narrow lanes of a poor country town, thought about robberies and kidnapings, fastened the coach doors, and urged the driver to hurry on. The lower classes in particular were excoriated for cunning and avarice, a demeaning servility, and an insincerity of behavior. Margaret Fuller, staying for some time in the village of Rieti, at first found the peasants there simple and kind, but soon she discovered that they looked upon her as an *Inglese* of untold wealth and had become ferociously mercenary.[19] People seemed determined to get what they could from the stranger by any means whatsoever. "From every person we had any thing to do with," reported another visitor, "we received attention like the spider's to the fly." [20]

The people of the lower orders obviously were victims of great poverty, but more than that, in the eyes of some observers, that poverty had destroyed something of their essential humanity. George Hillard thought that a group of men engaged in excavating some ruins in Rome were themselves sadder ruins than those in which they were working. Want and poverty had left the mass of people dispirited, with a lifeless expression. Badly fed and often forced into unhealthful employments, they seemed all the more miserable in contrast to those somewhat better off, who made such an ostentatious public display.

The prevalence of begging among the lower orders reinforced the American's stereotyped view of Italian character and social conditions. Often the tourist discovered that almost everyone with whom he came in contact — not only people of the lowest class — was involved in the custom. Tradesmen from whom he had purchased something would ask for a small additional sum when paid. Gentlemen, masked for penance, visited the cafés, shaking a money-box in the visitor's ear. Begging monks stopped him on the streets. Destitute nobles and stranded travelers — including one said to be an American — petitioned for aid. In the smaller villages the whole populace engaged in the practice. The visitor could not ask for a drink of water or for directions to the next town without a demand for *qualche cosa*. Even children too young to speak held out their hands. Occasionally beggars fell down prostrate as if in worship at the feet of the potential giver, a stratagem that sometimes startled the American into unexpected largesse. Along the roadside decrepit old men, ragged young women, and diseased children sometimes ran for miles beside the carriage, clamoring for coppers and imploring the traveler to relieve their all too evident misery.

Each locality had characteristic types skilled in the art. Beggars in Florence made use of bright-eyed young girls to waylay strangers. The Tuscan government licensed the blind and the lame, who apparently then felt their medals gave them the right to peremptory demands. Every blind or lame beggar had a helper who shared in the profits and steered him to possible givers, and on Saturdays they made the rounds of stores and households to collect their due.

Roman beggars, always ragged, often deformed, but usually dignified, were considered to be, of all Italians, the most averse to working. Many beggars came to Rome from the country villages of the Abruzzi to spend the winter months haunting the church porticos and the streets along which the well-to-do passed. For many years Beppo, the king of the Roman beggars, presided on the Spanish Steps. He easily spotted newcomers and warmly welcomed old clients as they passed through his territory, shuffling up to them on hands and knees to ask for his toll, and always prepared to give change.

Neapolitan beggars specialized in amusing the passers-by with tricks and antics or in arousing pity. "They have a jaunty air about them, as they implore charity, which would make a miser laugh." [21] Along the leading promenades, the *lazzaroni* petitioned for handouts, while the maimed, the diseased, and the starving lay beside the pavement, groaning and wailing. Emerson thought that the streets of Naples looked like the wards of a hospital.

Not far off, at Sorrento, Fenimore Cooper discoverd how systematized begging could become. As he was walking on the terrace of his villa one morning, Cooper noticed a lame old beggar waiting for someone to come out of the front door below, and he threw the man a small coin. The next day at the same hour the beggar was back, and he continued to come daily at the same time. Soon a second petitioner joined him, and then the number began to grow. On the day Cooper left Sorrento ninety-six people stood in the street waiting for him to toss down the coins, but he was pleased that he was no longer bothered at all outside his house.[22]

The farther south the tourist went, the greater was the poverty and the more pitiful the beggars. During 1806 on his way to Greece, Nicholas Biddle, later famous as president of the Second Bank of the United States, was stranded temporarily in Messina, where he was assailed on every street by the piercing cry of *mori di fame*; he thought the people had fallen to the lowest point of human wretchedness possible, little superior to brutes.[23] To the north, in Venice, one group of Americans were so astonished when they were stopped by a beggar in a gondola that they gave willingly.[24]

Another form of begging arose in dealings with servants and attendants. Bribes and gratuities were always useful in gaining admission through locked doors, and customarily on the day following a visit to an important private house, a servant called on the visitor to solicit a fee. Some of these servants, it was said, received no wages, only the fees they might claim from guests. Even servants from the papal establishment came to those who had been presented to the pope for an expected gift. Annually, too, at Christmas or New Year's, servants made the rounds to the homes of those who visited regularly in their establishments to extract a sum for their services. If the money were refused, the visitor might not be admitted in the future.

The explanation for the profusion of beggars was simple. Although a few visitors suggested that the beggars could work if they really wanted to, most accepted the view that the individual Italian himself was not responsible for his poverty and his need to beg. Instead, as with the low level of morality, the fault lay in the socio-religious system.

Basic to this system, in the view of Americans, were governmental policy and the practices and teachings of the Roman Catholic Church. The governments of the states of

Italy were seen as narrow-minded and conservative, opposed to commerce and industry and all modern improvements. Where these illiberal conditions were least prevalent, as in Turin or Florence, there begging was at a minimum. But behind the governments — and constituting the political authority itself in the Papal States — lay the Church, which honored the system by its example and teachings. Whole communities of monks did nothing but beg on the streets, and the Church taught that the act of giving was a duty that each good Christian must perform. That many of the beggars were practicing an imposition on society appeared obvious, for in the leading cities there were many hospitals and charitable institutions for their relief.

Even though the American usually felt that social and religious conditions explained the practice of begging, and even though he often expressed compassion and pity for the victims of such poverty, he frequently responded with annoyance and anger. From time to time he resolved not to give at all, but he soon discovered that his resolution was hard to keep because of the beggars' pitiable appeals and practiced insistence. Occasionally an American proudly boasted of his ability to rid himself of these importuners, his heart becoming "as obdurate as a paving stone." The Reverend George E. Ellis discovered that the most certain way was to shame the beggars by taking off his hat and begging himself.[25] Samuel Topliff, proprietor of the Merchants News Room in Boston, guessed that the beggars he met on the road between Venice and Florence did not know that he was a Yankee or they would not have tried to get anything from him: "I had no wooden nutmegs to sell or give, or leather coppers to bestow: but I reckon I outgeneraled them." [26]

The American had little opportunity to learn about Italian family structure and domestic living conditions.

ARCH OF TITUS by Frederick Church, Jervis McEntee, and George
Peter Alexander Healy. Courtesy of The Newark Museum,
Newark, New Jersey.

MR. AND MRS. RALPH IZARD by John Singleton Copley. Courtesy of the Museum of Fine Arts,

Since the Italian seldom invited guests into his home, there was little chance to see the family at first hand. The few travelers who reported domestic visits usually noted a closeness among the family members, but the home, the visitor soon discovered, meant something different to the Italian from what it did to the American. Householders did not seem to take the pride in their dwellings that Americans did. Like the ancients, the Italian put less stress on domestic comforts than the visitor was used to. Life centered out of doors, on the streets, and in the cafés, rather than in the bosom of the family, and frequently men attended social occasions while their wives stayed at home. "Bad policy in a Government," Fenimore Cooper moralized in his journal, "not to encourage domestic life, as it clearly has a tendency to make good citizens" — a sentiment many others echoed.[27]

Every tourist had something to say about the place of women. First of all, the traveler — particularly the male visitor — was struck by the attractiveness of Italian women. The peasants of Tuscany were noted for their personal beauty, although the Venetians were reputed to have greater sexual charms. Most Italian women had a remarkable gracefulness and vivacity, though they faded rapidly, especially the poor. Standards of appearance for the home and for the street differed. At home, James Jackson Jarves reported, Italian women tended to be untidy and slipshod, poor housekeepers, indifferent to everything but their appearance outside the house. But Jarves was unquestionably moving against the tide of general opinion when he accused them of lacking good taste in dress.[28]

The position of girls was curious. The strict way that young girls were watched and the limitations on their activity surprised the American. Wealthy families often placed their daughters in convents, where they remained, always under the eye of a guardian, until a marriage had been arranged. English mothers, it was pointed out, customarily preceded their daughters on the street, but Italian mothers always followed them. As a result of this training, young girls were badly prepared for marriage and for the world; their education was poor, and they had seen little of society.

Marriage was commonly contracted by the parents without consideration for the feelings of the two parties. Marriage brokers sometimes arranged these unions, taking a percentage of the dowry in return. Monks or priests, acting the role of broker, could gain access to houses when the interested suitor could not. The American felt that this system of arranging a marriage was wrong, though it helped to explain the frequent infidelity that resulted from such alliances. Each partner followed his or her own inclinations and was willing that the other do likewise. It was even said that husbands, for the sake of money, sometimes abetted the wife's dishonor. Happiness within the marriage, the American insisted, seldom existed.

Although the practice of *cecisbeism*, whereby a woman was constantly attended by a man not her husband, was declining and by midcentury had largely gone out of fashion, it was still in evidence during the first half of the century and attracted much attention. The man served as confidant and counselor to his lady, waited on her in her private room and at the theater, accompanied her to church and on drives, and usually, it was assumed, was her lover. The extramarital alliance was sanctioned by the husband, who himself might be serving as cavalier to another married woman. James Jackson Jarves even reported that fidelity was measured by faithfulness toward this extramarital union, and that such an alliance was hedged with a strict morality of its own. "As for children — why legitimacy like justice is blindfolded — they are born, named, and no questions asked." [29]

Respect for women, it seemed to the American visitor, was remarkably low, and this factor, like begging, was an important element supporting the traditional view of the Italian character. A woman out alone on the streets was prey to any number of men who followed her, passing and repassing, uttering compliments or lewd remarks directly to her face. To go about without this impertinence, a carriage was essential. At the theater or opera, an attractive woman was sure to be stared at. Mrs. Hawthorne was upset one day in St. Peter's to find a man dogging her steps, suggesting good places for her to stand and pointing out things of particular interest. Unable to get rid of him, she hurriedly left the church and went home. He must have been a spy, she thought.[30]

A few visitors joined in the chase. At a convent in Syracuse, Washington Irving and some companions felt it was a shame that such pretty girls were shut up forever from the world, and they flirted openly with the nuns. Some days later when the group visited another convent, the abbess had taken precautions to keep the more attractive nuns out of sight.[31] The spirited William Preston recorded in his journal how immediately upon entering Italy at Susa he spied a beautiful girl sitting at a window beside the road. He was so taken by her looks that he jumped from the carriage and entered the room where she and her mother sat, declaring that he was a foreigner and had come to look at the beauties of Italy, the present individual being the first that he had seen. With the aid of a French-Italian conversation book, he was able to keep talking for half an hour, but was interrupted eventually by his traveling companion who remonstrated that they would never get anywhere if

Preston felt compelled to stop for every pretty thing along the road.[32]

The heavy work that females of the lower classes were obliged to do always made an impression on the American. Almost every traveler commented upon the sight of peasant women carrying enormous loads on their heads or backs, driving sheep and goats through the fields, and doing all kinds of strenuous labor. Women had seemingly been degraded into mere beasts of burden, their position particularly deplorable in contrast to that of the men beside them. It was especially distressing to find women carrying heavy baskets of sand on their heads to mend a road, while men played ball nearby and priests looked on, or to find women harnessed to the plough pulling it through the earth, while men merely guided the share.

As the American looked at Italian society and attempted to define the national character, he constantly made comparisons with what he knew at home. Observing the rigidly established class structure, he reflected how uncertain class position was in his own country. All Americans, he realized, were involved in the race for class status, and while in this competition they lost much in repose and contentment, along with the security of a clearly indicated class position, they also gained in self-reliance and individual initiative. The gains, he generally felt, were worth the sacrifices. Though some Americans, it must be admitted, were attracted to a rigid social hierarchy, the visitor commonly expressed gratitude that his country did not have a nobility, whose vices and oppressions he considered partly responsible for the extremes of splendor and misery in Italy. The magnificence of upper-class life was impressive, but it also indicated excess, age, and decay. Americans, in contrast, had simplicity, youth, and virtue.

The visitor was surprised by the extensive intermingling

of luxury and misery. Accustomed to American towns and cities either of uniform economic level throughout or of diverse neighborhoods physically contrasting and distinctly separate, he was startled to see wealth and poverty so closely mixed together both in dwellings and in personal contacts on the streets and in the churches. Somehow the inter-mingling of classes in public places only set off more sharply the class distinctions. Some observers, in fact, believed that the closeness of such extremes was not right, and that classes should be more separated.

The sight of beggars usually brought an expression of thanks to the American's lips that such people were not found in his own land and that the want leading to such a condition was something that he did not know at home. "Let us rejoice," wrote one observer, "that while Italy so far surpasses us in objects well calculated to delight and improve taste, we have — what she has not — a thousand avenues wide open for the employment of adventurous industry." [33]

The visitor took pride in the strength of his family bonds. "The domestick picture of our country is inferiour to none, is indeed *superiour to any in the world*," wrote an anonymous visitor.[34] Family ties, he firmly believed, were a solid basis for individual happiness. Knowing little of the Italian family, he contrasted his family position with what seemed on the surface to be the loose domestic ties of Italy. American life centered in the home, and American women, the visitor felt, were treated with the proper esteem due the female sex.

While observing the components of Italian character, the American observer frequently tried to analyze his own national character. Italian indolence seemed to him in sharp contrast to the industry and activity of his countrymen, who appeared to value work for its own sake. The low standards of honesty and truth, too, were not what he knew at home, though it must be emphasized that this charge was principally directed against customs' officers, hotelmen, carriage drivers, street vendors, and beggars, groups that the traveler ordinarily saw less of in his own country. He found Italian tendencies to crime much greater than his own, but he believed that social conditions explained a great deal and that, with judicial procedures often distant and uncertain, the Italian was sometimes forced to take what he considered justice into his own hands.

Although the American often disapproved of idle lounging and considered it unseemly that so many people should be unoccupied, he generally responded in a positive way to the pace of life and to the art of living the Italian had cultivated. He envied the people for their apparent contentment, and he came to realize that the Italian knew better than he how to make the most of what he had; the Italian was a specialist in the economy of living. Fenimore Cooper, for one, speculated as to whether Americans should now change their habits and stress more the enjoyment of the passing moment, but he decided that the American people yet had to acquire certain arts and tastes before they could be ready for such pleasures. In fact, he asserted, "nations in their decline enjoy more true happiness than nations in their advance." [35]

The visitor saw himself as less forceful in emotional expression, as lacking something of the Latin's freshness of passion. Perhaps he had become too versatile and accommodating and had lost something of the primitive vigor that Italians had retained. "It is ill with a nation when the cerebrum sucks the cerebellum dry, for it cannot live by intellect alone," suggested James Russell Lowell.[36] Others, however, decided that the Italian was less vigorous than the American in things other than the expression of feelings.

Both directly and indirectly, travelers insisted that American moral standards were far higher than those of Italy, and the reasons they accepted were that the United States had a form of government that necessitated a high individual moral standard, a religion that emphasized conduct and action rather than form, and a family structure that preserved the purity of domestic relations. Because he had certain political and social institutions, a man in America could fulfill himself better than in Italy or anywhere else in Europe. "Notwithstanding the faults that freedom brings out in him, it is much more gratifying & satisfying to the mind, to the affections, to the soul to live in our state of society than to live in any I know of on this [the eastern] side of the Atlantick." [37]

In summarizing the American appraisal of the Italian people, the infrequency of extended and meaningful personal contacts must again be emphasized. The American visitor's estimate was a limited one, based both on the inherited view and on his own observations of people in the mass. Striking practices, such as the heavy work that women did or the omnipresent begging, reinforced this traditional external view and reassured the visitor in his judgments. The stereotypes he carried with him helped him to adjust to the people and their ways, but the traveler was nevertheless often jolted into a realization that his patterns of belief were inaccurate. The Italian whom the traveler occasionally did come to know well appeared to be an exception to many aspects of the picture the visitor had formed of the national character. For example, he was not so rigidly constrained by the barriers of class, nor was he dishonest or indolent, and he apparently enjoyed a happy domestic life. The final result, then, especially among the most perceptive observers, is a curious two-sided attitude that condemns, yet hesitates to condemn, praises and yet cannot help but disparage at the same time.

Bound closely to the American's estimate of the Italian people were his responses to their social customs and institutions. His views, on the whole, were again those of the outside observer rather than those of the participant personally involved. What he saw, of course, always was important in giving him a better perspective on his own society and institutions.

CHAPTER V

SOCIAL CUSTOMS AND INSTITUTIONS

ITALIAN social customs and institutions usually made a sharp impression on the American visitor. He commented on the varieties of dress, on the peculiarities of regional dialect, and on the sights of local celebrations. He took notice of the distinctive types that he encountered on the streets — the public letter writers, the storytellers, and the wandering *pifferari*, or piping shepherds. He observed the ways in which the different classes sought entertainment. On rare occasions he saw something of domestic customs and usages, especially among the upper classes. He investigated institutional life, visiting schools, hospitals, and charitable organizations, motivated by a desire to learn something of value to bring back to his own country.

Social life in Italy ordinarily centered about the coffeehouses and the wine shops, institutions unfamiliar to most newcomers. Men regularly gathered in these places to refresh themselves, meet their friends, and exchange gossip. Sometimes they listened to the improvisations of a witty street singer. Alcoholic beverages other than wine were not readily available, and though the atmosphere was animated, outright drunkenness was rare.

The life of the café usually pleased the visitor, who found it relaxing after the tiring business of picture galleries, churches, or ruins. Occasionally he looked with suspicion on the wine consumption, believing that this habit was partly responsible for the country's misery, but he lauded the general level of temperance and wished that his own country could do as well.

Some of the coffeehouses enjoyed international fame. Even before he came to Florence the American had perhaps heard of Doney's, which he visited regularly, sometimes making it a second home. Here he could find newspapers and journals from abroad, meet his friends, and pick up his mail, and here, according to the Florentine custom, flower girls sought him out each morning and presented him with small bouquets, expecting to be generously reimbursed before he departed. Occasionally a local poetaster would wait on the newcomer and declaim verses honoring his visit.

The most famous coffeehouse of Rome was the Caffè Greco, a large establishment that had long attracted an artistic clientele. It had been founded in the middle of the eighteenth century, and during the following century it became an important center of liberal political activity. Through the dense smoke of its crowded and dingy rooms, the newly arrived customer saw a surprising array of strange costumes and unusual faces, for there were many painters and sculptors who regularly met there after dinner each evening, and he heard a babel of tongues, since each of the major nationality groups in Rome had taken over one of the rooms at the coffeehouse. German artists generally dominated the assemblage; Italians, in fact, were far less in evidence than were visitors from other countries. Toward the end of the century, even Buffalo Bill and his road company of cowboys and Indians visited the Greco.

The name of only one restaurant, the Lepre in Rome,

has come down in many different travelers' reminiscences. Like the Greco just across the Via Condotti, the Lepre had rooms traditionally taken over by clients from different countries, and it catered especially to artists. The menu of five hundred items, of which a hundred were prepared each night, invariably proved confusing to the newcomer. For the rest, it has to be remembered that restaurants were far less numerous than they are today. As a rule, the visitor took his meals in a small *trattoria* or had food sent to his chambers.

Italian eating habits surprised the American, who was used to a large breakfast as well as a substantial afternoon dinner and an evening supper. The Italian ate little beyond one large midafternoon meal, and he usually took nothing in the morning but a cup of coffee. He tended to lavish his money on clothing for the street, for public display, and to economize at home on food. Even at a café, he spent almost nothing.

The few Americans that were actually initiated into Italian domestic social life have left vivid reports of their impressions. The upper classes customarily entertained with evenings of "conversation" or with balls. On the evenings of "conversation," usually several rooms in the household were opened; in one the guests might play cards, in another they found billiards, and in a third they could listen to music. Light refreshments were served, and sometimes the guests joined in impromptu plays and country dances, but the elaborately decorated rooms frequently were so cold and poorly furnished that despite the display of jewels and the parade of nobility, the evening was unpleasant. Good conversation, in fact, was often lacking.

When John Cogdell, on his way to Rome, asked his hotel landlord at Viterbo for entertainment one evening, he was sent to a private house nearby to join in a *conversa-*

zione. Cogdell thought it strange that he and his companions should be so casually introduced, but the evening went well, even though Cogdell knew no Italian and he lamented that it fell to his lot "to be uninteresting and unintelligible." [1]

A frequent form of diversion during such evenings was a performance by an *improvvisatore*, an entertainer who was given a topic by members of the audience and who then improvised a rhymed song on the subject, accompanied by a musical background. The Marchese di Negro, whom many Americans met at Genoa, was one of the great *improvvisatori* of his day, and when Joel Tyler Headley visited him, the old Genoese obliged Headley's request with an ode on liberty. The American realized, however, that such a feat, because of the rhyming quality of the language, was easier in Italian than it would be in English, and that not all the performances were so spontaneous as they appeared.[2]

The balls were more elaborate. Visitors in Florence usually attended the grand duke's ball in the Pitti Palace, and many Americans in Rome went to one of the dances given by the Torlonia banking family. No individual invitations were issued by the grand duke; instead, the foreign representatives of the various powers were notified, and they in turn selected those of their countrymen who might attend. Since Americans had no diplomatic representative in the Tuscan capital, they had to apply personally to the duke's chamberlain. At Genoa the American consul was given a free hand to bring to the social events of the governor any American tourists and visiting naval officers. Prince Torlonia in Rome invited everyone who had a banking account or did business with him, and his guests were always numerous. Dr. Samuel Gridley Howe was of the opinion that the Torlonia party he attended was "a vulgar, tawdry, stupid affair," with such a crowd that he could scarcely breathe.[3] A few of the Americans living in Rome also infrequently entertained with dances. Christopher Cranch considered the Storys' ball in the winter of 1859, with dancing in four or five rooms and a great seasoning of nobility, "the most brilliant party of the season." [4]

The balls, however, often seemed overly ceremonious and formal to the American, who complained that too much attention was paid to dress and manners. He was struck as well by the presence of many older people at the Italian affairs, for in the United States younger persons so dominated social occasions that they had thrust the older generation aside. The mingling of youth and age contributed a solidity to society and ought to be encouraged in the United States, believed Grace Greenwood, for one. She was impressed, too, by the presence in society of clergymen, who were usually considered out of place in American social gatherings.[5]

The theater and the opera also were important recreations. Some of the opera houses, such as La Scala in Milan, San Carlo in Naples, and La Fenice in Venice, were world-famous, and even many small towns had regular musical seasons provided by local or traveling companies. The opera houses tended to be imposingly decorated and so designed as to provide a large number of private boxes that were rented by families for an entire season. One box at La Scala, Edward Everett recorded, even had a private bedroom attached. At Florence, a box at the opera was considered essential to social acceptance; a box cost from $125 to $150 for the season and could be rented out on nights when not being used.

Although the American was generally disappointed with theatrical performances (in part due to unfamiliarity with the language), more often than not he was enthusiastic about the opera. He was, however, surprised to find that the opera house served a function different from what he had expected. He sometimes felt that the opera did not receive the respect it deserved, for he regarded the opera as an instrument of "culture," as something removed from daily concerns, to which he should bring an appropriate attitude of respect. Going to the opera or the theater, or visiting an art gallery, was a ceremony like worship in a church — something of significance partly because it was removed from everyday activities. In contrast, Italian families who had boxes not uncommonly received guests during the performance, and often paid little or no attention to the spectacle on the stage. Instead they kept up a constant chatter, punctuated by silent attention to a particular aria or the ballet. Since boxholders customarily went almost every evening and had probably seen the same performance a good many times, there was, of course, a good reason why they paid so little attention to the stage. Italian audiences took great delight in the ballet, but the American, not accustomed to this type of entertainment, was sometimes shocked. An "obscenity," wrote the novelist Catharine Maria Sedgwick, "I cannot call it by a more compromising name." [6]

Many Americans cautioned that the opera, along with the ballet and the theater, held dangers for the unwary. Samuel F. B. Morse, for example, felt that the governments of Italy encouraged the theater largely in order to take men's minds off politics and religion. Americans, he urged, should have nothing to do with theaters and the waste of time they entailed; instead, domestic duties should absorb the American family. The artificial stimulations of such entertainment could only lead to a craving for renewed indulgence and an eventual apathy and listless indifference. [7]

A more informal type of amusement was the promenade, either on foot or by carriage. Regularly, at a fixed hour,

fashionable personages assembled to stare and be stared at.
While promenading they met their friends and often listened to music. In Rome, the Pincian Gardens, the Villa
Borghese, and the Corso served as places of promenade.
In Florence, the carriages moved slowly through the Cascine, the grand duke's dairy farm, along the Arno River.
At Milan, the promenade was along the ramparts; at Venice, in Piazza San Marco; and at Naples, the Chiaja, along
the edge of the bay. Elaborate English coaches dominated
the fashionable promenade in Florence and frequently were
seen in other cities as well.

For a visitor who had no pressing duties, promenading
merged imperceptibly with perhaps the most characteristic
of Italian amusements — lounging about and doing little
or nothing whatsoever — *dolce far niente.* Along the street
he might stop to see a Punch-and-Judy show, listen to an
orator or a popular ballad singer, observe a lively game of
bowling, the antics of a street juggler, or the wild gesticu-
lations of men playing *morra,* or simply sit in a café and
watch the passers-by. He could observe the excitement of a
lottery drawing and perhaps become involved himself in
the curious ways of choosing numbers. He might stroll
about looking for prints or antique objects, and, once beginning to bargain for something, find himself the object
of interest of a dozen other loungers. Or he might accept
the solicitations of the seldom-encountered ladies of the
street and visit a local house of prostitution. If he happened
to be in Venice, he might idly drift down the Grand Canal
and perhaps, like George Ticknor, might even discover gon-
doliers who could sing. But wherever he might be, whatever he might be doing, he had to endure the stares of those
who were unoccupied and leading "the purely contempla-
tive life," something that he had not known before in the
United States.[8] Often he expressed disgust with the many

who idled away their days on the streets, but just as often he discovered the mood was contagious, and he enthusiastically joined in. He even suggested that such a habit would be a good way to counteract the overly strenuous pace of life at home.

Americans almost always responded enthusiastically to the public festivities at carnival time and periodically during the rest of the year, throwing themselves wholeheartedly into the revelry. The carnival brought balls and parades, with the principal streets the scene of a constant crushing assemblage. Many participants were in costume and masked, and they pelted one another with confetti (made of lime), sugarplums, or flowers. An inventive American, it was reported, had even devised an instrument shaped like a sugar scoop with a spring handle for shooting off a quart of confetti with tremendous force. The Roman carnival surpassed Margaret Fuller's expectations, though she found it too exhausting to go for more than one visit to the battle on the Corso and to an Italian masked ball and the German artists' ball.[9] At a masquerade ball in Palermo, Washington Irving reported the curious sight of "a walking Vessuvius that vomited flames & had red hot lava represented very ingeneously." [10]

Everyone took part in the festivities. In Naples the king was discovered throwing sugarplums at his subjects. In Genoa a group of American naval officers dressed as women romped through the streets. In Rome, Francis Parkman, a most proper Bostonian, joined the crowd and discovered that tossing flowers at the young ladies on the balconies along the route was "no contemptible amusement." [11] Even the Unitarian clergyman Theodore Parker participated in the fun, throwing almonds at the priests, then drawing himself up with an air of innocence, but his victims got their revenge, for one missile hit him square in the face and broke his glasses.[12]

Visits to social institutions were a more serious pursuit. In several cities the traveler customarily went to see the universities, especially the old, historically important schools at Bologna and Padua. At Bologna he visited a large university library, a museum of natural history, an art gallery, and rooms filled with scientific instruments. William Berrian noticed a kind of perpetual motion machine on his visit to Bologna in 1818, but he was most struck by the decline in the number of students from the great days of the past.[13] Nathaniel Hazeltine Carter found the University of Genoa little worthy of notice, though he did observe in the reading room some new American periodicals and other publications.[14] At Padua, several years later, Benjamin Silliman, professor of geology at Yale, was surprised to find how much of the school term was interrupted by religious observances; he counted 160 days during the scheduled term on which there were neither lectures nor recitations.[15] James Jackson Jarves criticized Italian professors for their remoteness from current life, feeling that they paid no attention to the needs and tastes of the public to whom they lectured.[16] Somehow the universities had declined from their former greatness, living on their reputations alone.

Visits to lower schools often elicited disparaging comments on the whole Italian educational system. Availability of public, popular education was an important tenet of the American's creed, and the backward state of lower education in Italy, compared to the school system in the United States, was obvious. The contrast between the lavish sums used for decorating churches and palaces and the small amount spent for educating the common people constantly aroused the traveler's ire. The schools were almost always judged bad. "There is not a school in Rome which must not be considered as a beacon to warn rather than a light to guide the inquirer," wrote Dr. Samuel Gridley Howe, himself an educator.[17] Only one school was widely praised during these years — a Florentine institution conducted on the Lancasterian plan by Marchese Carlo Torrigiani, who had traveled in the United States and had absorbed American "liberal and philanthropic views." [18] In the latter part of the century, after the union of Italy, educational conditions seemed to be improving.

Not only education but science as well was a significant concern to many Americans, increasingly so toward the middle of the century. Professional scientists, like the geologist Benjamin Silliman or the chemist John Griscom, made a point of visiting scientific institutions throughout the peninsula. Silliman, especially, displayed an active interest in all fields of knowledge and went to see the scientific departments of several universities. When the famous American astronomer Maria Mitchell met Father Secchi, director of the observatory of the Collegio Romano in Rome, and asked permission to see the telescope, she was immediately refused both because of her sex and because of her religion. Through some behind-the-scenes maneuvering, however, she was eventually given permission and was taken by Father Secchi to the monastery where the observatory was located. Though she could not use the telescope, she was shown some recent examples of celestial photography, but rules could only be adjusted so far for a foreign, female visitor, and she had to terminate her visit before darkness fell.[19]

The American was somewhat uncertain if his own country were ahead or behind in scientific investigations. In any case, he was sure that the future in this realm lay with his nation. He nevertheless admired governmental patronage of scientific and other institutions, and looked upon this practice as one that the United States ought to imitate. Even the most despotic monarchy of Europe, he realized, patronized science in ways that the American republic did not.

The Italian press proved a great contrast to what the American knew at home. Newspapers were tiny sheets containing little besides notices of Church activities and celebrations. There was scarcely any foreign news, and almost nothing was written about local affairs other than those of the Church. In Rome, few foreign journals were available, and those at hand were only of a neutral character. Concerning this dearth of published news, the newspaperman Horace Greeley found that he "could not learn to relish such a state of things," and he was happy to depart from the Papal domain.[20] Other observers, though, found the moderation of the newspapers a welcome relief from some of the excesses of their own journals.

Open to the foreigner in Florence and Rome were public circulating libraries and reading rooms. Vieusseux's library in Florence was an important center of liberal activity. Here the visitor could read several New York papers, and here he might meet the influential Marchese Gino Capponi and foreign literary celebrities. In Rome there was Monaldini's library, the shelves of which were well stocked with French and English novels. Particularly in Rome, however, the traveler had a hard time finding modern and liberal works, for the censorship regulations were severe, and the Index was strictly enforced. "The Index," wrote Theodore Lyman, "has excluded nearly every book that does not sing to the glory of the cross, the glory of the throne of St. Peter, or the still more harmless glory of a Roman column." [21]

Publishing was also severely restricted. Cooper, for example, could not get *The Water Witch* printed in Rome because of one offending sentence about the decline of ancient Rome. There the Court of the Inquisition was still active in combating schism and heresy. The Kingdom of Sardinia and the Austrian dominions of the North generally accorded greater freedom in publishing than was the case in the South, where censorship was often arbitrary and dictated only by the caprices and prejudices of the censors. Such restrictions on the free expression of ideas were, quite naturally, a major element of the visitors' indictment of the society and its government.[22]

The hospitals of the principal cities, the American discovered, were large and clean, with good care provided for the patients. But he sometimes felt that like other institutions, such as orphanages and poorhouses, the hospitals were badly managed, in that the rich endowments had been squandered on lavish establishments for the ecclesiastical dignitaries in charge. Despite the good care that the hospitals gave, the American often expressed a low opinion of the state of Italian medical science.

Provisions for care of the insane, on the other hand, commonly impressed the visitor favorably. The asylum at Genoa was shaped like a wheel, with a central section and wings radiating outward like spokes; exercise areas were provided between the buildings for the various classes of the mentally ill. Though some of the insane in Genoa were chained to their beds, this practice was unusual, and a great contrast to such an asylum as that at Aversa near Naples, in which there was an atmosphere of freedom and where the patients were encouraged to work and were soothed by music. Treatment at Venice was humane and mild, the institution clean and well managed. At the female asylum in Venice, one traveler found the insane busily employed in large workrooms and "quieter and happier than the same class with us." [23] Occupational therapy and constant kindness were also the treatment in the well-run asylums at Palermo and Milan. At Rome, however, care for the insane was bad. Dorothea Dix managed in 1856 to gain an audience with Pope Pius IX, who was sincerely shocked by her revelations of the conditions of Roman asylums. He promised to make a personal inspection, and after an unannounced visit to a local asylum he saw Miss Dix again to thank her and promise to reform the abuses; a new asylum was subsequently erected making use of more enlightened methods of care and treatment.[24]

The poorhouses, or "inns of the poor," in most cities were magnificent palaces, accommodating several thousand persons, who were employed in manufacturing carpets or beads or in studying reading, writing, ciphering, and often a trade. The poorhouse in Florence even set aside a certain part of the earnings coming from the inmates' labor for their assistance in old age.

Although the American was struck by the many provisions for public charity, he entertained some doubts about the value of these undertakings. Sometimes he expressed the feeling that such alleviation merely encouraged greater indigence. Usually, however, he was aware that the extensive areas of distress justified extensive measures of relief, though he still objected to the ostentatious forms that such measures often took. To some visitors, foundling hospitals were an obvious and glaring sign of immorality, a spur to prostitution and sexual promiscuity.

Penal institutions and devices also interested the visitor. But many Italian laws relating to crime seemed unnecessarily harsh, and some methods of punishment inhumane. That a Neapolitan who brandished about a knife that did not close and with a blade more than three inches long could be condemned to the galleys for life was scarcely just. At carnival time provision was made for the immediate public whippings of disorderly persons. Even more disturbing was the spectacle of prisoners condemned to spend their lives chained together and employed in heavy labor for public works. Particularly in Tuscany, such inhumane treatment seemed out of keeping with the comparatively mild government of the state. The sight of these criminals was a bitter one, but it seldom led the American to reflect on the practice of slavery in his own land.

Visits to prisons were not unusual. Most prisons, it was discovered, were overcrowded, and the care of the inmates was bad. In 1819, Stephen Grellet, a Quaker enthusiast, personally reported his observations on the prison at Naples to the Neapolitan prime minister, and on the prisons at Rome to the powerful papal secretary, Cardinal Consalvi, with the hope that such conditions as beatings and chainings as well as the general misapplication of funds could be alleviated. In the prisons, the outspoken Grellet preached repentance to the inmates, but he felt that his words had little effect.[25]

In two customs especially — the way the Italian dealt with animals and the manner he treated the dead — the American found what seemed to him a curious insensitivity. Although the Italian seemed to be a passionate man of deeply felt emotions, he somehow lacked appropriate feelings for certain important subjects. His sensibility appeared strangely limited to the American.

The New World visitor was constantly upset by the treatment of animals. He saw the donkeys he used to get to the lower slopes of Vesuvius or the waterfall at Terni mercilessly beaten. Post horses were invariably whipped to unnecessary speeds, and pack animals were commonly overladen. Neapolitans frequently decorated their animals with flowers, bells, and gay trappings, but for this trouble they seemed to flog the beasts all the more. Madame Le Vert and her party, immediately after arriving in Italy, were so disturbed by the beating their *vetturino* gave his horses that they reported the driver for cruelty and were promised that he would be dismissed at once.[26] Even the way Italians captured small birds for the table was held against them.

A revealing test of the American's feelings toward animals occurred at the Grotto del Cane near Naples. To amuse and enlighten the visitors a small dog was placed in the poisonous gas on the floor of the cave. When the fumes had rendered the dog unconscious, he was thrown on the ground in the fresh air, and soon revived and trotted off. Almost all the Americans coming to this place pitied the animal but still went through with the experiment. Thus even though Americans believed they had a kinder attitude toward animals than Italians did, in this case at least they usually made little attempt to transform these feelings into action. Some rationalized their behavior by saying that the dogs undoubtedly were used to the situation anyway. Only a few tourists declined to have the experiment performed, and then usually because the custodian wanted too large a fee and not because of sympathy for the dog. Washington Irving and his party threatened to withhold the custodian's fee if he went ahead with the performance, although they suggested as an alternative that he might hold his own head in the vapor.[27]

The American saw little of weddings, but he often commented on funerals and the usages of death. He was surprised at the prevalent attitude toward death and truly shocked by some of the burial practices. To come upon bodies exposed in churches or to see funeral processions in the dark of night, with the corpse borne to the grave on an open bier, made a strong impression on him. The fear of death, he learned, was so strong that bodies were never kept in the house overnight and the chambers of the dying were quickly stripped and fumigated. Members of the family or friends of the deceased seldom accompanied the body to the place of burial. Decency, the visitor felt, was slighted and the dignity of death outraged in the manner of burial of all except the well-to-do, whose families could afford costly space in a church.

The cemetery at Naples was the most famous in Italy, but some others were like it in design. The Naples cemetery had 365 pits, one of which was opened each day of the year to deposit the bodies of the poor brought for burial that day. The bodies were dumped together into the chamber, and quicklime was then poured down to hasten decomposition. The traveler invariably gave the guard a small tip to lift one of the stone slabs so that he could look within, and he invariably reported the most horrible sight of decaying forms that he had ever seen. The practice seemed particularly indecent, moreover, since men, women, and children of both sexes were all tossed into the same pits together, the bodies stripped of all clothing. Samuel F. B. Morse was horrified by what he saw there: "Death is sufficiently terrible in itself, and the grave in its best form has enough of horror to make the stoutest heart quail at the thought, but nothing I have seen or read of can equal the Campo Santo for the most loathsome and disgusting mode of burial. The human carcasses of all ages and sexes are here thrown in together to a depth of, perhaps, twenty feet, without coffins, in heaps, most of them perfectly naked, and left to corrupt in a mass, like the offal from a slaughter house. So disgusting a spectacle I never witnessed. There were in sight about twenty bodies, men, women, and children. A child of about six years, with beautiful fair hair, had fallen across the body of a man and lay in the attitude of sleeping. . . . We were glad to turn away and retrace our steps to our carriage. Never, I believe, in any country, Christian, or pagan, is

there an instance of such total want of respect for the remains of the dead." [28] Sometimes added to the indignities
of the burial was the behavior of the officiating priests, who
laughed and talked with each other during the funeral
ceremonies.

Just as shocking as this common mode of interment were
the Capuchin convent burial chambers, which the traveler
went to see in Rome, Syracuse, and Palermo. Here he found
mummified bodies lined up against the walls, often clothed
in the dress which they had once worn when alive. At
Palermo, Francis Parkman bought a Mass for fifty cents to
be said in the vaults of the Capuchin monastery at four
o'clock in the morning. He joined the monks for the service,
passing between rows of grinning mummies, men, women,
and children. "The virgins," he noted, "all wear crowns of
silver paper, from beneath which they grin and gape in a
most alluring fashion." [29]

Social life and customs in Italy thus provided the American visitor with some striking contrasts with what he knew
in his own country. He found the life of the café and the
promenade curiously appealing, and he enjoyed the colorful public festivals and ceremonies, so different from similar events at home. Domestic entertainments remained
largely closed to him, but his occasional excursions into
private society gave him a more penetrating view of Italian
life. The Italian opera opened up a new world of music to
him.

His feelings toward social institutions were mixed, for he
found some things that he felt his own country might well
emulate, as well as other things that must be avoided. Charitable institutions, he discovered, were far more extensively
organized in Italy than in his own country. Governments,
the Church, societies and confraternities, and private persons
all appeared to have a sense of responsibility for relief of the

unfortunate unlike anything the American had known before. Hospitals, insane asylums, and poorhouses were conducted on a scale that astonished him, and the care, he found, was usually good. Treatment of prisoners, by contrast, he thought far less humane than in his own land. Although the traveler was certain that the institutions and the organization of Italian society were responsible in the first place for so many people having need of assistance, he saw that such charitable associations were socially necessary and might well be models for his own country to follow.

Italian social customs and institutions were significant to the American traveler in the formation of his over-all response to the country, but the areas of art and religion occupied his attention still more. Art often was the main attraction drawing the visitor to Italy, and art filled the days of many who came. Art pervaded the Italian cultural fabric and frequently became the visitor's primary concern.

CHAPTER VI

THE WORLD OF ART

OR MANY nineteenth-century Americans, Italy represented, beyond any other land, that country which
most fully and most perfectly embodied the greatest
achievements in the Western tradition of the fine arts.[1]
Certainly this inheritance — the architectural remains surviving from antiquity and the Renaissance, world-famous
pictures, statues, and art objects, an atmosphere stimulating
artistic creativity — was a major force drawing foreigners
to Italy. Others, previously indifferent to art, found that
the characteristic way of life and the physical remains of
the past added something new to their lives, and they, too,
turned to art. "It is impossible to live in Italy long," wrote
the Reverend John A. Clark, "without becoming at least a
profound amateur in the fine arts." [2]

Art permeated the country. An intense appreciation of
art appeared at all levels of Italian society, though the lower
classes' love of art and ability to talk about it sometimes
struck the American as incongruous. Works of art in public places were regarded reverently and apparently seldom
defaced or mutilated. The governments of Italy honored
art and considered it an important source of public edifica-
tion and pleasure. In fact, painting and statuary in galleries

and churches served as a kind of free art education for the public. Sometimes the visitor even suggested that art was responsible for the refinement of manners and cultivation that the Italian commonly displayed.

The atmosphere stimulated the visiting layman as well as the professional, and many Americans, under the influence of Italian scenery and galleries and the example of their fellow countrymen working in the arts, took up painting or modeling or began to compose verse. Young George Bancroft on his first visit wrote a group of poems, which were printed in a slender volume in 1823. Edward Everett began lessons in drawing and took to writing verses. Bayard Taylor, later to become America's most famous professional traveler of the century, hired a studio in Rome on his visit in 1868 and secretly worked there each morning on figure painting. Even Washington Irving, tempted by the life of the artist and seduced by the beauties of Rome, considered turning to painting as a profession and staying on in Italy. Certainly many illustrated journals and water-color sketches must still be lying today, dust-covered and forgotten, in American attics, recording nineteenth-century visits to Italy.

Although art experiences meant a great deal to the American traveler throughout these years, his interest in art was decidedly greater toward the end of the period, and as it increased, his attention to contemporary social life and institutions declined. Furthermore, he was more concerned with sculpture during the earliest years, but by the 1850's he ranked painting as high. Near the end of the century, his taste markedly changed, and sculpture definitely lost appeal for him as compared to painting. Unlike painting and sculpture, architecture was seldom discussed in any detail.

Despite his general interest, however, the American took a rather dim view of the state of contemporary art; modern works seemed only to emphasize the decline of the country from her past glory. The Danish sculptor Thorwaldsen and the Italian sculptor Canova alone among contemporaries received universal acclaim. "The other artists," reported Ticknor in 1837, "make abundance of long-legged things that they call nymphs and Venuses and Psyches, and a plenty of chubby boys that they would pass off for Genii; but all poetry is wanting." [3] The painter John Gadsby Chapman attributed the low state of the arts to the long training and routine required of academic artists, so that "dull & spiritless imitation becomes [their] first and last effort." [4] James de Veaux, on the other hand, believed that this decline had been caused largely by the fall in monetary incentive; the churches were already well stocked with pictures, the decline in commercial wealth had reduced governmental and private patronage, and foreigners usually wanted only copies of the old masters. [5]

Immediately after the American Revolution and continuing at least through the first two decades of the nineteenth century, most American painters went to London for training and inspiration. Italy gradually began to attract more painters, however, and until after the American Civil War it remained the mecca of the American artists. During the final three decades of the century, with changes in taste, Paris, Munich, and Düsseldorf drew American art students.

In the middle years of the century, then, Italy attracted both enthusiastic amateurs and established professionals. The country had much to offer. The artist quickly discovered that Italy was itself a whole school of art. The public gardens and private galleries had a wealth of the greatest works of sculpture and painting from the past. Here he could study what those before him had succeeded in creating, perhaps deriving general principles of beauty from what he saw around him. Here he met others closely involved in the same type of work, and from whom he could benefit by way of companionship, advice, and criticism. "No doubt," as Hawthorne put it, "they keep each other warm by the presence of so many of them." [6] And here the artist also found distinguished schools for training, especially in drawing.

The artist was further stimulated by the architectural remains, the people, and the natural scene. The portrayal of decaying ruins, goatskin-clad shepherds, or jagged rocks and lonely waterfalls was exactly what contemporary taste demanded. What better place to find remnants of the distant past, a people colorful in appearance, and an often mysterious and "sublime" landscape than in Italy? Italy, in fact, became for the artist of this period the nearest tangible approach to the realm of ideal beauty.

Furthermore, the country provided the artist himself with a stature and prestige he had not possessed at home. His work was highly valued, and he was given an honored place in the social hierarchy as well as freedom from social pressures. No longer was he considered an eccentric who did not fit into the accepted social categories. Here, artists could claim Raphael and Michelangelo as ancestors, while in America, they had no forebears. "In every other clime they are isolated strangers; in this land of art, they are free citizens." [7]

Italy, in addition, afforded practical facilities for the artist to maintain himself and carry on his work. Living costs, as we have observed, were remarkably low, especially for one who had become well acquainted with the country. Many sculptors settled in Florence because the cost of marble was less there than at Rome. Horatio Greenough even lived for a time at Carrara, where marble cost a quarter of the price in Florence and wages were about half of those paid elsewhere. Highly skilled stonecutters — men impossible to find in the United States — were available. Particularly in Rome, the artist had ruins in abundance to utilize as backgrounds and all the models he needed. The professional models, who stationed themselves on the Spanish Steps, specialized in certain roles — the Magdalen, St. John the Apostle, or Jesus Christ; two or three old, white-bearded men were even on call to serve as God. Finally, Italy offered the opportunity for public exhibits, as, for example, in a room near the Porta del Popolo in Rome, where painters could display their works for a fee of only twenty cents monthly. And in Italy purchasers flocked to the doors of the studios.

Most of the professional artists looked upon time spent in Italy as worth-while, though occasionally someone depreciated the value of study and work there. William Rinehart in 1859 expressed the belief that Rome was a good place for the sculptor, but not for the painter, who would do better in Paris where he could find "stile" in perfection.[8] Others realized that in Italy they were perhaps cutting themselves off from their native roots and wondered about the wisdom of long residence abroad. Horatio Greenough, for example, asked Fenimore Cooper to advise him whether he should remain in Italy or return to the United States, where he still saw may obstacles to his art.[9]

It is impossible to tell just how many American artists visited the country during the nineteenth century. With few exceptions, all the major painters and sculptors of the period spent some time traveling or studying there. Many artists today forgotten except for a brief reference in William Dunlap's *History of the Rise and Progress of the Arts of Design* or Henry T. Tuckerman's *Book of the Artists* are known to have worked in Italy.

They were a most diversified group. Some American artists went with serious study and work already behind them, determined to pursue their chosen careers in the foreign scene. Some enrolled in schools and academies for supervised instruction; most, apparently, did not. Others went with no background in art and set out to make a career in the field. William Story and William R. Barbee both turned from successful law practices to sculpture. Joseph Mozier gave up a commercial livelihood in New York City, and moved directly to Italy where he felt he could best prepare himself in art. Some of the artists remained for only a short time, during which they did little more than visit the leading galleries and sketch the ruins in the Campagna or medieval streets. Others spent the major part of their productive years, and though they seldom considered themselves as such, became in fact expatriates. Some came to Italy never to return home, struck down in the foreign land by disease and death. A few were fortunate enough to have patrons, so that they had no immediate financial worries. For most, money remained a nagging problem, and their letters are filled with concern over finding the necessary sums to continue their work. A small number became enormously successful, sought by international society, heavily commissioned, and well rewarded; others failed to interest the public and spent their days in poverty and obscurity, sometimes in misery. At least two Americans, Randolph Rogers and Thomas Crawford, were elected to the famous Academy of St. Luke, and Harriet Hosmer was uniquely honored by a sculptural commission for a Roman church.

One can discern certain patterns in the lives of these American artists abroad. The sculptors were comparatively restricted in their movements, and usually established themselves in Florentine or Roman studios where they spent the greater part of the year at work, perhaps leaving the city only for a short time during the heat of summer. The painters, on the other hand, had more freedom and frequently took extended trips through the country.

WILLIAM CULLEN BRYANT and HIRAM POWERS. From a photograph.

THE GREEK SLAVE by Hiram Powers. Courtesy of the Brooklyn Museum.

During the summer months the painters abandoned the cities for villages in the mountains. Many from Rome went into the nearby Alban Hills or to one of the villages in the lower Apennines. Those in Florence often moved to the north. Sometimes artists literally painted their way across the countryside. James E. Freeman, a painter, tells the story of two artists, an American and an Englishman, who traveled through the Abruzzi sketching portraits of prosperous peasants in order to pay for their trip; unfortunately, in one village, a charcoal burner who was to marry one of their subject-models became so jealous of their attention to the girl that he killed her and was in turn slain by the girl's father.[10]

American artists in Rome annually participated in the arts festival, which attracted representatives from all nationalities to a site outside the city, often an abandoned quarry. The artists wore extravagant costumes and generously partook of the local wines. A collection of paintings and drawings was sold for the relief of the poorer artists, and one of those present was selected to rule. The revels were joyously uninhibited, and the Reverend Joel Tyler Headley, for one, was shocked by the spectacle: "There were Americans among the rest, and I am sure if they could have dropped into their native towns at home just as they were mounted and dressed to-day, their friends would have clapped them in a lunatic asylum 'sans ceremonie.' " [11]

A characteristic daily routine was followed by Robert W. Weir, a painter who for a time shared rooms on the Pincian Hill in Rome with the sculptor Horatio Greenough. Early in the morning Weir either worked at home or drew from antique statues at the nearby French Academy. Following breakfast he went to the Sistine Chapel, the Vatican Museum, or a private gallery and continued to copy until closing time at three o'clock in the afternoon. After lunch, he either returned to his own rooms to work, walked on the Campagna, or went back to the French Academy. Dinner at a favorite *trattoria*, which had once been the painting room of Pompeo Battoni, was followed by coffee at the Caffè Greco, then by two hours at a life class, sometimes cut short by a moonlight excursion to one of the ruins of the city.

George Loring Brown was also typical in many ways. Washington Allston considered that Brown's copy of one of Claude's landscapes was the best he had ever seen, and Allston encouraged him to work in Italy. A group of wealthy Bostonians supplied Brown with commissions for copying, and advanced part of the money for the pictures. In Italy, he worked chiefly on landscapes, "full of poetical and Claude-like effects," which he turned out rapidly in his studio. For R. H. Winslow of New York, as an example, Brown promised on April 15, 1854, to have finished by the following November 1st, at a price of $250, "1 landscape, large trees — water — group of Peasantry cooking or with a fire — Animals — mountains in the back ground — Similar to the picture for F. G. Shaw." [12] The Hawthornes visited Brown in 1858 and were delighted both with the man and with his pictures. Free of all affectations, Brown seemed to them "a plain, homely Yankee, quite unpolished by his many years' residence in Italy," and Brown's paintings gave Hawthorne greater pleasure than any landscapes of the old masters.[13]

The pattern of rigorous self-discipline and hard work is repeated in the career of James de Veaux, who spent the final three years of his life in Italy. Coming to Florence in 1841, he customarily passed six hours each day copying at one of the galleries, while in the evenings he drew from living models. He discovered that to copy the most popular pictures he often had to wait a full year for the necessary

THE WORLD OF ART 131

permission, and he lamented that feast days cut deeply into his time. Although there were many American artists in Florence, he found them an envious and jealous lot and preferred not to associate with them. De Veaux recorded in his journal his admiration for the Italian people, his shock at the contrasts of wealth and poverty, and, though a Huguenot, his satisfactions in the Roman Catholic Church.[14]

American sculptors took the leading role in American society in Italy. In Florence, Hiram Powers, as we have seen, was the acknowledged leader of American social and artistic affairs during much of the century. Everyone called on Powers, and after leaving Florence most of those who met him continued to regard him as a friend. The visitor usually found the sculptor in his studio, clad in a linen apron, a pasteboard cap covering his iron-grey hair, working perhaps on a plaster model with one of the filing tools he himself had designed. Moving past workmen busily chipping away at large blocks of marble, the visitor might see "California," "America," "Eve," or one of the several copies of the "Greek Slave." The Danish sculptor Thorwaldsen praised Powers' bust of Daniel Webster as the best work of its kind executed in modern times, and the grand duke of Tuscany was so delighted by the bust of the grand duchess that he allowed the sculptor to take a cast of the "Venus di Medici," a favor that other artists had long sought in vain. Although some travelers criticized Powers' imaginative gift, his work impressed American buyers, for it was in accord with the current canons of taste, and orders increasingly flowed in. His technical gifts, particularly his ability to give a delicate finish to a stone surface, were considered superb. The "Greek Slave" was the most famous American statue of the nineteenth century.

The first American sculptor to go to Italy was Horatio Greenough. Immediately on arriving in Genoa in 1825, he caught sight of statuary that went unnoticed by the passers-by but was better than anything he had ever seen before. Greenough was moved to tears, persuaded that he would never be able to do so well. He went on to Rome, but soon fell so ill that he was obliged to return to Boston. In 1828, Greenough returned to Italy, this time staying in Carrara and in Florence, where he ultimately decided to make his home. Fenimore Cooper, then living in Florence, gave him his first commission — a group of two angelic figures copied from the foreground of Raphael's "Madonna del Baldacchino." The "Chanting Cherubs" was the first marble group executed by an American. Although it was generally well received on exhibit in the United States, some viewers objected to the nudity of the figures, and others complained because the cherubs did not actually sing. The outcries of protest, however, were louder yet some years later when Greenough's "George Washington," scantily clad in a Roman toga, was set up in the national Capitol.

To Greenough's studio on the Piazza Maria Antonia came a great many visiting Americans. The sumptuously designed studio included a spacious exhibition room, a gallery of plaster casts, a vestibule of pictures, and a library, as well as Greenough's own workroom and a large area for his workmen. With small groups of visitors the sculptor was at his best, his conversation revealing his extensive learning and grasp of artistic principles. His writings advocating functionalist ideas have given him an important place in the limited community of American aestheticians. Greenough's statuary, nevertheless, did not receive the popular acclaim granted to the work of his friend Hiram Powers. Unlike Powers, Greenough participated extensively in Italian society, and in the midyears of the century he took part in the manifestations of Italian liberalism, joining the

Civic Guard of Florence, and putting the courtyard of his Florentine palace at its disposal for military drill.

In Rome, William Wetmore Story was the best-known resident American artist and the acknowledged leader of American society. Although some of his statues were enthusiastically received at a London exhibition, much of his work was greeted with awkward embarrassment even at the time. Mrs. Henry Adams, to take one example, was shocked at the way Story "spoil[ed] nice blocks of white marble." In his studio she found nothing but "Sibyls on all sides, sitting, standing, legs crossed, legs uncrossed, and all with the same expression as if they smelt something wrong." [15] Story's conceptions were literary, not plastic, a point driven home by the verses he wrote to accompany the statuary. Perhaps his most famous work was "Cleopatra," who sat in her chair, solidly massive, weighing at least a ton, and contemplating her fate — the storage room of the Metropolitan Museum.

When Thomas Crawford arrived in Rome in 1835 he was warmly received by Thorwaldsen and given a place to work in his studio. Soon Crawford was joined in Rome by James E. Freeman and Luther Terry, both painters, and Crawford's own studio presently evolved into another nucleus of American artist life. The sale of a statue of Orpheus to the Boston Athenaeum in 1840, through the help of Charles Sumner, who raised a subscription, aided Crawford immensely by attracting new commissions. He was obliged to expand his facilities and hire new workmen. Crawford brought to Italy as a bride Louisa Ward, sister of Julia Ward Howe, and their home in the Villa Negroni near the Baths of Diocletian became a popular center for visiting Americans. Like Greenough, Crawford supported the liberal movement, and, like Greenough, he joined the republican Civic Guard during the short-lived revolutionary outburst at midcentury. His career was cut short in 1857 by a painful cancer of the eyes. After Crawford's death, Hawthorne visited the artist's studio to look at the casts of various statues, and he dismissed them with the sour remark: "They are but commonplaces in marble and plaster, such as we should not tolerate on a printed page." [16]

Harriet Hosmer, the sculptress, provided still another focal point for American creative activity in Rome. She first came to Rome in 1852 and for several years studied with the Welsh sculptor John Gibson, who was well known particularly because he tinted his statues in imitation of ancient Greek practice. For a time she shared a house with the actress Charlotte Cushman and her friend Emma Stebbins; later she occupied a studio near the Storys, overlooking the Piazza Barberini. Harriet Hosmer, like Amy Lowell after her, was fond of wearing men's clothing, and was notorious for her suspiciously emancipated ways in general. When, contrary to custom, she appeared on the streets of Rome all by herself, on horseback, the disturbance was so great that the police had to intervene and forbade her to ride about in such a fashion. Both Nathaniel and Sophia Hawthorne, nonetheless, took an instant liking to the young sculptress on a visit to her studio in 1858, but William Story frowned on these independent females, who struck him as a distasteful crowd of Bohemians.

Among the important American painters in Italy was Washington Allston, who, during the first half of the century, was regarded by his countrymen as the greatest artist America had yet produced. Allston, who passed the years 1804 to 1808 in Italy, was considerably influenced in his art by the natural scenery of Italy, especially the landscape around Rome. His paintings reflect a preoccupation with the passage of time, the past seen through a dim and

dreamy veil of obscuring distance. In Rome, Allston became intimately acquainted with Samuel Taylor Coleridge,
and he was greatly impressed by Coleridge's originality.
Allston painted his portrait, and the two kept up a friend-
ship for more than twenty-five years. In Rome, too, Allston
advised and encouraged John Vanderlyn, the painter, who
lived for a short time in Salvator Rosa's house.

With Washington Irving, Allston explored Rome and
the surrounding countryside. Irving was so taken by the
beauty of the scene and the pleasure of artistic pursuits that
for a time he considered turning to painting and remaining
in Rome. The thought of going back to the study of law,
for which he had no relish and, he feared, little talent, inclined Irving to look with even greater favor on the kind of
life Allston was leading, "surrounded by masterpieces of
art, by classic and historic monuments, by men of congenial
minds and tastes, engaged like him in the constant study of
the sublime and beautiful." Allston eagerly seconded Irving's artistic aspirations, and suggested that they share
lodgings, while he gave Irving instruction. But doubts
grew, and the force of circumstance made Irving abandon
the idea.[17]

The American painter in Italy attracting the greatest
attention during the middle years of the century was William Page, who had studied with Samuel F. B. Morse, himself a pupil of Allston. An experimenter in painting tech-
nique and, like Hiram Powers, a Swedenborgian enthusiast,
Page was hailed by his compatriots as the latest in geniuses.
But Page's champions uncomfortably sensed that somehow
his talent had been led astray. For all his undeniable technical facility and a fine feeling for his craft, his paintings
were, in fact, largely failures. Page had a theory that the
Venetian colorists had originally utilized the dark patina
which their pictures came to have, and accordingly he

strove for a similar effect by working in middle and dark tones, but his process so far failed to come off that his canvases quickly deteriorated to an indistinguishable darkness.

Given so many American painters and sculptors in Rome and Florence, even the most indifferent American visitor turned to contemporary art as one of his principal diversions. Visits to the studios — especially toward the middle of the century — became a fashionable necessity, and the purchase of pictures and sculpture came to be one of the lesser reasons for making a trip to Italy.

Strangers were freely admitted into the painters' and sculptors' studios without introductions. The American visited several of the studios of his countrymen and occasionally inspected the work in progress of one of the better-known German or Italian artists. Brochures listing the names, nationalities, addresses, and specialties (portraits, historical, or literary) of the artists in Rome were regularly issued. At the Roman studio of Joseph Mozier, near the Spanish Steps, the visitor might see a statue of "Truth" striking off the mask from the face of "Dissimulation"; at the studio of Miss Lander, the statue of "Virginia Dare" kept company with "Evangeline Sleeping." A few sculptors specialized in New World themes, and Henry Kirke Brown, William Henry Rinehart, Horatio Greenough, and S. V. Clevenger all carved in Italy statues of American Indians. Most Americans managed to take studio visiting in their stride, but Hawthorne found it "a terrible business" to look at works of art in the presence of the artists who had made them.[18]

Somehow, stimulated by the very atmosphere of art in which they were caught up, Americans who had never before displayed any interest in paintings or statues were "infected by the contagion of the place" and began to make purchases on a grand scale. Conversation, William

Cullen Bryant reported, turned not on the money market, new enterprises, public measures, or the flow of trade, but only on art and artists.[19]

American art works created abroad were acquired on a mass scale. Obviously, because of the emphasis on art in Italy, the traveler's interest was turned in this direction. Often he merely wanted souvenirs of his foreign journey, and so painters brought into their original work some reference to the country, either in the present or the past. John Singleton Copley, for example, in painting Mr. and Mrs. Ralph Izard in Rome in 1774, surrounded them with objects associated with the city. G. P. A. Healy represented Henry Wadsworth Longfellow and his daughter Edith standing under the Arch of Titus, and William Page painted his wife planted solidly in front of the Colosseum. Such associations added to the sentimental value of the paintings.

Art objects served as well as recognizable status symbols and helped to show those at home what the traveler had been fortunate enough to experience. The works he brought home were unusual, things not commonly seen, and their mere possession helped to differentiate the owner. Certainly snob appeal was partly responsible for the many portrait busts that visitors had American sculptors carve for them. Powers was considered the most fashionable, though Crawford and Greenough also had distinguished clients.

Earlier, even Canova, the most famous sculptor of his day and considered by his generation worthy of standing with Phidias and Praxiteles, had been sought out. Although the Italian declined Joseph Sansom's request in 1802 that he execute a portrait bust of George Washington, declaring that he would work only from real life, he later carved for the North Carolina state capitol a large statue of Washington penning a message (in Italian) to the people of the United States. This curious statue, for which a portrait bust made by Giuseppe Ceracchi was used as a model, had been ordered on the advice of Jefferson through Thomas Appleton, American consul at Leghorn, and was finally shipped from Italy in 1821. It was destroyed by fire in 1831. Edward Everett, like many others, was much impressed by Canova's reputation and in 1818 wrote to the sculptor to arrange to have one of his pupils make Everett's bust, just so he could say back home it was a product of Canova's workshop.[20]

Since many American visitors, unsure of their taste and even of the artists', preferred to buy objects sanctified by familiarity, the production of copies, many of decidedly inferior quality, supported many artists. Copley had made copies on commission in the previous century, and a large number of American artists during the nineteenth century continued to provide the desired imitations. The competition to sell copies among artists of different nationalities who were based in Italy was intense, and an occasional critic deplored a situation that in the long run threatened to destroy the incentive for doing original work.

Old copies and old originals, too, were found in great abundance. Everywhere pictures were for sale. On the lookout for works of art for Robert Gilmor of Baltimore, Horatio Greenough wrote that he had discovered a Tintoretto copy of a Titian, "a grand original rendered with a fact, feeling and impetuosity of execution rarely met with." He thought that he would give as much as fifty or sixty dollars for it, though he was ashamed to say that earlier it had been offered to him for thirty, and he had rejected it because of a coating of dirt and grime. Thomas Cole, Greenough hastened to add, thought the picture "a masterpiece in its way."[21]

When Samuel Cabot of Boston visited Italy in 1833 he was commissioned to buy statuary for the wealthy Boston merchant Thomas Handasyd Perkins. He selected a "St. Jerome" in Rome, and in Naples found a copy of a statue of Aristides, taken from Herculaneum, which he succeeded in bargaining down in price. He wanted to have a copy made of a Raphael in the Pitti gallery, but, surprisingly, could not find a qualified artist to do the work. Price was the most crucial factor in his selection, though he also took account of size and subject. Cabot rejected the purchase of other statues on the grounds that none was "of so high a character in Sculpture except Venus's & naked figures which we did not like to venture upon." [22]

Some critics felt that Americans were being cheated, that in their untutored and uncritical concern for art, they were being loaded down with bad copies and manifest fakes. Charles Eliot Norton was irritated to discover in Italy that "the worst pictures are purchased by Americans, or for the American market." [23] James Jackson Jarves, himself a collector, cautioned the American public to be wary of picture dealers and artists; he cited instances of fraudulent dealers displaying a framed picture on the back of which the purchaser signed his name, only to discover later that the picture he received was not the one he thought he had bought, another having been placed in the frame on top of the one sent. Dishonest picture dealers bought old pictures at wholesale rates, touched them up a bit, and sent them to the United States to be sold as neglected masterpieces. Americans, Jarves warned, could not expect to find works by the great masters, though many good original pictures were still to be had, and at reasonable prices. The prospective purchaser, however, was cautioned not to believe the owner's tale of origins but to be guided solely by his own taste. The dealer would lower his price when he found the purchaser was interested only in the picture and not in its supposed lineage.[24]

Even if the American had been clever enough to make an advantageous purchase, he still had to face the difficulties of getting his treasure back to the United States, and transporting statuary especially posed some formidable problems. One first had to get the pieces to Leghorn, the usual port of debarkation; then came loading, which often delayed transport for a considerable time. A few pieces were lost at sea in shipwrecks, the heavy marble itself perhaps even contributing to the accidents. Powers' statue of Calhoun sank at Fire Island in the vessel on which Margaret Fuller Ossoli and her family were coming to the United States, though the statue was later recovered and set up in Charleston, South Carolina.

During the first half of the nineteenth century, the currents of taste of Americans visiting Italy reveal a great many different eddies, though the travelers, both artists and non-artists, were in general accord about what they saw. Despite this consensus, however, one has little feeling that most travelers had any great depth of understanding of the works of art or that the works had much aesthetic meaning to them.

Sometimes a visitor pointed out that the exposure to such dazzling areas of art might have its distressing effects: sooner or later surfeit was bound to set in as the viewer lost the primary capacity to be stimulated. Repetition of the same subject matter — usually religious — inevitably proved tiresome. On the other hand, a visitor sometimes suggested that one's taste could be improved by prolonged exposure to the masterworks. For example, one New Englander, viewing the galleries while on her wedding journey, came to find Carlo Dolce, her early favorite among the painters, boring and monotonous, and ended by ranking others far higher.[25] From time to time someone complained that a great many of the pictures and statues in the galleries were so hideous that the eye was actually offended.

It was suggested that some background of study and experience was essential to derive the most benefit from the art works. Oliver Wendell Holmes, the autocrat of the breakfast table, felt that the copies and casts of famous statues he had seen in the United States gave a good idea of these works, but as for paintings, one had to experience the actual works in order to appreciate them.[26] Another traveler, Erastus C. Benedict, similarly suggested that some background was necessary for real appreciation; he cautioned that Americans were too often led by national vanity and an iconoclastic tendency to depreciate the old pictures. Such works, he reminded his readers, had been created in a different period and had grown out of a different spirit from the present.[27]

Although interest in the Middle Ages was growing in European art circles during these years, the American was almost completely indifferent to all art works created between the late Roman Empire and the early fifteenth century. Rarely did he condemn anything Romanesque or Gothic; usually he just ignored it. Except for Thomas Jefferson Bryan and James Jackson Jarves, who brought collections of Italian primitives back to the United States, Americans showed little interest in artists before Raphael.[28] The work of the late seventeenth and eighteenth centuries suffered from indifference as well. Nor did the visitor have much interest in realism in painting; a few travelers turned with relief from religious to genre paintings, but most gave these pictures little attention.

For the American, one old master led all the rest. Raphael was the greatest painter of all time, indisputably. His personal life might indeed shock the Reverend John A. Clark, who thought him a "degraded sensualist," but that was almost beside the point.[29] With respect to his art, Mrs. Hawthorne spoke for all: "Every day I grow more and more amazed at the genius of Raphael. It gets to be miraculous. . . . We know him, because he is superior to all, and there is no fault. We may find some lesser or greater shortcomings in others; but Raphael cannot be criticised." [30] Somehow, it was felt, Raphael was able to speak directly to the viewer; the faces he painted were vivid and distinctive, each picture pervaded by grace of form and color. The hand of nature alone could surpass the genius of Raphael.

One picture, Raphael's "Transfiguration," overshadowed all others. This very simply was the greatest painting in the world. The American's comments indicate how relatively unimportant was personal response compared with the handed-on convention of taste. Before he ever saw the picture, he was prepared to regard the "Transfiguration" as the world's foremost painting, not only in reputation but in fact, and if the picture fell short of his expectations, the American was far less inclined to blame Raphael than his own lack of taste. The picture, he roundly declared, surpassed the imagination. The Reverend W. I. Kip, for one, was at first disappointed: "Realizing that Raphael was the noblest of them all, I expected perhaps, when I looked upon his masterpiece, to see more than human genius can ever execute." The picture continued to grow on him, however, and eventually he gave it first place.[31] W. C. Preston, who found this painting filled his heart "with rapture and with a sort of adoration," always dressed up when he went to see it as if "going into some august presence." [32] Other paintings by Raphael were also widely praised, particularly the "Madonna della Seggiola" in Florence. Remembering the portrait of Pope Julius II, Hawthorne wished that Raphael might have been able to paint Andrew Jackson.[33]

Just below Raphael the American usually placed Guido Reni, two of whose pictures struck him as outstanding. On the ceiling of the casino in the garden of the Palazzo Rospigliosi in Rome, the American saw Guido's "Aurora"; the bright colors, lively horses, and elegant pageantry of this fresco pleased him immensely. Certainly as well known as Raphael's "Transfiguration" was the supposed portrait of Beatrice Cenci, then attributed to Guido. The young girl's horrifying story undoubtedly accounted in large part for the interest shown by this literary-minded generation. Hawthorne wished that someone of deep sensibility could see the portrait without knowing the history of the subject, but he still considered it "the most profoundly wrought picture in the world." [34]

The painter whose work stood third in this hierarchy of taste was Domenichino, though many American visitors placed his "Last Communion of St. Jerome" second only to the great pictures of Raphael. The Reverend Horace Bushnell judged this painting "by far the most faultless picture, and the most perfect in coloring," and Samuel Cabot purchased a copy for Thomas H. Perkins' collection.[35] George Bancroft found Domenichino's paintings "always energetic, chaste, and expressive . . . often pathetic, and often sublime," but he felt the artist tried to present too many passions rather than one "expressed in unity & fullness," which would touch the feelings instantaneously.[36]

Claude Lorrain and Nicolas Poussin were also in the group of painters the American most favored. These two, perhaps more than any others, influenced the work of American artists in Italy, whose canvases embodied something of the same dreamy, mystical qualities, the sensitivity to light, and the nostalgia for a dimly remembered past of the seventeenth-century painters. It was principally through Claude's eyes, as seen in reproductions of his paintings, that many Americans first became acquainted with Italy. For Thomas Cole, who established his studio in what used to be Claude's house, Claude was "the greatest of all landscape painters." [37] Salvator Rosa, too, appealed to the American; in his dark and wild forest scenes, Rosa seemed to express some of the same deep-seated feelings about the wilderness that Americans shared.

Titian, by contrast, was apt to arouse hostility. To Hawthorne, the Venetian's "Magdalen" in the Pitti gallery appeared coarse and sensual, scarcely the portrait of a penitent, though he still found it "a splendid picture." "Titian," he thought, "must have been a very good-for-nothing old man." [38] The Reverend Joel Tyler Headley echoed a common opinion when he condemned the Titian Venuses as disgusting from "their almost beastial sensuality," inferior to the white-marble purity of the "Venus di Medici." [39] But Titian's "Presentation at the Temple" and "Assumption of the Virgin" found more admirers than detractors.

The appeal of other artists was a more individual matter, varying from picture to picture and from spectator to spectator. The frescoes of Correggio at Parma impressed a few visitors. Daniele da Volterra's "Descent from the Cross," on view in the Roman church of Trinità dei Monti, was high on the list of favorites, and many travelers liked the work of Carlo Dolce. Francia and Perugino both appealed to George Hillard, the soft light in the background of Perugino's paintings reminding him of the work of his fellow countryman Allston. Veronese, Tintoretto, Pordenone, Bordone, and Giorgione all struck Hillard as important. A Gentile Bellini painting seemed "very curious," though it gave a good idea of the costumes and architecture of the day.[40] Then again, Edward Everett in 1818 thought that the "Psyche" frescoes of Giulio Romano in the Palazzo del Té at Mantua were just a "coarse daub," nor did he like the fantasy of the "Fall of the Titans." [41]

The painters of the early Renaissance received little notice. Mrs. Hawthorne stood apart from the consensus (and from her husband's view) in her admiration for Giotto and Taddeo Gaddi: "I live better for even pale Giottos, and the whole quaint, devout old band, in any stage of ruin." She also liked the works of Sodoma and, in her praise for Gentile da Fabriano and Fra Angelico, she moved considerably beyond the standard taste of the period.[42] Theodore B. Witmer, who boasted of savoring many of the forbidden pleasures of European life, was one of the few who even bothered to mention Fra Angelico, but he could see nothing in the monk's pictures "worth wasting time over," and found the "Annunciation" so ludicrous that he could not help laughing at it.[43] The art historian Charles Eliot Norton, professor at Harvard and a disciple of Ruskin, within a few years was to take Fra Angelico more seriously.[44]

The American commonly had little to say about statuary, except for a half dozen or so ancient works. As with paintings, the visitor had been prepared in advance to know certain pieces, and these were the statues about which he commented most. Ordinarily, his remarks did not concern the plastic quality of the works but only their literary or historical associations: viewing a bust of Augustus usually led to a search for physiognomic indications of such characteristics as the American knew about the emperor. A few visitors explored the sculpture galleries solely to conduct phrenological investigations. Dr. Samuel Gridley Howe and George Combe, the famous phrenologist, for example, spent long hours in the Vatican gallery trying to discover something about the characters of the various ancients by analyzing the shapes and proportions of their sculptured heads.

The foremost statues of Italy were housed in the Capitoline and Vatican museums, and to the American the most important of these works was the "Dying Gladiator." The "Dying Gladiator" promoted tears on a large scale. "Nothing of all I had seen in Rome affected me so deeply," wrote one visitor. "The tears dropped like rain as I stood before it." [45] Joel Tyler Headley, one of the few who did not shed tears outright, at least barely refrained from weeping as he thought of Byron "and of the intense feeling with which he gazed upon [the "Gladiator"]." [46] The association with Childe Harold was inescapable, so that the American may be said to have wept at second hand. This capacity for artificially induced emotions remains one of the standard *curiosae* of our American pilgrims.

For some reason the American felt a slightly infantile need to rank the art objects he saw. Just below the "Dying Gladiator" on his list of masterpieces he placed the "Apollo Belvedere" and the "Laocoön." John Lothrop Motley found "more of the godhead, in the Apollo than in any [other] ancient statue. . . . The figure expands into life, into immortality while you are gazing." [47] William C. Preston thought that the Apollo had transcended his imagination of the object and was "a perception of the Perfect." [48] Still another enthusiast endorsed the statue as surpassing the "perfection of manly strength and beauty. . . . It is action, life, grace, music, perfume in stone!" [49] On the "Laocoön," opinion was less unanimous. The statue was evidently too violent, too naturalistic, to captivate the same tastes that found pleasure in the "Apollo." Cooper judged it "the noblest piece of statuary that the world possesses," but William Ware thought the subject "loathsome." [50] Headley, though expressing the appropriate horror, felt no sympathy for Laocoön, who seemed such a weak man, so overcome by fear, that he could not die decently.[51]

Finally, among the big four, the "Venus di Medici" beckoned to the American from the cabinet of the Uffizi. The traveler, all prepared to compliment her on her charms, usually did not like her quite so much as he felt he ought to — and, once again, found it necessary to apologize for his failure to approve the universally approved. Hawthorne, who acquiesced in the general praise, called the statue "very beautiful, very satisfactory . . . standing in chaste and naked grace," [52] but others complained about Aphrodite's disproportionately small head and her vacuous facial expression. One gallery-goer liked Canova's Venus better than the Medici "because there is more of it" — whatever he meant by that.[53]

The "Moses" of Michelangelo at the Roman church of San Pietro in Vincoli, elicited frequent comment. Margaret Fuller enthusiastically revealed that the statue was "the only thing in Europe, so far, which has entirely outgone [her] hopes," while Emerson saw in it "the Jewish Law embodied in a man." [54] Unlike most visitors, Emerson also responded happily to the "Last Judgment" of Michelangelo. Other American critics found the large fresco ludicrous. Charles Eliot Norton censured the subject as inappropriate for an artist and complained that the painting revealed nothing more than Michelangelo's skill as a draftsman.[55]

Architecture, unlike painting and sculpture, interested the traveler surprisingly little. Except for descriptions of St. Peter's, the cathedral at Milan, and a few ancient structures, he seldom commented extensively on the buildings he visited. Occasionally a tourist described interior decorations, and usually he was impressed by size, but form, the relation of spatial elements, and the intricacies of ornament in architecture held as little interest for him as they did in the other branches of the graphic and plastic arts. The journals and travel accounts give almost no idea, for example, of the nature of the lavish designs and of the structural elements involved in the baroque churches of Rome and the South. The American visited what seem today some of the most striking architectural works ever conceived; yet he visited the churches to look at altarpieces and statuary, conveniently labeled works of art, while the architectonic whole generally failed to make much of an impression. Gothic structures in the North, except for the cathedral at Milan, meant nothing to him, or next to nothing. Even at Milan it was the roof with its hundreds of statues, rather than any general feeling for the exterior form or interior space, that struck the visitor. Those who visited Vicenza and the surrounding region often mentioned Palladian buildings, but they apparently had little understanding of these structures. Although Cooper found he did not like the Palladian style as much as he had anticipated, it was, he thought, "not without the noble," and reminded him, in general outline, of Bostonian buildings.[56]

The Etruscan remains fared a little better. At Volterra, William Cullen Bryant carefully examined the Etruscan walls, gates, and tombs, and "gazed with exceeding delight" on the cinerary vessels; while at Perugia, Margaret Fuller found the frescoes of female figures in an Etruscan tomb "dignified and calm." [57] Joel Tyler Headley was filled with "strange sensations" when he reflected that Etruscan ruins had been ancient when Rome itself was young: it seemed to him a sad comment on human fame that posterity could not even read the epitaphs on these tombs.[58]

Finally, the American felt the impact of music in the most musical of countries. He heard it everywhere on the streets — the singing of itinerant merchants, of children at play, of soldiers on the march — and it was not all good music, by any means. On the other hand, he did go to the opera, often responding with a passionate devotion to spectacle and sound. In journals, letters, and travel accounts, the visitor repeatedly comments, with an initiate's enthusiasm, on this completely new realm of experience.

Emotionally more important than any other was the music he heard in the churches. At Santo Spirito in Florence, Horace Bushnell heard an organ "for the first time in [his] life," and reported that he had never before known what "this instrument is capable of." [59] The *Miserere* sung in the Sistine Chapel or in St. Peter's was one of the customary entertainments of Holy Week. Here, jammed tightly into a crowd of foreigners, the tourist stood for hours while the chanting went on, and candles — the only lights in the room — were extinguished one by one. The music, for one listener, "was the sigh, the wail, the supplication of mortality unto God, yet breathed the profound sweetness of his eternal harmonies. . . . Never had immortality, holiness, and heaven been more eloquently proclaimed . . . than through that cry of the human for mercy and redemption." [60] Another memorable musical experience took place in Rome at the convent church of Trinità dei Monti, where the cloistered nuns sang behind an iron grill. The sound of these voices, within the impressive setting of the church ritual, often awoke the American for the first time to the powerful appeal of Catholic rite and Catholic liturgy.

The American thus arrived in Italy bringing with him the standard taste of his period, a taste basically inherited from the late eighteenth century. Coming to works of art without previous direct acquaintance, he largely judged them in terms of this tradition, rather than in any immediate or personal way. He accepted the judgments and the reputations he already knew, and discovered little for himself. Certain objects were labeled art; to them he directed his attention. Fundamentally his standards were literary. He was interested in the story behind the painting or statue, and in how well the artist had shown appropriate emotions in the figures. He especially liked to find a unity of emotion expressed in the subject, and he was concerned to discover the concrete representation of abstract qualities. Such aesthetic elements as the uses of light, color, space, and form seldom were of much concern to him.

Above all else, art served for him a moral purpose. Art was thought to educate the mind and to elevate the feelings, raising men above the problems and clashes of the ordinary world into a higher realm of ordered form. Man was believed to have both animal and spiritual needs, a base nature and a divine one. Art, like a magnet, could draw men upward so that the higher nature might be more fully realized. A new dimension would then be added to men's lives; their feelings and understanding would grow; and their actions would reveal a corresponding moral improvement. Just as art could elevate the soul and make men as individuals better, it could also help to raise the level of virtue on a national scale.

Unfortunately, aesthetic contemplation offered its threats, too. For though most masterpieces could be trusted to elevate the soul, some works of art might have just the opposite effect and stimulate what were considered the baser passions. The greatest danger thus lay in the representation of nude forms, especially in statuary. That Italian morals were corrupt was a common American complaint, and to the moralistic visitors one obvious reason was the prevalent depiction of the naked human figure. Though the beholder's natural delicacy might at first be repelled by what he saw boldly exhibited in gallery and church, this delicacy tended to be blunted under repeated exposure.

The blunting of the higher senses thus encouraged the sharpening of the appetitive ones. Besides, Hawthorne rationalized, nakedness was not a fit subject for sculpture, since modern men all wore clothes.[61] Moreover, artists and models were often allegedly depraved, and spectators who looked at their pictures and statues might well "advance to a sympathy with vice itself." [62] Italy thus could serve as a lesson for some things that might be avoided in art.

Visitors were astonished to see how matter of factly Italians themselves accepted the naked representations, and how casually men and women mingled together while viewing these works. Even in the presence of gentlemen, a group of ladies would surround a Venus or an Apollo and discuss the merits of the statue "with the same un-blushing firmness of look and speech, as if they were coach wheels." [63] Americans, the critics discovered, as readily as any others fell into the habit after a while. Clearly, they were becoming acclimated.

On the other hand, the American was warned not to succumb to the dangers of hypersensitivity to certain forms and subjects. Prudery could be carried to such lengths that it no longer spelled modesty. "An artist of pure aim," cautioned James Jackson Jarves, "should not be held an-swerable for the imagination of the spectator." [64]

Beyond these different attitudes toward certain specific art forms, the American came to realize that the world of art generally had a wholly different significance for him and for the Italian. Other activities in the United States — organizing social institutions, producing goods, expanding trade, for example — were more important than creating beautiful works of art. It was because of this different focus of energy, he believed, that little good painting or sculp-ture was created in America, that architecture was bad and taste was crude. The ordinary Italian, it was suggested, appreciated the arts far more than did the American, for he had lived with art all his life and had had greater opportunity to develop his sensibilities. Charles Eliot Norton criticized Americans for their presumption in judging works of art without having previously studied the subject and without having grasped artistic principles. The American's ignorance and low state of taste only showed how little art actually meant to him.[65]

How could the situation be improved? The atmosphere of the United States, critics suggested, was still not congenial to any significant cultivation of the arts. In the United States the artist found mainly the distractions of hurry and change; his mind might be stimulated, but he needed a more tranquil atmosphere in which to work. Undoubtedly, however, with the passage of time and the growth of national wealth, more possibilities for a quiet leisured life and more patronage would come, and art would flourish as it had in the past in Italy. Eventually the time would come when the American passion for utility and native forms of beauty would complement each other, and society would be the better for it. Moreover, American art would surely be dedicated to nobler purposes than those of the past. "The Ideal will succeed, as the rainbow doth the sun and shower. We are following the true order of nature." [66]

Even so, current indifference to the arts was repeatedly deplored as unfortunate, no matter what the future prospects might be. For now, while American life was in a formative stage, the arts were surely of great importance. That so many sculptors and painters were working abroad was in itself, some critics believed, not a healthy sign. Artists obviously could learn a great deal in Europe, but their absence hindered the development of the arts at home. By extended residence abroad, too, artists' morals and

ideals might be corrupted, and in Italy there was the constant danger of slavish worship of the past. The artist
could learn from the past, but his meaning would have to
lie in his relation to the present. Like the ancients, who
created for their own times, the finest American art would
have to spring from contemporary taste, philosophy, and
social interests. The United States, as a fresh and new country, must have a fresh and new art.

Time and again the American in Italy lamented the
dearth of public art galleries in the United States. Somehow, the poorest Italian was able to enjoy experiences that
even the wealthiest American had to forego in his own
country, since in Italy the churches and many galleries,
both state-owned and private, as well as extensive parks and
gardens, were open to all. Young America might well
adopt as her model this openhearted liberality of old Italy.
And democracy might go further yet in commissioning
painters, sculptors, and architects, taking its cue from
Athens and Florence in their prime. Academies of art in
the major cities of the United States should undertake to
establish permanent galleries, which in themselves would
stimulate creative activity. Wealthy private citizens should
also take heed and use their resources to form art collections, which they should then make available to the public
free of charge. As the knowledge of art increased, as taste
improved, widespread patronage would surely follow. Fenimore Cooper hoped that his commissioned work, the
"Chanting Cherubs," when exhibited in the United States,
would stimulate general interest in the arts. Artists, he
believed, had to be encouraged, if only because they tended
to contribute to the national prosperity.[67]

Art in Italy was to a considerable extent devoted to the
service of the Church. Most of the paintings and much of
the sculpture were religious in subject matter, and either

had once been or were still found in churches. Perhaps religion was the element of Italian life that struck the American with greater emotional force than any other, and without question religion strongly influenced his over-all judgment of the country and its people.

CHAPTER VII

RELIGION IN ITALIAN LIFE

R ELIGION was the component of Italian life that the visiting American viewed with greatest disfavor, and the practices and beliefs of the Roman Catholic Church antagonized him more than anything else he found in Italy. To the Protestant American his own religious practices and institutions were among the most important influences that had shaped his society. Protestantism, he felt, not only had brought the individual in the United States to a serious communion with the divine, through conscience and understanding, but had also promoted morality and fostered certain virtues of character. Religion he regarded as a significant basis for the prosperity and happiness of his own society.

Judged by its social results, religion in Italy, by contrast, had somehow failed. Poverty and misery were everywhere evident; economic activity was backward; morality appeared to be decaying; and the character of the people often seemed debased. Unrivaled though she might be as a curator of the past, Italy obviously was not a success in the modern world, and for Protestant Americans the blame rested in part with the Church and its practices.

Religion in Italy was all-pervasive. Each locality had its

periodic Church festivals, devotions were carried on even in the midst of business activities, and everywhere the traveler came upon churches, shrines, and crosses.

The piety of the people was not without its impressive touches. At all hours worshipers flocked to the churches. People of every age and condition had made the church an intimate part of their lives. "The poor mother brings her babe in her arms, and before it can lisp or go alone, teaches it to respect sacred objects and to imitate her acts of religion." [1] Most Italians undoubtedly knew little of dogma and theology and merely worshiped as their fathers before them had done, but such worship probably was no less devout for having been handed on by custom.

But the American observer commonly responded adversely and was certain that religious practices were not deeply felt and had little meaning. The use of a tongue most people did not understand, as well as the endless bowings and incessant repetitions of movement by the priests seemed mere conventions in which true religious feeling and devotion played no part. The bands and banners, the musicians and marchers, the candles and canopies obviously lessened the daily monotony, but the American questioned whether or not they aroused real religious feeling. The forms of Church worship and the dogma had apparently pushed some communicants into superstition and had turned others to skepticism and atheism. From time to time the visitor charged that religious indifference was openly revealed, even during Church ceremonies, as when he noticed worshipers on their knees before the altar conversing with one another or priests taking snuff and chatting while supposedly engaged in the Mass. William H. Rinehart, the sculptor, believed that he had never met a people on whom "a true religious sentiment" had such a slight hold. [2] Crosses were often painted on walls not from spiritual motives but merely to prevent those walls from being defiled. "Their religion is a cheat," affirmed one American, "and no man in his sober senses can deny it." [3]

The social effects of Roman Catholic belief and rule seemed to be far-reaching. By its doctrines of charity, its surfeit of festival days, and its public ceremonies and processions, the Church, critics charged, encouraged idleness and indolence. Great sums were spent to amuse the masses and keep them under control. The Church absorbed most of the fruits of economic effort, while the clergy produced nothing in return, many cutting themselves off completely from the responsibilities of the world. As a result, personal enterprise was weakened by being chained to the clerical weight. Men were held in ignorance and superstition, "that they may be subjects for priestly and political deception." [4] The system had, in fact, led to "a puerile fatalism"; men were discontented and bitter, but so distrustful of one another and even of their own capacity that they could do little to oppose ecclesiastical rule. [5]

The Church was held to be an obstacle to the progress of mankind. Catholicism seemed to the American to restrict liberty of speech and freedom of the press and to deny the free play of truth. Education was often condemned as merely a systematic indoctrination into superstitiousness and fanaticism. The habit of slavish submission to Church dictation, moreover, had spread into the political arena. Looking to eternal welfare, the Church neglected the temporal, even when its kingdom often seemed to be conspicuously of this world. Wealth that should have been spent to rescue the poor from starving in the gutter was all too often channeled into the Church. Italy had built up a vast array of magnificent buildings and had brought forth great works of art, but at the cost of infinite misery.

"It is the wretchedest, princeliest land on earth," as Mark Twain was to express the paradox.[6] The desolate Campagna surrounding Rome clearly symbolized the barren waste of society under Catholic rule.

The relation of the Catholic Church to personal morality was difficult for the non-Catholic American to understand and often became a matter for critical indictment. Roman Catholicism not only seemed to neglect personal morality in the practice of ceremonial forms, but actually to encourage immorality by the agencies of priestly absolution and imposed penance and by certain so-called "charitable institutions." The Italian apparently was unable to conceive how good morals and social stability could exist without the papal authority.

Many activities of everyday life were, as we have seen, morally questionable to the American: wine-drinking, card-playing, frequent use of oaths, the loose system of pricing, Sunday dancing and theatergoing. What was worse, these activities so often took place close to sacred images or religious shrines. Indeed, to some Americans of rigid Puritanical cast, the Italians were undoubtedly well along the road to hell. Servants stole from their masters, and, it was said, were relieved of their guilt by penance, not by returning the money or goods. Cases were even reported of servants who stole candles to burn before a shrine. At the entrance to a church, Mrs. Hawthorne encountered a pickpocket, who, failing to take her purse, went inside and paid his devotions, perhaps, suggested Hawthorne, praying that he would have better luck the next time.[7]

The American also had difficulty in adjusting to the uses to which Sunday was put. "My ideas respecting the proper method of spending the Sabbath," wrote Ezra Stiles Gannett, a Unitarian clergyman from Boston, "have undergone a great change." [8] After the morning's religious observances,

Sunday was devoted to relaxation and public amusement. Shops were open, and the theater did a big business. The visitor frequently lamented that the day was desecrated, that its true purpose had been violated. "They have turned the word of God into a lie." [9]

For the Catholic Italian, true morality appeared to lie in faithful adherence to the rule of the Church; for the non-Catholic American, true morality was strictly a personal affair, a matching of individual action to an absolute moral standard. For the Italian, in the view of these nineteenth-century Americans, morality was thus primarily concerned with certain actions he performed inside a church, while for the American, morality was something having its basis in the word of God and affecting character and carried into action in all areas of life. Under Catholicism, the American Protestant believed, even men who were dishonest could look to eternal salvation if they were pious, for their religion stood apart from their action in life. It was a wonder that there was as much honesty as there was! Catholicism appeared to relieve the individual of personal responsibility, and instead of the vague and difficult task of seeking virtue, he had only to perform certain tasks and exercises. The confessional was, in fact, a safety valve for conscience. The man who sinned was easily forgiven, and, it was said, was soon ready to sin and be forgiven again. Life became simple, for everything was weighed and balanced, religious duties were specifically set forth. "Thus all is plain and easy; no questions about faith; no doubts about duty; to obey, not to inquire, is the grand requisition; docility, submission, are the characteristic virtues of the Catholic system." [10]

The negative influence of the Church on individual morality thus seemed to be marked, and personal standards of truth, justice, and integrity appeared low. Individual responsibility scarcely existed, according to the American, who believed that the Italian's conscience was not developed to the same extent as his own. Since a lie was as good as the truth until it was found out, hypocrisy and suspicion were rampant. Matrimonial fidelity was the exception, not the rule. Religion in Italy, as far as the American was concerned, had failed to promote sound moral principles.

The absence of religious toleration further indicated the backward condition of society, and for the visitor provided another telling example of the way that Catholicism had impeded man's progress. All men, the visitor affirmed, should be free to pursue their religious practices, and toleration of religious belief (within certain limits) was something he stoutly advocated.

To the Catholic, however, toleration was an error that bred error. A man who had been given the opportunity to enter the Church and worship according to the prescribed practices, and who failed to avail himself of his glorious chance, was in grave danger of eternal damnation. Moreover, attempts by non-Catholics to interfere with the established religion were emphatically discouraged for political reasons. Not only were such activities bound to lead to adverse consequences for the Church but they were also regarded as threats to the stability of the state itself. In the first part of the century, Protestant congregations of Italians were liable to fines and imprisonment, and foreigners not belonging to the Catholic Church could only worship privately. Leghorn alone enjoyed general religious freedom, and had enjoyed it since the end of the sixteenth century.

The money spent by foreign Protestant tourists was considerable, however, and Protestant worship had unofficially come to be tolerated as an economic necessity. Then

VIA CONDOTTI, ROME. In the background the Piazza di Spagna, the Spanish Steps, and the church of SS. Trinità dei Monti. Luigi Rossini, *Scenografia di Roma Moderna* (Rome, 1850).

MRS. WILLIAM PAGE by William Page. Courtesy of The Detroit
Institute of Arts.

too, as a result of increased knowledge of the outside world, a growing liberalism and secularism, and more extensive contacts with non-Catholics, the nineteenth-century Italians themselves became increasingly aware of other beliefs and practices, and moved toward greater personal tolerance. Even in the early part of the century strangers were no longer expected to kneel before the Host in the streets or in the churches. One could attend services without being at once suspected of interloping or taxed with interventionism. Stephen Grellet, a Quaker zealot, was surprised that no one laid hands on him when in 1819 he lectured to the girls at a Neapolitan foundling hospital on the evils of Catholic practice and when he "had to expose pretty fully some of the superstitions of the Romish Church" to Cardinal Consalvi. "Surely it is the Lord's doing, in the very centre of Popery . . . to make way for one, who holds testimonies so contrary to them, to proclaim the Lord Jesus as the sole Head of the church, and the author of eternal salvation to all that believe in him." [11]

James Fenimore Cooper recorded an incident about a friend of his who had stopped on a narrow street to relieve himself. As he was rejoining Cooper, a crowd gathered around the place he had selected, and the Americans realized that a Madonna was fixed directly above the incriminating puddle. Though the friend prudently retired, Cooper waited to see what would happen. Eventually a priest appeared, bringing holy water to sprinkle on the wall. His companion's blunder, Cooper believed, might have cost both of them their lives thirty years earlier.[12]

Even toward the middle of the century, nonetheless, Protestants were considerably restricted in celebrating their faith. In Turin and in the valleys of Piedmont, the native Waldensians, drawing on a long Protestant heritage, enjoyed a certain amount of religious liberty, but few Americans visited these groups or (in spite of Milton's sonnet) had even heard of them. English-language Protestant services were held in Florence before 1827 in the residence of the British minister, and subsequently in the Protestant Swiss chapel. St. Mark's English Church was opened in Florence in 1881. In Rome, the British for many years celebrated services outside the city walls; no official permission was given, but papal soldiers kept Italians from entering the chapel. An American chapel was opened at Rome for a short time at midcentury, and services were held regularly in the American legation after 1859, though the room available would not accommodate all the Americans present in the city each winter. These meetings, quietly held in simple surroundings and in opposition to the official creed, reminded James Jackson Jarves, the art critic, of the secret gatherings of early Christians in the catacombs of Rome.[13] After the unification of Italy, toleration became an official policy, and in 1873, St. Paul's American Church was founded in Rome.

As early as the 1840's, American Protestant groups became actively interested in Italy. Through the dissemination of the Scriptures, Americans maintained, the Italian people would come to see how needless were the superstitious formulas, the elaborate ceremonies, and the grasping priesthood, and they could then begin to cast off their chains and reform their society. The American Philo-Italian Society, established in 1842, aimed to make Italy a Protestant republic. Reorganized as the Christian Alliance, it later formed a part of the American and Foreign Christian Union, which promoted "religious liberty" at home and abroad. By the 1860's, American Protestant missionaries were active in Italy. By the end of that decade two well-stocked Protestant bookstores were established in Naples and several schools flourished under Protestant auspices.

The Bible and tracts in Italian were distributed, and missions set up. Nevertheless the Catholic Church continued its opposition, and Lucia Alexander, wife of the American painter Francis Alexander and a long-time resident of Florence, discovered that the book of psalms she had given her servant had been quietly confiscated by a priest.[14]

Since by ecclesiastical law non-Catholics could not be buried in consecrated earth or in Roman Catholic churches, a burial place had to be found for them. The first known interment in what came to be the Protestant Cemetery in Rome occurred in 1738; previously, deceased Protestants had probably been taken to Leghorn or buried in the Campagna. The first American to be buried in Rome was a young bride of eighteen years, who, ironically, had come to Italy for her health and had died in Rome in 1803. Here, in the non-Catholic cemetery, near the graves of Keats and Shelley, William Wetmore Story, George Perkins Marsh, minister to Italy, Constance Fenimore Woolson, the novelist, William Stanley Haseltine, the painter, and Elihu Vedder, the poet and painter, found a final resting place. In Florence the English Cemetery was established just outside the city walls in 1827, and was used until a large cemetery was opened in 1877. Today the old Florentine Cimitero degli Inglesi stands like a quiet island in the midst of noisy traffic rushing along the boulevards built on the site of the old city walls. Eighty-two Americans, including Theodore Parker, Richard Hildreth, and Hiram Powers, are buried there.

Though they formed a minor element in Italian society, the Jews nonetheless aroused the interest of the visitor, who saw in their treatment another weakness of the Roman Catholic Church. Long treated with disdain and contempt in the Papal States, the Jews had greater freedom of occupation and of movement in the North, especially in Lom-

bardy-Venetia and at Leghorn in Tuscany. All disabilities
on Tuscan Jews had been removed by the early nineteenth
century, and they could hold civil and military offices.

In the early nineteenth century the condition of the
Jews in Rome was somewhat better than it had been in
the past. For example, they were no longer required to race
on foot through the Corso at carnival time, though they
still were locked up each night in the ghetto. Most occupations were still closed to them, and they were required to
listen to a sermon each Sunday directed against their religion. Only toward the middle of the century were the
walls of the ghetto in Rome leveled and permission given
to the Jews to reside beyond the area of that district. The
lot of Roman Jews was eased considerably when Pius IX
ascended the papal throne and removed many of the restrictions. But later, following the collapse of the short-
lived Roman Republic, after the pope's return from vol-
untary exile at Gaeta, the Church authorities quietly with-
drew the recently granted privileges, and the harsh treatment of the Jew was resumed. And it was the Church itself,
Protestant visitors charged, that was responsible for such
acts unworthy of the Christian religion: "Forbidden to
raise their head, the Church that has crushed them under
its decrees points at them the finger of scorn because they
creep and crawl beneath their burdens. The favours granted
them are hypocritical and visionary — the injuries alone
are real." [15]

Through the many religious ceremonies, the often suspicious foreigner was himself caught up in Church activities. With the faithful, he could attend the celebration of
the Mass or join in the pageantry of a religious procession.
Ignorance of the intended meaning of the rites was nearly
universal among American visitors, very few of whom
were Catholic, and incomprehension sooner or later yielded

to the belief that the ceremonies actually lacked all purpose and meaning, even for the participants. The American enjoyed the spectacles, nevertheless, and considered them excellent entertainment, something that one naturally went to see in Italy. Visitors crowded into churches as they would crowd to the theater or the circus. They stared, frequently disgusted and occasionally bored; often they openly jeered.

Sometimes the passive tolerance of Italian Catholics was strained to the breaking point by the outrageous behavior of foreigners. The English were the chief offenders. On Sundays it was the custom for the English to transform St. Peter's into a fashionable place of promenade, where they strolled, arm in arm, chatted and laughed aloud, met their friends, and displayed their finery. Some went so far as to bring food into the churches and even to toss chicken and ham bones on the floor of the Sistine Chapel during Lent. On one occasion at the height of the Mass in St. Peter's, when the Host was elevated and the congregation bent low, the worshipers were startled by the sound of popping champagne corks, coming from one of the tribunes where the English were seated.

Some American visitors condemned their fellow countrymen and their English cousins for this indecorous behavior. Coming voluntarily to a Catholic ceremony, the stranger was bound to pay it fitting deference, expostulated Fenimore Cooper. Protestants, he felt, too often mistakenly found merit in irreverence and intolerance.[16] If foreign visitors could be brought to understand that these were not spectacles put on for their entertainment, but religious ceremonies, they would not be guilty of such barbarism. When a young Frenchman tried to bring what he considered were English manners to the English Chapel and walked around during the services, curiously examining those present — especially the girls — as he had seen the English do in Catholic churches, he was quickly directed to sit down in the farthest corner. Obviously this was a question of just whose ox was gored.

The Romans themselves complained that the crowds of foreigners at religious ceremonies were so great that the natives could not even join in the rites. Pasquin, a mutilated fragment of a statue invested with sibylline wit, which long served as an outlet for popular feeling, was questioned one night, "How shall I, being a true son of the Holy Church, obtain admittance to her services?" The following night the answer appeared, "Declare that you are an Englishman, and swear that you are a heretic." [17]

Christmas commonly found the American visitor in Rome. Theaters were closed before Christmas, and on the streets the visitor encountered the *pifferari*, who came annually from the mountain villages of the Abruzzi or Calabria to earn money for the winter months. Midnight Mass on Christmas Eve in Santa Maria Maggiore or Santa Maria d'Aracoeli and the papal Mass at St. Peter's on Christmas morning were traditional. A few days later came the Epiphany fair at Piazza Navona, with great crowds milling about, and everyone blowing on a horn or whistle. Soon it was carnival time, and horse races, maskings, and costume balls were the order of the day. Then, during Lent, the theaters were again closed, and an atmosphere of restraint fell over the cities. At one Roman church during Lent, the American who had a taste for the unusual might even indulge in flagellation.

The most important ceremonies occurred during Holy Week. The celebrations began on Palm Sunday with the blessing and distribution of palm fronds. On Wednesday afternoon at the Sistine Chapel and in the evening at St. Peter's the famous *Miserere* was sung, an experience that the American found uncomfortable because of the crowds but still intensely moving. Holy Thursday brought the ceremony of the washing of the pilgrims' feet in St. Peter's and afterwards the feeding of the pilgrims, the washing of the altar, and the exposure of the most venerated relics (part of the true lance, St. Veronica's handkerchief, and a piece of the true cross). On Good Friday special Masses were said in the Sistine Chapel; and at Trinità dei Pellegrini the Roman nobility washed the feet of pilgrims and then served them dinner. The traditional baptism of a Jew was held at the basilica of St. John Lateran on Saturday, but most Protestants were skeptical of this performance and repeated the rumor that the converting Jew looked suspiciously the same each year. The week reached a climax on Easter Sunday, with a pontifical Mass in St. Peter's and the papal benediction to the city and the world in the square outside. In the evening the outlines of the great church were illuminated by thousands of flares and torches, and the following night the *girandola*, or fireworks display, terminated the celebrations.

Not always was the American pleased with the activities of Holy Week. The crowding, pushing, and rushing from one place to another made these days tiring and uncomfortable; fistfights and ladies armed with needle-like hatpins sometimes made the expeditions dangerous, and some of the ceremonies seemed inappropriate to the occasion. Most of the visitors, for example, found the papal feet-washing ceremony ludicrous because of what they considered to be the mock humility of the pope and the high churchmen. They felt that the exhibition only served to emphasize the abuses of Catholicism and to show how far it had strayed from the simplicity of the primitive Church. At the dinner that the pope himself served to twelve men, William Story recounted, "It was with difficulty that the Pope himself could keep his countenance while he was performing this solemn farce." All in all, Story summed up Holy Week by saying that, except for one or two things, "the result has been 'bosh'." [18]

Several Americans attended the colorful ceremony of the taking of the veil, and the sight of a young woman shutting herself away from the world was usually a poignant one. George Ticknor watched a young countess receive the veil at the most fashionable convent of Rome. A cardinal celebrated high Mass, and the candidate partook of the sacrament, after which she asked and was given permission to enter the convent. She then pronounced vows of obedience and seclusion, her hair was cut off, and following the entire burial service for the dead, she arose a nun and was received by the sisters of the convent. Afterwards, "a tasteful breakfast and collation was prepared in the room of the Superior; those who chose went over the convent, and saw the room of the new nun, which was prettily and comfortably fitted up, and the whole affair was ended." [19]

Relics, which played an important part in the ceremonies, were a favorite target of the critical non-Catholic American. Veneration for such objects, he felt, easily distracted the mind and could lead to idolatry. Many of the objects connected with Church ceremonies, he discovered, were anachronisms, whose use was strangely rationalized by the Church. Then, too, the fraudulent pretensions of many relics defeated their claims to authenticity, but since relics brought in money from the pious, the credulous, and the curious, they obviously were valuable to the churches possessing them. Among the non-Catholic Americans, only Charles Edwards Lester, consul in Genoa, put up a limited defense of the possible authenticity of relics. Why, Lester

questioned, would it not be possible for a relic to have survived from such an event as the crucifixion, since certainly
many other things from the same period had lasted down
to the present? [20]

The true religious function of shrines and images was
also questioned. Most of the apparent reverence to images
and shrines, it was suggested, was not reverence at all but
merely a perfunctory gesture to ward off evil. At the
church of Aracoeli in Rome, the Holy Bambino, a small
doll lavishly dressed and bedecked with jewels, which was
taken out in a carriage to visit the sick, appeared to be a
particularly egregious instance of how religion had been
perverted. The incongruity of some sacred images was all
too evident. Theodore Witmer, a young traveler who considered himself an expert on such matters, revealed that
the leading assignation house in Naples had at the top of
the staircase a virgin in fresco with *ora pro nobis* written
beneath, and that the girls, before making love, always took
their rosary from their wrist and put it carefully aside.
"Incomprehensible compound of veneration and disobedi-
ence of God's laws," he sanctimoniously moralized, "the
prescribed form gone through with, and the sin-freed spirit
may wander again wherever it listeth. A convenient religion, both to live and to die by." [21]

The Holy Staircase (*Scala Santa*) at the Roman basilica
of St. John Lateran seemed another flagrant example of
Catholic credulity. A few Americans, such as the clergyman George E. Ellis, felt that when in Rome one might
as well do as the Romans, and climbed the staircase on their
knees in the approved manner. Others, eager to flaunt both
their disbelief and their contempt, tried to walk up, but
were usually stopped by irate guards. Just as James Jackson Jarves was asked by the attendant priest to stop going

up the staircase on foot, he was startled to be passed by a group of French soldiers having a race to the top on their knees.[22]

The attitude of the non-Catholic American toward the priesthood almost invariably was one of dislike and distrust, a feeling that increased in intensity by the middle years of the century. Priests were accused of stupidity, avarice, dishonesty, hypocrisy, charlatanry, fatalism, immorality, and depravity. Instead of exemplars of righteousness, the clergy had a reputation as inordinate immoralists. They were said to be willing to perform any "miracle" if only enough were handed over to set the machinery in motion; money was the key to getting anything done. They reportedly enlisted youths in their ranks before these youngsters were able to think for themselves. They frequently appeared contemptuous of their own rites and duties and often failed to maintain an appropriate gravity and decorum. Jesuits were considered especially despicable and crafty in their activities.

Even the appearance of the clergy was often attacked as repulsive. To William Dean Howells the cardinals looked like "a grotesque company of old-womanish old men in gaudy gowns." [23] Mrs. Hawthorne found the Florentine clergy so fat, flabby, and earthy-looking that she could compare them only to hogs: "They merely need to stoop upon their hands to be perfect likenesses of swine, so that the encounter of one of them in the street gives one a faint sensation." [24] Mendicant Franciscans and Capuchins were particularly singled out for their lazy ways and their coarse and dirty appearance. "The Franciscans are the ugliest, coarsest, and the most animal-looking set of men I have ever encountered, in or out of the church," wrote the author Grace Greenwood, though another visitor had difficulty in determining "whether the Capuchin or Franciscan monk, approached nearer in appearance to the lower order of animals." [25] Even William Story, whose enthusiasm for things Italian knew few bounds, had little good to say for the monks, and investigating their physiognomic traits he discovered bigotry, cunning, and narrow-mindedness.[26]

The hypocrisy of the clergy seemed all too evident, and plenty of tales about the sexual laxity (in one form or another) of priests always came to the traveler's ear. To Henry Wadsworth Longfellow, visiting Italy in 1828, it was obvious that "a young man who can have no wife of his own — is not scrupulous with his neighbour's!" [27] A Roman saying had it that if you wanted to go to a brothel you had to go in the daytime, because they were all full of priests at night. Even the statue Pasquin had something to say about clerical morals: when the rumor arose that Garibaldi was on his way to Rome and it was feared there might be a general attack upon the priests, Pasquin reportedly cautioned, "Beware, unhappy Romans! reflect that you may all become parricides!" [28]

Travelers likewise had harsh words for the monastic life. Confinement away from the world, they suggested, was unnatural, since it cut family ties and led to warped and frustrated minds. The solitude of religious community life was certainly all right for the scholar or for the person of great religious passion, but it turned the ordinary man or woman into a human vegetable. Men had need of the discipline of an active existence. Many Italians went into monasteries, Americans believed, not out of piety, but because they had difficulty in supporting themselves. Entering a monastery was, in fact, a desertion of the world, though in shunning temptations individuals might only fall into greater errors.

Despite this common view, a few non-Catholic Americans actually entered monasteries to stay for short periods. Artists often stopped in convents or monasteries while on sketching tours. Charles Sumner spent a few days with George Washington Greene at the Franciscan monastery at Palazzuola above Lake Albano. Here they lived comfortably in three-room suites and spent the days reading poetry, walking in the woods, bathing, and chatting with the fathers. Sumner looked at every book in the monastery library and found few that had been touched recently. He did not feel that his stay had led him to believe in the pope or in St. Francis.[29]

Francis Parkman wanted to see firsthand the life of a monastery in order to help prepare himself for future studies of the French in colonial America, the same motive that later led him to live in the Rocky Mountain lodges of Sioux Indians (whose company he much preferred to that of the monks). To a small cell in the Passionist convent near the Colosseum, he brought along Cooper's *Pioneers* for reading. The Italians at the convent expressed sympathy for his unhappy condition outside the Church, and a snuff-taking monk tried to convert him. Parkman was surprised to see how much better the laymen visiting the convent fared than did the clergy. At mealtimes, the monks ate and scowled, while the laymen ate and smiled at one another. He also stopped for a short time at the luxurious monastery of San Martino in Sicily, where the Benedictine monks, all nobles, lived superbly, enjoying a game preserve, excellent cooking, and comfortable rooms furnished in good taste. Ascetic privation and mortification, Parkman suggested, would have to be sought elsewhere.[30]

A few American critics felt that the Italian clergy had generally been maligned and that hypocrisy or licentiousness were no more true of them than of other men elsewhere. Ignorance and indolence were perhaps the worst charges that could be held against them as a group. Turned by their belief from modern progress, the priests neither knew how to nor could adjust themselves to the contemporary world. Yet the clergy commonly seemed devoted to their duties and were always courteous and helpful to the stranger, and on a rare occasion, an American traveler defended the monastic institutions. The vices attributed to the monks and nuns were not so prevalent as in the past, asserted Theodore Lyman, Jr. True, he went on, it was rare to find a monk bearing the mark of great penance or indulgence, since the restricted life chiefly contributed to carelessness about the world and a calming of all passion. Protestants, he believed, were wrong to associate gloom or austerity with the cloistered life.[31]

John England, an American Catholic bishop, feeling obliged to defend the Italian clergy from American attack, pointed out that most travelers received their information from guides and hotelmen who told these visitors what it was thought they wanted to hear of clerical avarice, tyranny, and misconduct. Guides, he asserted, delighted in recounting to each other how they had imposed on the tourists' credulity.[32]

Usually personal acquaintance with a particular priest or monk brought the American up sharply, for somehow this experience did not accord with what he had been led to expect. The individual cleric, whom the traveler encountered in a long-distance coach or at an evening's entertainment, generally turned out to be a superior person, often learned and well-traveled, and endowed as well with social grace and superior powers of conversation. One group of Americans were displeased when they found a Franciscan in their carriage, and they ignored him for some time, until, when one of the party asked him a question, they discovered that he was shrewd and well-educated and, all things considered, most interesting. Nevertheless they lamented that this man had been deluded into cutting himself off from society and leading a comparatively useless life.[33] At Turin, while walking beside the river, W. C. Preston met a bearded friar, who, engaging him in conversation and discovering that Preston was an American, threw his arms around his new acquaintance "with a sort of ecstasy as if he had found a treasure." The two new friends walked up and down the banks, each delighted by the other, and they continued to see one another for the length of Preston's stay. "I was his first American," Preston recounted, "and he my first friar." [34]

Attacks on the clergy often concentrated on the papacy itself, in which the whole Catholic system was focused. Although the pope was often blamed for the poverty, backwardness, and illiberality of the Papal States, the man himself was sometimes considered a prisoner of his ministers and of Church traditions and as a consequence unable to make needed changes. Many Americans had papal audiences, and, like the contacts with individual clergymen, most of these visits inclined them favorably toward the pope as a man.

The Protestant American visitor objected most of all to the fact that the pope's religious power was coupled to temporal sovereignty. Certainly the papacy had done much to promote the arts, and, admittedly, it served to focus spiritual feelings, but with secular power joined to religious authority, the enforcement of uniformity of religious belief without regard to individual conscience was possible and frequently did occur. These two areas, the American deeply believed, should remain separated, for by being joined there was danger that religion would be profaned and the state would become tyrannical. While probably not the corrupt organization it had once been, the papal establishment still was a bureaucracy, inefficient and sometimes unjust. The general feeling, however, was that the hold of the papacy was less constricting than it had been in the past.

The papacy itself was accused of extravagance, an opinion continually reinforced by the glaring contrasts of papal magnificence and lower-class poverty. Time and again the visitor wondered why some of the wealth of the pope could not be rechanneled for the benefit of the poor, or why so much money should be devoted to papal ceremonies, processions, and illuminations, when so many men were nearly starving. The visitor sometimes grew increasingly resentful of the papacy during his stay in Italy. Margaret Fuller, for example, recorded how her antagonism toward the Church mounted daily during her stay in Rome prior to the revolution of 1849.[35]

The papal ceremonies were filled with anachronisms, and though bringing much from the past often seemed to have little relation to the present. Deference shown to the pope by both ecclesiastics and laymen appeared ludicrous and even disgusting. Kissing the pope's foot was viewed as particularly degrading and inconsistent with human dignity, though one observer reported that the pope's foot was said to be "very clean" and "well washed beforehand."[36] And what a contrast was the ceremonial display of the pope to the simple life of Jesus himself!

The papal ceremonies, nonetheless, were highly popular. The American visitor rushed from one church to another to see the pope, eager to satisfy his curiosity about this man and to join in the best entertainment Rome had to offer, and an introduction and talk with the pope became one of the things for the newly arrived visitor to do. A few Americans were presented to Pius VII (1800–1823), and many to both Gregory XVI (1831–1846) and Pius IX (1846–1878).

George Ticknor and Joseph Greene Cogswell were

granted an audience with Pope Pius VII in 1818. Ticknor had long wanted to see this pope, who, he thought, during the Napoleonic troubles had behaved with strength and dignity. On entering the papal presence the two Americans, together with a Scottish scientist, knelt and kissed the papal hand. The pope received his visitors standing, wearing the simple robe of a friar, and they spoke entirely about the United States, the pope praising American toleration and showing great interest in the American population increase. Ticknor was much impressed by his good nature and kindness.[37] When Stephen Grellet visited Pius VII in 1819, he reported that the pope had already read the reports that the Quaker had prepared about Roman prisons, promised that the abuses would be attended to, and related how he was trying to reform the Inquisition. Grellet told the pope about the vices of many priests and monks he had met and also what the qualifications for the sacred office of a priest of God ought to be. Feeling the spirit upon him, Grellet then urged the pope to proclaim Jesus Christ the only head of the Church, believing that such a confession would do more to advance Christ's kingdom than anything preceding popes had been able to do. The pope responded kindly and respectfully to his suggestions, Grellet revealed, and gave him his blessing.[38] At Jonathan Russell's presentation to Pius VII in 1819, the pope held his hand for the quarter hour they conversed.[39]

Both Samuel Morse and Albert Brisbane attended the 1831 coronation of Gregory XVI; this pope, though respected as an honest and pious man, came to be widely condemned as an unusually bad administrator, who was spending the papacy to ruin.[40] Fanny Hall in 1836 was favorably impressed by Gregory, whom she thought mild and unassuming in manner, but she objected to the rules on formal dress for the presentation.[41] To Wilbur Fisk, then president of Wesleyan University, this pope expressed his appreciation for the toleration accorded to all religious groups in the United States.[42] The Reverend George E. Ellis in 1838 found Gregory XVI easy and pleasant, though untidy in appearance, his gown soiled and "his nose, hands, and breast being completely covered with snuff." [43]

During his long reign as pope, Pius IX was closely concerned with the events of the Risorgimento. Coming to the papal throne in 1846, he was immediately hailed by Italian liberals as one who could bring about reforms in the States of the Church and effectively advance the cause of a united Italy. Americans praised the consistory's choice and reported the genuine, widespread enthusiasm for the new pontiff. The pope's first public act was to grant an amnesty to political prisoners, a measure which increased his public following. Describing the Christmas Mass of 1847, George Hillard reported that the pope was "the object of a feeling hardly short of Idolatry — a feeling painted on the countenances of every Italian who was present." [44] A mass meeting at the Broadway Tabernacle in New York City in 1847 sent an expression of good will to the new pope, and President James K. Polk in his message to Congress in December 1847 recommended the establishment of regular diplomatic relations with the Papal States. A chargé d'affaires was soon sent to Rome.

As other reforms, including a constitution, followed, the popularity of Pius IX increased, but conservative groups within the Church establishment opposed change and reform. Even though the pope was urged to free himself from these forces, he reappointed the reactionary Count Pellegrino Rossi as prime minister. Events then moved quickly in 1848–1849, for Count Rossi was assassinated in November, a Roman Republic was declared, and the pope fled his capital, taking refuge in the Kingdom of Naples. The short-lived Roman Republic fell to French troops in July 1849, and the pope returned to Rome in 1850. Subsequently, the regime was more reactionary than before, losing power and prestige as the Papal States were gradually chopped away. The final blow came in 1870, when Rome was taken to become the capital of a united Italy.

As a person, Pius IX always made a good impression on his American visitors. Attractive in appearance, kindly and tenderhearted, and of irreproachable character, the pope was thought to have great spiritual worth. It was acknowledged that he had brought an improvement to the manners and morality of the higher clergy at Rome, but he was not considered to have the shrewd judgment and leadership of a good administrator. Particularly in political matters, he tended to be led by others. When the American consul in Genoa, Charles Edwards Lester, saw Pius IX in March 1848, he reported that the pope had advocated to him civil and religious liberty, including full liberty of conscience; though later disappointed, Lester still felt that the pope was "the best man I had ever seen." [45] G. P. A. Healy painted Pius IX's portrait and found him a pleasant but rather childlike subject; the pope constantly edged forward to see how the picture was coming along, and when requested to go back to his pose, "putting his hands together in imitation of a chidden and penitent child, he would patter back to his proper position." [46]

Sometimes American critics wondered how any man of sense could be attracted to the Church in Italy, where, of all places, the corruption of the clergy was so evident. Travelers were constantly warned not to be deceived by papal prestige and power or to be deluded into indifference or acceptance. But since Catholicism played an important part in Italian life, since the visitor spent much time going to churches, and since some aspects of the ceremonies obviously appealed to him, he often wanted to learn more. Sometimes, like the Reverend Orville Dewey, he became "a perfect church worshipper." [47] A few Americans went all the way to become converts.

Although there is little record of American conversions in Italy during these years, an occasional traveler from the United States is mentioned as having joined the Church. Jedediah Vincent Huntington, an Episcopal minister, who became interested in the Oxford Movement, was one such case; he went to Rome in 1846 and was converted there three years later. A pithy statement in the account book of Thomas Appleton, long-time American consul in Leghorn, reveals another conversion: "pd. Hospital for 90 days board & attendance on John Nile, Negro man, who died this morning, having previously been converted to the Catholic Religion — Pauls 270." [48] On a rare occasion, the convert went on, like the Reverend John Thayer in the eighteenth century, to become a priest, but probably most conversions went unnoticed by the American visitors.

The traveler's encounters with religion in Italy frequently moved him to reflect on Protestant practices at home. Finding religion such an all-pervasive component of Italian life, the visitor sometimes regretted that in America the influence of religion was not more widespread. Although the American often questioned the depth and sincerity of Italian religious practices, and although he often regarded the presence of religious artifacts and ceremonies as incongruous, he realized that constant reminders of the spiritual side of existence could help to enlarge man's experience.

Sometimes the visitor urged that Protestant churches in his own country adopt some of the external elements of Catholic worship. He suggested that a concerted attack on the senses through the setting of architecture, paintings, and statuary, the harmony of the organ and chanting choir, the

odors of burning incense, the display of dress, and the overtones of long tradition would have a powerful emotional
attraction. Though often warning that such appeals to the
senses and the imagination might distract the mind from
true religious awareness, he realized that these stimuli could
also have a salutary influence, especially on the minds of
the uneducated. Ex-clergyman Ralph Waldo Emerson revealed how much the churches had impressed him, and felt
it strange that Americans had not constructed a single building in such a magnificent manner. Americans, he felt, were
as padlocked in their own customs as Orientals and would
undoubtedly continue to build "mean churches with pews
for a thousand years to come." [49] William Ware, a Unitarian clergyman, who believed that Americans might benefit from more enjoyments on Sundays, enthusiastically approved of the way Catholic churches were always open so
that a worshiper could enter at any time and give himself
to private devotions. In these churches the individual might
always find peace and solitude.[50]

Some visitors stressed the effectiveness of Catholic practices. Although Catholic worship did not move the reason
or conscience in the way that Protestantism could, it did
cultivate faith and reverence better, asserted the Reverend
Theodore Parker.[51] It provided more liberally for the "instinct of worship which is a deep thirst of the human soul,"
and if its ceremonies helped to elevate the soul, the religious
person should accept this aid.[52] The danger of Protestantism
was that it reduced the mysteries of religion to vulgar com-
prehension and reasoned "God and all spiritual existences
out of the world." Credulity, indeed, was far better than
skepticism.[53] Other commentators, however, disagreed, and
the American by and large remained convinced that his
form of religion had fostered a superior national morality.
One traveler, Theodore Dwight Woolsey, a young minister

then studying Greek in Europe, lamented that his moral condition certainly had worsened during his Continental tour, "for who can grow better so removed and banished from the means of moral improvement and our wholesome state of society?" [54]

A few travelers believed that Catholicism had something else to offer American Protestants in showing how religion could reach the lowest levels of society. It was a common criticism that Protestantism, in fact, was not truly democratic in the way that Catholicism was. Rich and poor, aristocrats and commoners were all placed on a common level before the Mass, and this shared religious experience formed bonds of sympathy among the different classes. Protestant churches in the United States, on the other hand, sometimes tried to move toward a religious aristocracy, and in striving to be fashionable often failed the lower classes. The Roman Catholic Church held distinctions of race as odious, while the non-Catholic American in his attitude toward the Negro denied the brotherhood of man. Catholicism maintained the idea of a democracy of souls to be saved and distinguished only between priest and layman; men from all classes could rise up in the organization of the Church. Catholicism, however, it was also pointed out, was undemocratic in a different way, for the Church demanded absolute obedience and surrender of individual conscience to the priesthood. The road to salvation was not one that the Church allowed a person to explore on his own.

The American was cautioned about some of his own religious attitudes. Fenimore Cooper, for example, warned that Americans should be careful not to overlook their own ferocious fanaticism as they ridiculed Italian superstition.[55] If the Church was too authoritarian and continued to hold down the individual, it was perhaps no worse than the inquisition of public opinion in the United States. Perhaps, aside from religion and politics, a man had greater freedom to express himself in Italy than in America. As Hawthorne put it: "Rome is not like one of our New England villages, where we need the permission of each individual neighbour for every act that we do, every word that we utter, and for every friend that we make or keep. In these particulars the papal despotism allows us freer breath than our native air." [56]

Roman Catholicism in Italy, thus, both attracted and repelled the American visitor. The Church provided a great emotional stimulus in the colorful ceremonies and pageantry, the stability of hierarchy, and the sense of continuity with the past, all of which fulfilled needs that could not be similarly satisfied in the United States. Many of the practices seemed, however, to be an insult to reason and appeared to have been instituted to keep the people in slavish bondage to the priestly caste. Usually the American vigorously attacked Catholic usages and blamed on the Church many of the ills of society, continuing to maintain that his own religious practices were distinctly superior.

Intimately bound up with religion were political conditions. Ties between Church and state, indeed, seemed to be so close that opinion about one often involved a position about the other. The religious implications of the Risorgimento were perhaps as important to the American as the political, though the whole question of government was decidedly of less interest than art or religion.

CHAPTER VIII

GOVERNMENT AND
THE ECONOMY

THE AMERICAN's direct contact with government in Italy customarily was limited to the occasional soirees of a ruling monarch and frequent encounters with customs' officials. Nonetheless political conditions in the various parts of the peninsula were important to the visitor, for, like religion, government was something on which he placed precise responsibility for economic, social, and intellectual problems. The government of Italy as such was another focal point for certain of his attitudes towards the society as a whole.

The American's responses to political authority varied as he moved from one part of the peninsula to another. He looked with favor on the mild and benevolent rule of the grand duke of Tuscany and on the enlightened regime of the king of Sardinia; he contrasted them with the harshness of papal rule and the restrictive foreign dominance of Austria in Lombardy-Venetia. He ranked the government of the Neapolitan kingdom the worst in Italy, probably the worst in all Europe.

The most striking characteristic of the Italian political system was its particularism. Split into a group of small units having much in common but extremely jealous of their local traditions, the different states seemed hopelessly at odds with one another; during the first half of the century the outlook for national unification appeared dim indeed. The foreign dominance of France and Austria, the tight grasp of papal and royal authority, the dearth of educated and enlightened men, and the want of individual initiative and responsibility all seemed significant in hindering unity, but even more important was this narrow local allegiance. The long tradition of the city-states still closely circumscribed the Italians' loyalties: the man of Padua was considered a "foreigner" at Bologna and was dealt with, and expected to be dealt with, accordingly. Former regional feuds, now long past, were still remembered. Even the language varied so much from place to place that men from different sections often could not even understand one another. Napoleon had enforced unity on the peninsula, and at the cost of a certain humiliation had succeeded in moving Italy considerably along the road to the modern world. Some Italians viewed his downfall and the return of the old regime as great misfortunes; legitimacy had crushed unity and reform.

In the view of Americans the Kingdom of Naples and the Two Sicilies embodied the most deplorable features of Italian political rule. Taxes to support the king, the army, the Church, and the nobility were oppressively heavy; commerce was severely restricted; the condition of the masses was wretched. The kingdom lay under the hand of a rapacious ruling family, which knew that it was hated and feared and had to treat all suspicious activity as possible plots. The streets of the cities were filled with soldiers, many of them foreign mercenaries hired to keep the populace under control. At the upper levels of government independent judgment was strikingly absent. Conferring with an adviser to the council of ministers, Charles Sumner learned that even this high official "thought there was too much flattery and too little honest independence in the Cabinet — and that men gave up their real opinions in order to please the King." [1]

Things seemed almost as bad in the Papal States. Like the other governments, the papal authority was under no obligation to the people. It was a rule of power rather than of opinion, bolstered by soldiers, priests, and a decadent aristocracy. In Rome despotism was not even relieved by the desire of an hereditary ruler to gain good will for his heirs. Existing on a foundation of bigotry and general intolerance, the papal government forcefully maintained the *status quo*, fearful of change and progress. Education was aimed at inculcating submission to authority. The prisons were filled with political offenders. "Both justice and injustice are for sale; and the first price asked for either is often much larger than will be finally accepted; as is the case with that asked for most articles in Rome." [2] Even men's consciences were under the watchful eye of the Church through the confessional. On the other hand, the government made certain concessions to the people in order to gain their passive support; amusements and spectacles diverted the Romans from political matters, and capital punishment was seldom enforced.

Tuscany, in contrast, enjoyed the comparatively benevolent rule of the grand duke. The external evidences were all to the good: the economy was relatively prosperous, few beggars were seen, and the press enjoyed a certain freedom. During the early part of the century, Tuscany was considered the most enlightened state of Italy.

By midcentury, however, only in the Kingdom of Sardinia did the American find much hope for the future. Although earlier as repressive as the other states, Sardinia had established a popular assembly by 1848, reforms had been instituted, and freedom of religion and the press established. Sardinia came to take the lead in the Risorgimento, but since the traveler spent little time in Turin and Genoa, the liberal government of this kingdom meant much less to him than the reactionary governments to the south.

Perhaps more than in any other sphere — social, religious, artistic, or economic — observations on the conditions of government turned American thoughts homeward. Whereas in the realms of social organization, religious practices, and, especially, artistic achievement, the American felt that he could learn something from the Italian experience, his views on Italian political conditions left room for few lessons, except for negative warnings. The American government, he admitted, might well emulate the Italian example of the government providing parks and gardens as well as encouraging learning and the fine arts, but it was far more important that Americans should understand the evil fruits of particularism and of repressive governmental practices.

In the political realm the United States definitely could teach more than it could learn. The American believed his own political institutions had promoted the development of the individual to the fullest extent. His government was enlightened because it was based on the "beautiful and Benignant" Constitution, and because it sprang from religious principles and was sustained by them. His laws were uniformly applied to all men, and men were accustomed to obey them. He considered that his countrymen were well informed and that knowledge was widely diffused. His governmental institutions, he felt, fostered high moral standards and a pure personal morality. Moreover, he considered that he was freed from the heavy hand of prejudices of the past and "exempt from the miseries which follow in the train of arbitrary power." [3] His political institutions, in

fact, had brought him much further toward "true civilization." [4]

Sometimes the American visitor speculated how different,
how much better, life in the Mediterranean country might
be if only his own nation could gain political control. To
the beauties of the land and its artistic heritage such rule
would add the enlightening influence of free institutions,
thus releasing the powers of the Italian people and initiat-
ing a progressive and advancing development. Racial overtones occasionally crept into this view; as one writer put it,
a "nobler people . . . the Anglo-Saxon race," might make
it "a fruitful garden throughout." [5]

Many Italians, along with other Europeans, certainly
looked to America as a hope and an example. The United
States, it was suggested, had unsettled conditions in Europe,
for in America, even though the traditional European forms
of government were unknown, the citizens prospered to an
enviable degree. Established European authority feared
American institutions: "America rises like a great Sun before the eyes of the tyrants of Europe; and the one constant
struggle of their lives, is to keep out the rays of light which
she emits to all the earth." [6] Italians often expressed to their
visitors a wish to emigrate to America, where social and
political conditions approached those about which they had
before only dared to dream.

Again and again, Americans blamed the Italian states and
the institutions they fostered for keeping men in a condition of poverty, dulling their energies, paralyzing their ambition, debasing their minds. The impact of reactionary government had led to widespread cowardice, deceit, syco-
phancy, indolence, and immorality. Italians apparently
were dissatisfied with their political position, yet consider-
ing how downtrodden and debased they seemed to be,

visitors doubted if they had the strength of purpose and determination, the sense of personal responsibility, to undertake changes. They seemed to lack confidence in one another to carry on in concerted action.

Because the European religious and social foundations were alien to democracy, a long and difficult readjustment would be necessary, and the whole fabric of society would have to be remade. Perhaps change would first have to be imposed from outside. To be ready for democracy, Italians would have to be educated to it by the traditional American means — the town meeting, the church, and the schoolhouse. "It is only by the diffusion of information, political, religious, and general, that man acquires self-respect, and despises dependence." [7] Since the tradition of civic virtue in Italy had been inactive for centuries, Italians had to realize that readjustment would take a long time, "that all valuable institutions in government and politics have a law of organic growth and that they must be waited for, like pine trees." [8]

Eventually when government was changed for the better, the character of the people would itself improve. "A government, in which the mass of the people would be admitted to some share of power, would elevate the tone of publick feeling, and cure that shameless relaxation of morals, which, at present, disgraces their nobility." [9] Ideas would be widely disseminated, men would search out the truths of religion and government for themselves, and society would move progressively onward.

Although the sympathies of the American were exclusively on the side of the liberal Italian nationalists during the Risorgimento, these sympathies were only vaguely directed. Few Americans took a knowledgeable interest in the political events, and only a limited number became personally concerned. The events of 1848–1849 and of

1859–1860 involved a handful of Americans; the political movements earlier in the century went largely unnoticed. The American's lack of personal contacts, his often severely critical attitude toward social and religious institutions, and his frequently low estimate of Italian character account in part for his limited interest in such events. Perhaps even more significant was the visitor's perspective on the meaning of Italy, since for him Italy was, above all, a land of the past in which the great events of antiquity and the Renaissance had once occurred. The present, correspondingly, was of lesser importance.

The American showed some concern, nonetheless, for the course of nationalism in Italy, and many articles on political conditions in the peninsula appeared in American journals. Reports home in letters to local newspapers and published travel observations helped arouse interest and increasingly made political conditions a subject of comment. A few writers in the United States actively promoted the liberal Italian cause. Mrs. Andrews Norton translated Silvio Pellico's story of his imprisonment and revealed Austrian tyranny in a dramatic personal way. Thomas Parsons, William Cullen Bryant, and especially John Greenleaf Whittier, among other American poets, also kept the Italian cause to the fore.

The Story family and Margaret Fuller were in Rome during the short-lived Roman Republic of 1849 when French forces coming to reinstate the papacy beat down resistance and brought the fall of the new government. Mrs. Story's notes, as recorded by Henry James, reveal a curious detachment during the days of waiting, preparation, and fighting, the attitude of a spectator watching the latest act of the Roman drama. (One had come to Italy expecting to be entertained, but this — it was far better than one had even hoped for!) When the siege of the city began, the Ameri-

cans in Rome gathered in one house, prominently displaying an American flag. The day the attack reached a climax,
the situation grew very exciting; Margaret Fuller, who had
been tending the wounded, came by to tell of the casualties,
and rumors of all sorts kept the group in a continual state of
alarm. Late in the afternoon when the firing stopped, they
all walked to the Pincian Gardens to gaze upon the distant
French positions. And at night they "kept looking at the
watch-fires of the enemy as they blazed in the distance, and
. . . got little sleep." [10]

It was during the siege of Rome that Margaret Fuller revealed to Mrs. Story how deeply she had become involved
in the fortunes of the Roman Republic. After her years as
editor of the *Dial* and as reviewer for the New York
Tribune, Margaret Fuller, vigorous and intellectual, had
come to Europe in 1846 to report on men and conditions.
She first visited England where she met many celebrities of
the day, including the exiled Giuseppe Mazzini, whom she
came to admire passionately. Early in 1847 she arrived in
Italy, and after travel in various parts of the peninsula, she
settled in Rome for the following winter. Her sentiments
were strongly on the patriot side, and in Rome her acquaintance with Mazzini was renewed when he arrived to head
the new republican government. By a chance meeting in St.
Peter's, she became acquainted with a young, handsome,
amiable, and impoverished Roman nobleman, to whom in
December 1847 she was secretly married and whose child
she later bore. Her husband, Marchese Ossoli, was a captain
of the insurgent Roman Civic Guard, and when the siege
began she joined him in the defense of the city, tending the
wounded in a military hospital and accompanying him to
his battery on the Pincian Hill. At this time she revealed her
marriage and entrusted her child to Mrs. Story in case she
should not survive.

With the fall of Rome to the French troops, the Ossolis fled to Florence, where they remained for several months, while Margaret wrote a history of the recently expired Roman Republic. Though they had strong forebodings about an ocean voyage, the Ossolis were eventually forced by financial need to the decision to go to the United States. During a violent storm off Fire Island, just out of New York, the *Elizabeth* was wrecked and the entire family was drowned.

Other disturbances occurred in Florence in 1848, though this Florentine revolt remained only a minor episode in the turbulence of the Risorgimento — an uprising such that Mrs. Browning had written: "Every now and then a day is fixed for a revolution in Tuscany, but up to the present time a shower has come and put it off." [11] Horatio Greenough in Florence, like his fellow sculptor Thomas Crawford in Rome, took an active role in the newly instituted Civic Guard. Soon after the grand duke of Tuscany had fled his realm, fearing for his personal safety, the Austrians brought the monarch back, and the new constitution was withdrawn, the Civic Guard abolished, and strict censorship instituted. With this reaction, Florentines felt betrayed at the hands of the formerly popular grand duke. At this time Greenough was annoyed by the quartering of Austrian soldiers on his premises, but a nominal diplomatic office soon rid him of the bother. Nonetheless, he felt that the atmosphere of Florence was spoiled, and in 1851 he returned to the United States with his family.

The failure of the liberal movement deprived the city of some of its appeal. Many Florentines surprisingly had welcomed the foreign conquerors, an event that seemed to William Story an indication not of the lack of a popular base for political change but only an illustration of just how fickle Italians really were. The weak encouragement the people of Rome gave to the later Roman Revolution showed the same tendency. Support for the Roman Revolution, one American discovered, was limited almost exclusively to the educated. "The people," he wrote, "had no understanding of political questions and remained outside of the political agitation." [12]

Events of 1859–1860 involved Americans little more than those of a decade before. Some visitors expressed hope for the outcome of the movement toward Italian unity, but only a few became personally engaged in furthering this endeavor. When Garibaldi undertook his Sicilian expedition in 1860 he was aided by William De Rohan, a Philadelphia ship captain, in whose name were purchased three steamers, which then flew the United States flag. De Rohan also helped bring the vessels to Sicily. Garibaldi obtained powder from some American merchant ships in the Palermo harbor, perhaps through the agency of Captain Palmer of the warship *Iroquois*.[13] Several Americans served with Garibaldi as volunteers, and by collecting funds, as well, Americans aided his campaign. Sympathy meetings were held in New York City, Newport, and Cincinnati for the red-shirted leader.

At the time of the Sicilian conquest in 1860, Henry Adams went to interview Garibaldi at Palermo. Though the Italian leader had little of interest to say to Adams, the New Englander nonetheless thought Garibaldi looked "in his red shirt like the very essence and genius of revolution, as he is" — far more capable than his followers. Meeting Garibaldi seemed, in retrospect, for Adams, another failure in his own education, for the man hid what he really was under an impervious exterior, uttering political commonplaces, and showing himself simple and almost innocent.[14]

Economic activity, on the whole, was of secondary in-

SARAH MARGARET FULLER, MARCHIONESS OSSOLI by Thomas Hicks,
engraved by M. Haider. *Century Magazine*, April 1893.

ITALIAN LANDSCAPE by Washington Allston. Courtesy of The Addison Gallery of American Art, Phillips Academy, Andover, Massachusetts.

terest to the American visitor. Overwhelmingly an agricultural country with limited commerce and almost no industry, Italy presented little of note in this realm. The traveler, furthermore, had journeyed to Italy in order to view the famous monuments of the past, to pursue a life of artistic creativity, or to study social organizations, not to see how Italians made a living. Through casual observation, in any case, it often was difficult to tell just how many people actually did earn a livelihood.

The traveler often had sharp words for the Italian governmental attitude toward economic development. Except for the Kingdom of Sardinia and to a lesser extent Tuscany, the various states did little to encourage commerce or industry. For many years the Papal States even forbade the construction of a railroad, objecting to the expense involved and fearing the changes it might bring. Certainly Italy had tremendous potential natural resources, which went unused for lack of governmental enterprise. Horace Greeley pointed out what a good basis there was for a textile industry — infinite water power, a large supply of cheap labor, inexpensive food, a good supply of wool, and land and climate suitable for growing cotton. If these governments would undertake to promote industry, the energies of the populace might well revive, and the country would feel a new vigor.[15] As it was, the people had no incentive to develop their country, and because of the system, the American maintained, Italians had themselves become unambitious, deficient in enterprise, and indolent, certainly lacking in qualities desirable for entrepreneurs.

Agriculture suffered from the traditional, age-old landholding system. Most of the land in the South was owned by large proprietors who leased it for a share of the crops, the tenant working the land and furnishing the tools. Often the lease continued for a lifetime and was passed on from one generation to another. Not owning the soil, the farmer usually made little attempt to maintain it for the future. He continued his traditional ways of cultivation, which meant that production was comparatively limited, despite the richness of the soil. Most of the agricultural tools, the Americans found, were awkward and inefficient, the same as those used by the ancients: crude wooden plows were drawn by a cow or a woman, the spades and scythes were heavy, and the adz a waste of effort. William Story did not find "a single utensil employed, even on the farms of gentlemen, that would not be jeered at by the most ignorant American labourer." Roman agriculture, he went on, had not progressed "since the days of the Georgics." [16] Sometimes the property was leased to factors, who furnished capital, managed the cultivation of the crops, and sold the produce. The prosperity of the farms and the abundance of the crops to the north in the Po Valley, in contrast, astonished many foreigners. This was indeed a region well blessed. Tuscany, too, was rivaled by few parts of Europe, and the fertility of the area close to Naples was as great as it had been in antiquity.

The crops were chiefly grains and fruits. Wheat, barley, oats, rye, and potatoes were raised extensively, and the vine was seen everywhere. The unfamiliar sight of groves of olive, citrus, and mulberry trees, and the great rice fields made a strong impression on the visitor. Samuel Morse sent back cuttings of grapes to the United States, and Jefferson, as we have seen, made a special trip to Italy in 1787 to procure rice seed. Coming upon cornfields, the American often expressed pleasure and homesickness at the sight. Corn, though, he thought, was poorly grown in Italy, for it was so thickly planted and highly cultivated that the ears did not have a chance to fill out, and he was surprised that it was not used as a food for humans.

The traveler had less to report concerning the state of manufacturing and commerce. Seldom did the visitor even mention the shops or the produce markets, except to complain of overcharges. Only considerably later when the small single-product shop was beginning to disappear in the United States did Americans revel in the color, sounds, and activity of foreign markets. In Genoa, the visitor sometimes went to see coral works, where beads and other ornaments were fabricated, and he visited the small-scale weaving establishments. In Milan he saw silk fabrics woven. At Florence he found locally manufactured mosaic work, furniture, silver, straw goods, marble and alabaster objects, and textiles. In Rome and the Papal States, he discovered manufacture of cloth, rope, and paper; but to the American, accustomed to a multitude of labor-saving devices, the craft and industrial processes were crude: "It seems as if everything is done in the hardest possible manner, and every body goes the most round-about way to work." [17] Clinging to the traditional ways, the Italian was unable to see that production could be improved in any way.

Commercial exchanges among the states of Italy or between Italy and foreign countries were limited. In most regions agriculture was near the subsistence level, with the little in excess going to the local towns. Transporting products from one place to another was difficult, and borders were jealously guarded. Commercial taxes on imported products also discouraged exchanges, but where foreigners were present, there commerce was stimulated. Even at Syracuse, Washington Irving discovered, the money that American naval men had brought to the city had increased business activity. Italy obviously needed all the money that foreigners could bring.

The American often expressed the belief that, as with political conditions, he and his countrymen, if given the opportunity, could vastly improve the economic situation of Italy. There was much that Italians could learn from efficient American agricultural, commercial, and industrial practices. Railroads were needed, and if built by "an enterprising company of Americans" could bring profit to such an operation, for example, as the Carrara marble quarries. With efficient methods Americans could even regain the wastes of the Campagna. If this region were given to a group of Yankee emigrants, suggested one visitor, they would in a few years get rid of the malaria, restore "republican liberty," and make it "one of the finest countries in the world. . . . Industry and enterprise would perform greater miracles, than even the Romish church has ever witnessed." [18] With increasing economic opportunity, a new set of impulses would be awakened, and men would begin to develop new powers.

Some Americans suggested that their own country could benefit, nonetheless, from some elements of Italian agricultural knowledge. More intensive cultivation similar to that in Italy ought to be encouraged in the United States. Irrigation and treeplanting practices could form a profitable example for the American farmer. Strong Italian oxen might be imported. Vine cultivation, moreover, might be encouraged, for, as one writer suggested, it would increase the value of the land, promote temperance, and give American businessmen suitable leisure-time activity.[19]

The American, it was felt, could learn something even more important in the economic realm — a sense of perspective concerning his values. Though the United States surpassed Italy in commercial activity, many Americans devoted themselves so exclusively to commerce that they had lost sight of all other values. In American commercial towns there was a want of taste, an absence of leisure and refinement, and an excess of worry and ostentation. Looking only to its own interests, to temporary expedients, and to the policies of the hour, the American business class treated moneymaking as the chief end of human affairs rather than as an incident in life, and the influence of these men was such that their opinions dominated American thought. The American could well take a lesson here and place economic activity in its proper place.

Italy, everything considered, was obviously past her glory. The full greatness of America, on the other hand, was yet to come, and the American believed his country would surpass everything done before. After some time in Italy, as the excitement and newness wore off, the traveler began to look back to his homeland, usually ready to return where he knew his own future lay and where he was sure the future of the world lay. "It was with a throb of exultation," as one American asserted, "that we recurred to the new world in the west: its institutions, its prosperity, its inhabitants." [20]

CHAPTER IX

THE MEANING OF ITALY

CERTAINLY the visit to Italy was highly meaningful to many nineteenth-century Americans. Again and again the letters and travel journals eloquently reveal that exposure to the country had greater significance than visits to other places. Sometimes the American looked back on his Italian tour as one of the most important events in his entire life.

Although the traveler frequently responded negatively to specific social, political, and religious conditions, his overall response to Italy was almost always enthusiastic. George Ticknor wrote in 1817 that he had enjoyed himself "more in Italy than in all the rest of Europe, and . . . Rome is worth all the other cities in the world. . . . I am sure I shall leave it with more regret than I have yet left any spot in Europe." [1] George Bancroft in 1822 wrote: "Everything conspires to make a journey in Italy the most interesting in the world." [2] Often the American used almost the same words in reporting that Italy had added a new dimension to his existence. "In sober sadness," revealed Nathaniel Parker Willis, "one may well regret any country where his life has been filled fuller than elsewhere of sunshine and gladness; and such, by a thousand enchantments, has Italy been to me. . . . You can exist elsewhere, but, oh! you *live* in Italy." [3] Ephraim Peabody, minister of King's Chapel, Boston, agreed: "Till a man has seen Italy and breathed it . . . he cannot be said to have lived." [4] Margaret Fuller, with her gift for self-dramatization and epigram, said flatly: "Those have not lived who have not seen Rome." [5] And Henry James in Rome a few years later on his first visit: "Que vous en dirai-je? At last — for the first time — I live!" [6]

Sometimes the American went so far as to pronounce Italy, and especially Rome, his real home. "Of all places in the world [Rome] is the true spot for us," wrote William Story to James Russell Lowell. [7] On departing from Rome in 1867, James A. Garfield, then congressman from Ohio, recorded, "Rome is indeed 'my country' — dead, but alive forevermore." [8] Fenimore Cooper found that he had never left any other country with half the regret with which he left Italy: the departure, he wrote, was like "quitting his own home." [9] Conversely the professional traveler Bayard Taylor, poetically recalling his first impressions, saw his arrival as an end to exile, a homecoming. [10] Charles Eliot Norton said that if he were ever given a new life, he would choose to be born an Italian. [11]

Such feelings, it must be emphasized, were not unique to Americans. One finds the same enthusiastic response and the same sense of personal fulfillment among the English and other peoples of northern Europe. Walter Savage Landor, who spent much of his life in Florence, expressed the common attitude when he had one of his imaginary conversers declare: "It is worth all that remains of life to have lived one year in Italy." [12] Goethe reckoned a new birth from the day he entered Rome: "All the dreams of my youth I now behold realized before me." [13] But the experience of Italy was even more significant to the American than to the European, for the elements of Italy and Italian life that the American found important were certainly present to a lesser degree in other parts of Europe. Perhaps in the same way that Rome concentrated the experience of Italy, Italy itself summed up the essential meaning of all Europe to the American.

During these years, the first six decades of the nineteenth century, the American was probably better prepared for a visit to Italy than to any other foreign country except England, whose literature, history, and culture he most particularly shared. In the early years of the century, Byron, Madame de Staël, and the eighteenth-century English writers exercised the greatest impact on him, and it was through the eyes of these authors that the newcomer usually viewed Italy. By the middle and later years of the century, however, the visitor was not only prepared by the countless English, Continental, and American volumes of Italian letters and travel, but also by a deluge of paintings, drawings, and reproductions of Italian scenes. Margaret Fuller recalled how popular the collecting of Italian scenes had been in the United States around 1839 or 1840: "Our walls were hung with prints of the Sistine frescoes; we were all petty collectors; and prints of Correggio and Guercino took the place, for the time, of epics and philosophy." [14] The photograph album had also come into its own. Thus the American frequently looked at the luminous skies, the colorfully dressed peasants, the grass-covered ruins through the refracting lens of remembered descriptions and illustrations. The visitor's expectations were aroused long before he arrived, and part of his enjoyment of Italy came from this long anticipation and the pleasures of recognition.

A tour of Italy was important for the American, too, because of the emotional associations he brought with him.

The visitor often came as a former student of the classics. During the impressionable years of adolescence he had studied the literature of ancient Greece and Rome, and long before seeing the Mediterranean world he had formed mental pictures of what he might find. Such youthful images had the strongest emotional content, embodying bright hopes for a horizonless future and the achievement of any possibility. A visit to what was left of the world of Rome aroused evocative overtones of these early feelings. At such moments "the present is forgotten. The weary cares of manhood fade away, and 'the heat and burden' beneath which we are now laboring, is unfelt. The Spring of life returns in all its freshness." [15]

Closely connected with this, Italy offered continuous and fascinating entertainment. Increasingly, by the mid-decades of the century, the American found an important meaning in the spectacle the country provided. The picturesque scene delighted the traveler, stimulating his imagination, and the effect was intensified by his remembered associations. The reality of Italy, he discovered, often looked just like animated pictures, nature imitating art. The country was like a vast theatrical performance. "Every thing here has a kind of stage effect," one observer put it.[16] "It seems as if the world had indeed turned into a stage, and the men and women into players," reported another visitor.[17] And yet another wrote: "Their country has become, as it were, one vast exhibition." [18] Indeed, a trip to Italy had become a visit to the best show the nineteenth century had to offer.

For some Americans Italy had primarily a moral meaning. This was a land blessed by nature, promising a comfortable living for all, and yet a great many people enjoyed little more than the bare necessities of life. The contrast of the glories of ancient Rome and the High Renaissance with the decay of modern Italy kept obtruding itself on one's notice. Instead of finding men who reminded him of the statesmen and orators of antiquity, the traveler saw only "a poor, superstitious priest ridden race having no affinity to their heroic ancestors."[19] Immorality was widespread. Even the malarial wastes of the Campagna were viewed as divine retribution for the sins of the people.

Why had Italy fallen so? American travelers had a ready answer. Men had been crushed by the burden of their own inherited institutions. A false system of religion and a false concept of government were chiefly responsible. Ancient Rome, in its failure to follow the Christian God, had had no fitting aim or goal, no hope for immortality to brighten its course, and it had gone down as a result of its disbelief. Probably in any case Rome got what it deserved, for the evidence of ancient immorality that survived in a place like Pompeii was overwhelming. Then came Catholicism, which the Protestant American believed had eventually perverted Christianity from its original aims, fostering idolatry and inevitably leading to irreligion and licentiousness. On this framework was placed the baneful influence of a hierarchy of nobility. The results were the all too apparent deterioration and wreckage of humanity. Yet if the institutions of Church and state could be changed so that conditions of living might be altered, there was certainly hope that men would improve and that Italy might be regenerated. Italian life thus could serve as a warning.

In the nineteenth century, as today, a visit to Italy sometimes meant escape from the problems of one's own society and from the responsibilities of personal decision and moral choice. Away from home and the customary complex of social relationships, moving in the midst of this great spectacle, visitors often expressed feelings of release, "the delightful freedom from the common cares and business of life." [20] Old duties fell away, and the pressures to act and to achieve in certain prescribed ways were lessened. Perhaps this feeling as much as anything else was involved in the response of those who declared that in Italy at last they were "alive."

Italy shared with all foreign lands a further meaning in the opportunity that a visit afforded the traveler to take a fresh look at American social institutions, religion, art, and government, and the whole scheme of American values. He discovered, importantly, that the Italians put a different estimate on time. Life flowed along in slow movement, and men did not hurry about trying to "save" time; instead they savored and enjoyed each moment to the fullest for its own sake. In this new perspective the American often came to question what the worth of many of his daily activities actually was. Despite this questioning and despite his praise for many elements in the Italian scene, he nonetheless usually came away convinced of the superiority of his own way of life. "An American," reportedly said Father Taylor, "does not know the value of the blessings of his native country till he comes to Italy." [21]

Removed from familiar surroundings, the traveler saw his formerly unquestioned sense of identity, based on accepted assumptions and on a specific role in the society, fall away, and the problem of who and what he actually was became an important one. The American was forced to define himself to himself, and in doing so, too, he perhaps came to a better understanding of his own values and ideals. Often self-consciously feeling himself culturally inferior, for example, he also had to consider what this difference in cultural achievement really meant.

National allegiance was simple. "Every American devoted to his Country, feels his national attachment expand with every mile of remove from his native shores." [22] The

question of nominal identity was always raised at the passport and customs' offices, as the traveler passed from one
state to another, and his nominal identity was strengthened
when native Italians reacted positively toward him, a foreigner, merely because of his nationality. Long-time American residents clung to their native tongue as an assertion
of identity and never really became proficient in Italian.
They closely followed events "back home" in newspapers
and periodicals months out of date, and they usually
planned to return to the United States, though many never
did. The children and even the grandchildren of Hiram
Powers considered themselves Americans and always spoke
of the United States as "home." [23] The American's sense
of his own national identity, furthermore, was strengthened
by his visits to the many different states of Italy (and of
Europe generally) and by the realization that the residents
possessed only local allegiance to the particular town or
region they inhabited. In touring abroad he was recognized
and treated and increasingly thought of himself as an
American, not as a New Yorker or a Virginian.

In part as a reassurance of their identity, in part as a
nostalgia for their homes, Americans loyally gathered together wherever they were to celebrate such national holidays as the Fourth of July or Washington's Birthday, toast-
ing their homeland and their national heroes, and expressing
suitable patriotic sentiments. The painters Samuel F. B.
Morse and Amasa Hewins, to give only one example, found
themselves the only Americans present in Venice on July
4, 1831, and the two met to celebrate the day, Hewins
proposing a toast to "the political and religious regeneration of Italy" and Morse calling for "success to our principles throughout the world." Morse felt that this particular
year had impressed upon him more than any before a
thankfulness for having been born in the United States
and for the blessings he enjoyed.[24]

In the process of self-identification, the American became involved in the problem of differentiating himself from the English, the most numerous of the foreign groups in Italy. The American's dislike of the English, whom he considered haughty, avaricious, and ambitious, was almost universal. George Hillard put it simply: "The natural and unadulterated English is an unrefined animal." [25] Proud of his homeland and at bottom ashamed of his British cousins' behavior abroad, the American had to show the Italian (who tended to class all foreigners as *Inglesi*) that he was not the same as these people. When Neapolitan street musicians serenaded William Preston and a companion with "God Save the King," the two Americans strenuously objected and instructed them instead to play "Yankee Doodle." [26]

The English were blatantly inconsiderate in their attitude and responses, and they often shocked the Italians by their lack of respect and by their indifference to public opinion. On one occasion Francis Parkman heard an Englishman in St. Peter's complain, "How long does this damned Pope expect us to stand here waiting for him?" When admonished by an English-speaking priest that he should refrain from such insults, the Englishman answered with an insolent stare, turned his back, and proclaimed "The English *own* Rome!" [27] In the same vein, James Russell Lowell reported on the difference between English and American behavior at the church of Trinità dei Monti: "The moment the singing was over, while the priest was continuing the service & the people were on their knees, the English rose in a body & scuffled out of the church talking & laughing as they went. The Americans all remained seated quietly till the services ended." [28]

The eccentricities of English dress, manners, and activities stood forth everywhere; as a people they seemed far less adaptable to foreign ways than the Americans. An epitaph in the Protestant Cemetery at Rome to one Thomas Dessoulavy, who died in 1869, reads that he "painted the classic scenes of Rome — with truth and beauty — and never ceased to be an Englishman." [29] But the English apparently frowned on the Americans as much as the Americans did on them, and they wanted equally to dissociate themselves from their foreign cousins, making it clear that though they spoke the same language they were an entirely different breed.

Just as Americans criticized the English, they were often displeased with one another in this foreign environment. Sometimes an American critic warned that his countrymen abroad were puffing up their own importance in ways that the European could not accept. Margaret Fuller, for one, cautioned that all was not the best in the United States, where political ambition was frequently sullied, social laws were often weak, and the nation was eaten by the cancer of slavery.[30] Inward-looking Nathaniel Hawthorne wondered about the quality of the American's patriotic feeling and how in fact it was possible for an American to feel any love for his land at all, when the limitlessness of the country and its want of oneness were considered. He concluded that the singular form of government, separating Americans from people of other nations, was responsible for their kind of patriotism.[31]

A few critical travelers felt that most American tourists were so unprepared for what they saw and so cut off from Italian life that they gained nothing at all from the visit and merely displayed their own vulgarity. Margaret Fuller concluded that her fellow nationals abroad either became servile, spending their money and indulging their tastes in their anxiety to associate with titled persons, or else became conceited, contemptuous of the court and the Church and of all things old. Only a few were "thinking

Americans" who could learn something for the benefit of
their own country.[32] Henry James a few years later was
even more severe on his countrymen: "There is but one
word to use in regard to them — vulgar, vulgar, vulgar."
Secure in their own limited standards, ignorant and defiant,
they reacted grudgingly toward everything European. "It's
the absolute and incredible lack of *culture* that strikes you
in the common travelling Americans." [33]

By and large the midcentury American in Italy thought
of himself as one liberated from the prejudices of Europe,
from the hold of outmoded social forms, from the grasping
hands of priest, king, and soldier. He saw himself as one
who had been able to build up a new society and help in
the formation of new institutions. He believed that this
society was based on the proposition that each man must
have full scope to develop his powers, that it gave all men
an opportunity to partake of the material goods of the land,
and that his country would continue to be able to make
changes. He was proud of his democratically oriented government and of the separation of religion from the state.
Traveling abroad, he felt foreign governments had no right
to prevent him from speaking and acting just as he would
speak and act in his own country. Were a slogan necessary,
it would read: When in Rome, do as you do at home. Nonetheless, he did not flaunt his own ways to the same extent
as the English.

He considered himself morally superior to men of the
Old World. He prided himself on his realism, on his acceptance of hard work, and on his honesty in dealing with
other men. He showed perhaps less pity than contempt for
others who had not succeeded in doing what he had done.
Intensely patriotic, he assumed that what he had accom-
plished in his country had been the greatest achievement
of modern times. Did he not see the proof of the worth of

his ideas and actions in the rapid expansion of his new nation? He had a missionary fervor to bring what he had achieved to the rest of the world, and, especially toward midcentury, was far more eager to teach than to learn. He was convinced that the future lay with him and his ways, though he had the duty to help speed up this change. But at the same time he was extremely self-conscious, for he was aware that all Europeans did not regard him in the same light as he saw himself. He sometimes feared that his country did not yet have the power and respect commensurate with its guiding position. He was, furthermore, rather uncertain of his national cultural achievement, and hence doubly flattered when the work of his Fenimore Cooper or his Hiram Powers was praised. To be an American, then, to the man of the first half of the nineteenth century, was to be a trail blazer, a discoverer of new patterns for living. To be an American meant to be an exemplar for all men.

Beyond all these elements, Italy had yet another and more profound meaning: she gave the American a sense of the past, a feeling for the passage of time and for his own place in history, that no other land could provide in just the same way. Coming from a youthful country, the visitor from the New World seemed to feel a particular need for tangible evidence of the flow of time. Of all the European countries that he visited, Italy had the longest continuous past. Admittedly, the remains of ancient Greece were older, but the bridge between past and present had been more thoroughly annihilated. In Italy, on the other hand, civilization had been continuous from antiquity, and physical evidence from most periods still remained. In the successive layers of these architectural remnants the American could witness the development of Western civilization itself. At every step he met the past, so that it became as real as the present. Italy, as Henry James suggested, was "thick with the sense of history and the very taste of time." [34] The rich historical associations thus provided the American (whose historical knowledge was usually rather meager) with a new life dimension.

The concept of time the American had brought with him was sharply jarred, for what had appeared old to him in the United States was as yesterday in Italy. Buildings and art objects of the sixteenth century were close at hand, and nothing really seemed old that came after the Emperor Constantine. The Egyptian obelisks put even Augustan antiquities to shame, and the American was startled into a realization of how young he really was. "What a speck does the history of America become in this long vista of events," exclaimed Fenimore Cooper at Paestum. [35] A certain humility attended these observations, sometimes not without an equally patriotic hope that the United States, in coming thus far, might still move a great deal further, surpassing — if the issue were to be pushed quite far enough — even Rome at her mightiest.

That a land unknown to the ancient world could now be compared in achievement to the Roman Republic was astonishing and glorious. Often, in fact, the American saw himself as one of the new Roman people. "Our art, our literature," Lowell was to write, "are, as theirs, in some sort exotics; but our genius for politics, for law, and, above all, for colonization, our instinct for aggrandizement and for trade, are all Roman." [36] Sooner or later, however, the sobering question forced itself: just how far could the analogy to ancient Rome be pushed? Obviously, the United States had a great future to look forward to, but would the same fate overtake America that had crushed Rome? Was America, similarly, bound to fade away and to present to some future Gibbon a spectacle of desolation such as the sight that the Englishman had contemplated amid the Capitoline ruins? The American realized he might profit from the lessons that ancient Rome had to offer, but the fear remained that nonetheless the path for his country might inevitably be the same.

The impact of this new and extended sense of time appears in passages from the painter Thomas Cole's journal, in which he recorded his visit to Volterra in 1831. Though far declined from its former glory, Volterra still retained traces of the important Etruscan city that once stood on the precipitous site, as well as many structures from the late Middle Ages. Sitting below the ruins of an Etruscan wall one hot afternoon, Cole was meditating on "the great scene of desolate sublimity" before him, when suddenly the deep stillness was shattered by the bell of an ancient convent mournfully ringing "as if wailing for the hour whose departure it announced." To Cole then came a profound awareness of the transitory nature of all things. "Brief are the limits of human life," he lamented. "Man measures time by hours & minutes: Nature, by the changes of the Universe." The great gulf before him seemed "an hourglass of nature" through which men and events had passed, and he realized that the sounds he was then hearing had run on for ages and ages past and would continue for countless ages to come.[37]

This expanded sense of time, then, helped to fulfill a certain emotional need for the American, who in his New World home had lost a feeling of continuity with what had gone before. He had been born into a family that had moved out of the neighborhood where all the old ties were found. Visiting Europe meant a return to the old home, a realization of what this inheritance, from which his family had been separated really involved. To the uprooted, a visit to Europe could convey the awareness that he did have a past to which he could look back. Even though he did not establish new roots physically, such a visit could give him a new sense of belonging.

The visit to Italy, moreover, was a characteristic American version of a characteristic nineteenth-century phenomenon — the flight from modernity. Just as Byron turned to Greece and Wordsworth to nature, the American sought and found in Italy a sense of stability. Coming from an environment that emphasized social and physical mobility, "progress," and the future, the American could find in European lands, and most particularly in the continuous past of Italy (above all, in Rome), a resting place, where change rarely intruded and where he could reunite himself with the past from which he had been cut off.

Yet a certain attitude of repulsion from the past is also to be noticed. Some critics believed that the atmosphere of Italy was bad for the American, since in it his creativity often withered away: the weight of the past was simply too great. This becomes a common theme in nineteenth-century American fiction set in Italy. In *The Marble Faun*, Hawthorne described Hilda's turning in Rome from original work to copying. Henry James similarly depicted the drying up of the creative springs in the artist Roderick Hudson. James believed, too, that William Story might have done better work elsewhere, in a place where distractions were fewer and the past was less obtrusive. Bayard Taylor, who had been almost everywhere, became convinced that in Italy "the Past is too powerful," so that men tended to become indifferent to the present and unable to work, narcoticized by the atmosphere.[38] William James, on a visit to Italy in 1872, likewise complained of the burdens of history, and suggested that if one remained long he would cease to use his own active powers and become a mere parasite on the past. "The ancients did things by doing the business of their own day, not by gaping at their grandfathers' tombs, — and the normal man of today will do likewise. Better fifty years of Cambridge, than a cycle of Cathay." [39] The American's destiny obviously lay at home in the present.

Finally, Italy meant the place where the ideal world of art and beauty could best be appreciated. Perhaps more than anywhere else, Italy epitomized "culture," which some Americans so often and so determinedly pursued. From the bustling world, this land provided a refuge where all things associated with culture were found. The individual life took on new meaning, old problems vanished, and personal energies moved to creative self-expression or the acquisition of new knowledge. The traveler seemed to become more civilized just by being there, and, as always, these reactions were intensified in Rome. "Nothing, verily," as Henry James expressed it, "used to strike us more than that people of whom, as we said, we wouldn't have expected it, people who had never before shown knowledge, taste or sensibility, had here quite knocked under." [40] Just as past and present had been woven together in a richly textured fabric, natural beauty and the work of man had also been united more fully in Italy than elsewhere. Sensations were multiplied, and life, indeed, became richer.

THE TRAVELERS' BAGGAGE

IN HIS remarks on the many components of Italian life, the American traveler revealed a great deal about himself. Many of his responses led to comments he was quite ready to articulate; others led him to express ideas he had not completely thought out before. After encountering the attitudes, the assumptions, and the prejudices of others, he was often better able to see his own. Taken as a whole, however, the American's statements do reveal significant presuppositions and popular ideas of which he was not always totally aware.

Although the visitor coming early in the century had less idea of what to expect and fewer preconceptions than the midcentury tourist, both shared a surprising consistency of response over these years, a consistency based in part, of course, on stereotypes of Italian religion, government, art, and national character they brought with them. Beyond these specific stereotypes, the American held other more general determining ideas, or underlying assumptions, that formed a basis for his attitudes and led him to conclusions about what he saw. His preconceptions were not entirely unique, however, and some were shared generally with northern European people.

Some of the ideas that were held by nineteenth-century Americans as the immutable truth, the natural values of all men, now seem both charmingly innocent and incredibly naïve. It is, in fact, the quality of their minds, their ways of thinking, their cultural assumptions, that most cut these men off from us today. Their unquestioned faith in the value of hard work, the inevitability of progress, or the truth of absolute moral standards seem to place them more in a far and distant land — never again to be inhabited — than do any subsequent changes in the economy, institutions, or techniques of living. One must emphasize this break in ideas strongly, for too often today we continue to think of ourselves as differing from our grandfathers and our great-grandfathers only in our greater environmental controls. These differences in ways of thinking help to show us how enormous the gulf actually is.

The American believed that a tightly-knit family was commendable. Lacking long-standing communal traditions, physically mobile, and often new to his own community, the American undoubtedly found in the close bonds of the immediate family unit something of the same emotional and social support that the long-established, stable European community, with its extended family relationships, gave its residents. A closely united family life, he was convinced, promoted good morals and personal virtue; loose family ties, on the other hand, could only lead to immorality and individual depravity. Marriage ties were absolutely binding, and though a man might occasionally transgress, for a woman to do so was unthinkable. He saw that family life in Italy centered much less in the home than was the case in the United States; the coffeehouse, the wine shop, and the open street took over a share of the role of the American domestic dwelling. Unlike the Italian, the American believed, he himself sought physical comfort in the home, took pride in the appearance of his residence, and was delighted to entertain his friends there. His observations of the different social function of the home and of the extramarital alliances and his infrequent opportunities to meet Italians in their homes and so view the domestic situation close at hand led the American to feel that his own family ties were far stronger than those in Italy. Convinced of the importance of family bonds and of his own superior position, he concluded that his own nation in this respect morally was far superior to Italy.

For the American, women were guardians of morality, elevated creatures who were dependent on men for their support. Deference was due them in public as well as in private, and the American was surprised to see how rudely women were sometimes treated on the streets of Italy. A particular class of women might be accorded different treatment, but they had set themselves apart. For the rest, premarital virtue must be assured and marital fidelity unquestioned. Girls, he thought, should be educated so that they would be prepared to participate in the world. The American was shocked to see lower-class women doing the work that he considered only men or animals ought to perform, for not only was this disrespectful to the sex, but it took women from what he accepted as their acknowledged role as mistresses of the household, and even led to confusion over the social role of the male. For two reasons, perhaps, the American visitor became so exercised over the place of women in Italian life. The value of women in the United States, in the first place, had been enhanced by the relative scarcity of the sex in many parts of the country. And secondly, the place of American women was changing, as their importance in schools, factories, and commercial life was manifestly growing. Believing that the factors of reason and perfectibility were common to all human beings, the

American man could see that he had not yet extended to women in his own society a full opportunity to develop their individual capacities. With some uncertainty over what exactly the economic function of women should be, the American male took a very strong position about the completely different role of the sex (particularly among the lower classes) in Italy. His stand was moral, and he condemned Italian society for denying the distinctiveness of women by allowing them to do what he saw as man's work and preventing them from developing their talents.

The American tended to approve of a hierarchy of social distinction and was willing to grant respect to certain people for their position alone — and this despite his strong affirmation of the principle of equality; nevertheless, he had firm ideas about the origins of class and rejected rigid barriers that prevented a man from changing his condition. That a man could not better himself appeared both wrong for the individual and harmful for the society. Upper-class position, he believed, should arise from natural talent and personal achievement. Each man thus had a duty to try to improve his condition, and the community was obligated to foster an environment in which this was possible. Especially among the large group of those Americans traveling for pleasure, usually men of standing in their own communities, possessing wealth and leisure, there was a tendency to look with favor upon a clearly structured society, in which persons of the upper group provided social leadership. For some Americans the trip to Italy itself was one of the accepted symbols of status achievement. Perhaps the reason why many Americans looked so favorably upon a definitely structured society was the difficulty they themselves were having in forming recognized social groupings at home. With the absence of old families and traditions and the difficulty of maintaining distinctive badges of status, the American social structure remained fluid and undifferentiated. Italy, thus, provided a social model, the rigidity of which the American (with his democratic beliefs) vigorously rejected, but in the class lines of which he sometimes found an appealing stability.

The American also firmly believed that men had a duty to work and to work hard. Coming from a land having an abundance of natural resources and an almost perpetual shortage of labor, growing up in the Protestant-Puritan tradition, which emphasized the duty and value of work, often gaining his fortune through his own hard labor, the American stressed work as an important tenet of his creed. Work was of definite value not only for the goods or services it produced, but also for its effect on the individual, developing in him qualities of industry and creativeness. While extolling the virtues of work, thrift, and activity, the American vigorously condemned begging. This practice was a personal annoyance, and in addition it was bad for the beggar's character and dangerous for society. Worst of all, the beggar usually did not even feel any shame. There was something wrong, too, with men who chose not to be active in the world. The American looked with disfavor on members of religious orders who had withdrawn from the world for contemplation and prayer, as well as on idle aristocrats, whose activities had been circumscribed by tradition, and lower-class loungers, who wandered aimlessly through the streets or did nothing but sit and talk. He objected to the overabundance of festival days, which seemed to encourage idleness, and to the reliance on the saints rather than on individual exertion. He believed, however, that as an observer acquainting himself with works of art, the history of the past, and varieties of social organization, he was not himself wasting his time. And he was curiously attracted to the life of the lounger-observer, which often came to symbolize to him the pace and value of the Italian way, so different from his own.

Commercial activity was important, the American felt, even though he esteemed it less than the "higher life" of religion and art and the influential work of government. By means of commerce, honestly conducted, both the individual and the nation would prosper. Commercial relations, he believed, should be built on a clearly understood foundation of agreement as to price, quality, and services. He was willing to give a fair price for goods and services, though he naturally favored spending as little as possible, but the variations from a uniform price that came in bargaining struck him as wrong. By the middle of the century, the commercial market of the United States had largely moved to a national scale, so that goods and prices to a large extent were uniform throughout most of the country. The American at home thus usually knew what he was expected to pay for a specific article. Somehow in Italy, the land of culture and cultivation, the land in which he was taking a holiday from the ordinary, business concerns of living, this haggling over prices was strangely out of keeping.

The American's system of government was perhaps his greatest pride. Government, he felt, was a concern for all men responsibly working together. While to the Italian, government was "they," to the American it was "we." The major function of government, he affirmed, was to bring about social conditions that would enable men to develop their powers to the fullest. By and large, the governments of the states of Italy, in the hands of a few, had restricted education, limited the free expression of ideas, allowed little individual political participation, and hindered economic development. Men had been denied their rightful natural liberty. In the face of this situation, the

American's faith in his own political philosophy and governmental processes was strengthened, and he sincerely felt that he had the duty to bring the virtues of his own system of government to foreign peoples. He was intensely and loudly patriotic, "stinking with national conceit," proud of his own country, which had come so far. Indeed, it often seemed inevitable, a Manifest Destiny, that this form of enlightened government would spread to other lands. He became even more sure that the future lay with him.

Art and religion, for the American, were found in a special realm, the "higher life," to a large extent apart from everyday concerns, though elements of this life extended down into mundane activities and drew men upward. The American considered these two fields eminently important.

Art, he felt, dimly mirrored an ideal world of ordered form in which the principles of beauty (usually only vaguely conceived) held sway. At their best, works of art could serve as a magnet attracting the individual to this higher realm, elevating feelings and providing moral uplift. On the other hand, since art could also appeal to man's baser emotions and thus degrade him, it held certain dangers. For the American the world of art was largely new; he had known few artists at home, and he had certainly not seen many masterpieces. He realized that his own society had not yet had the time to encourage art and had much to learn of its traditions and of artistic creativity in general.

Religion, he felt, could also elevate and better the individual by bringing him closer to this realm of the ideal. Religion, the Protestant American affirmed, should appeal primarily to reason and the understanding rather than to the heart or the emotions; through the word of God as revealed in the Bible men could best see what religion really meant. The Italian Roman Catholic, it seemed, concerned himself primarily with external forms and not with true inward religion. Catholic ritual and ceremonies appealed dangerously to the senses and the imagination, and the celebrant did not always show a proper attitude of reverence.

Religion was intimately bound up with morality for the American, and sometimes his religion seemed to have more to do with mundane concerns than with eternity. Religion, he believed, both gave men faith in the world to come and helped them with their activities in this world. All action was important, since all action involved a moral choice between good and evil. An absolute and unquestioned moral law was embodied most fully in the word of the Scriptures, and access to it was gained by the conscience or "moral sense" of the individual. Each man possessed a moral sense, which could unmistakably guide him in his actions; in part this sense was innate, and in part it was acquired by training and association. The Italian's moral sense, the American felt, had been corrupted by the institutions of despotic government and the Catholic Church. The Italian people constantly transgressed the moral law, as, for example, in violations of the sanctity of the Sabbath, in marital infidelity, or in superstitious religious practices. Coming from a new nation without old institutional forms and customs, the American saw himself as uncorrupted and morally superior. He was seldom modest about his feelings of superiority, believing himself far more honest in business, more sincere in social relations, and more devout in religious observances. In this sphere he was sure he could better teach than be taught.

During these years the American also showed considerable faith in progress. His own society, he believed, had moved a long distance in a very short time, and was itself a remarkable proof of the meaning of progress. By continuing under the forms already established in the United States, men would inevitably advance toward an increasing perfection of the individual and of the larger social order. The right course, he felt, was development toward something new, and education was the most crucial social element directing that movement. Through education all men could be improved; through the best education would come the "best" men, the leaders of society. In Italy he could see the dangers of oppressive institutions; men had not worked for change, and education had been neglected. Americans could profit by this example to advance their own society.

Underlying these several controlling beliefs were other ideas even more general, which seldom came out explicitly and yet which seemed to be implicit in the American's thought. For example, he had moved completely away from the earlier Puritan estimate of human nature; no longer did he find the individual innately sinful, but instead he saw man's nature as good and perfectible. He had a profound faith in the reasonableness of the individual and his freedom to act and to plan his own future. The American's interests, too, were secular; he was primarily interested in this world now and in what it might be in the future.

Institutionalism was another important element of his underlying beliefs. Men had the capacity to shape their society, and it was through social institutions that personal character was formed and behavior determined. With proper institutions, the old social problems would be solved, and men themselves could move toward perfection. The American thus believed that the individual Italian himself was by no means responsible for his own character traits or for the declining condition of his society; once institutions had been changed, men themselves would change. Perhaps the chief reason why the American in Italy wanted government and private individuals to promote art activities at home was not to provide aesthetic pleasures for the citizen but to establish another type of institution that could also help to improve society through impact on character. With respect to his own country, he did not consider that the abundant natural resources, nor his private enterprise system, nor individual character had been particularly significant in bringing about present conditions. He saw instead the development of his country as strongly affected by the primary institutions of government, religion, and the family. These three institutions, it must be admitted, were all called into question in his tour of Italy in a way that his economic system was not. Having been called into question, they were thereupon examined and defended and perhaps given a more positive valuation than they otherwise might have had.

Americans also tended to compartmentalize the areas of human activity. Art was associated with specific works that had been agreed upon as worthy of inclusion in the category. Art was something distinctive to which the individual turned on particular occasions. The life of art was something that he approached self-consciously, knowing that it was "higher," not integrally involved in the ordinary concerns of living. Learning, too, was something found in books or the university. Art along with learning largely made up "culture," something decidedly apart from daily life, toward which he had a reverential attitude. Religion as well was in a special category, though morality brought the consequences of religion into different areas of everyday life.

Finally, related to compartmentalization was a sense of appropriateness, of consistency of behavior and situation. The American had a strong sense of the fitting, and felt uncomfortable when what he considered the appropriate was not observed. Morality itself frequently seemed to be a category of appropriateness, and he often found something immoral when action fell outside the appropriate category, as, for example, when business dealings took place close to a religious shrine. He found it odd that the rich and poor mixed so closely together in the cities. He objected when the nobility did not possess the trappings that he believed nobility ought to have. At the opera, a category of culture, he was annoyed when the respectful attitude he felt fitting was not forthcoming. He thought it ludicrous when guides dressed in rags would learnedly discuss antiquity. The sight of priests casually chatting when engaged in devotions seemed very much out of keeping with the attitude of reverence due religion. Italian funerals did not bring fitting solemnity and dignity to the ceremonies of death. He frowned on a discrepancy between showy appearance and indigent reality; for a poor man to make a public display was not right. Men ought always to present themselves as they actually were, not cringing to those above them in the social scale or striking at those below.

Thus in their responses to Italy, Americans of the first half of the nineteenth century painted a boldly defined portrait of their own minds. Interacting with an alien culture, which offered much that they deeply admired and a great deal they wholeheartedly rejected, they revealed a great many facets of the ideological structure of their own culture. A visit to Italy usually confirmed Americans in their most basic attitudes and beliefs; it provided

them with a justification of their own national experiment;
and it led them to see better just who and what they themselves were. But the experience of Italy did something more
as well: it commonly brought to these fortunate pilgrims
a new awareness of the variety and richness of life itself
and a profound sense of personal fulfillment.

FOR FURTHER READING

NOTES · INDEX

FOR FURTHER READING

THE RESOURCES for study of Americans in Italy in the nineteenth century are vast and varied. Not only did many Americans write travel books specifically about Italy, but also to a considerable extent those Americans who wrote accounts of general European travels included sections on Italy in their books. Some of the discussions of Italy are in the form of a daily journal or diary of impressions; more often they tend to be impersonal descriptions of the leading sights of the country. A few of the travel works are truly perceptive studies of the land and the people; many, however, are little more than repetitions of the comments and responses of earlier travelers. Some of the books are actually guidebooks, with detailed information as to how the visitor might best utilize his time and get along on his journey. Further sources for study of this subject are American periodicals of the last century, which frequently included such articles as "Letters from Naples" or "Impressions from Italy," as well as reviews of new books on Italy. Besides the travel writings, a great many biographies, autobiographies, and collections of letters of nineteenth-century Americans provide additional insights on the American experience in Italy. These works often give a more profound sense of the significance of this experience than do the travel accounts, since the Italian journeys can be better seen in the perspective of the individual's entire lifetime and career. Unpublished letters, journals, and diaries are another important source of information on this topic; in such private papers one often finds a more immediate and personal response to the Italian scene than is the case in the accounts written for the public eye.

Among the books and articles concerned, either in whole or in part, in a general way with the nineteenth-century American experience in Italy, the following have proved most useful for this study: Van Wyck Brooks, *The Dream of Arcadia* (New York, 1958); James Thomas Flexner, *That Wilder Image* (Boston, 1962); Albert Ten Eyck Gardner, *Yankee Stonecutters: the First American School of Sculpture, 1800–1850* (New York, 1945); Emilio Goggio, "Italy and Some of Her Early American Commentators," *Italica*, X (March 1933), 4–10; Angelo F. Guidi, *Relazioni Culturali fra Italia e Stati Uniti d'America* (Rome, 1940); Angelina La Piana, *La Cultura Americana e l'Italia* (Turin, 1938); Howard R. Marraro, "American Travellers in Rome, 1848–50," *Catholic Historical Review*, XXIX (January 1944), 470–509; Howard R. Marraro, *Relazioni fra l'Italia e gli Stati Uniti* (Rome, 1954); Giuseppe Prezzolini, *Come gli Americani Scoprirono l'Italia, 1750–1850* (Milan, 1933); Edgar P. Richardson and Otto Wittmann, Jr., *Travelers in Arcadia: American Artists in Italy, 1830–1875* (Detroit, 1951); Madeleine B. Stern, "New England Artists in Italy, 1835–1855," *New England Quarterly*, XIV (June 1941), 243–271; Giuliana Artom Treves, *The Golden Ring: the Anglo-Florentines, 1847–1862*, trans. Sylvia Sprigge (London, 1956); Henry T. Tuckerman, *Artist-Life: or, Sketches of American Painters* (New York, 1847); Henry T. Tuckerman, *Book of the Artists: American Artist Life* (New York, 1867).

American travel writings on Italy from the earlier decades of the nineteenth century number in the hundreds of items. The most popular book on Italy written by an American was George Stillman Hillard's *Six Months in Italy* (Boston, 1853), published in two volumes. Probably the most perceptive American study of Italy during this period was James Fenimore Cooper's *Excursions in Italy* (Paris, 1838), though certainly close to it would be a few other volumes, such as Rembrandt Peale's *Notes on Italy, Written During a Tour in the Years*

1829 and *1830* (Philadelphia, 1831); Henry R. Tuckerman's *Italian Sketch Book*, 3d ed. (New York, 1848); and J. W. De Forest's *European Acquaintance: Being Sketches of People in Europe* (New York, 1858). Later in the century, the various Italian studies of Henry James and William Dean Howells are especially significant.

Among the other outstanding volumes all or in part on Italy written by American travelers and concerning the period 1800 to 1860, the following should be mentioned: William Berrian, *Travels in France and Italy in 1817 and 1818* (New York, 1821); Matthias Bruen, *Essays, Descriptive and Moral: on Scenes in Italy, Switzerland, and France. By an American* (Edinburgh, 1823); Nathaniel Hazeltine Carter, *Letters from Europe*, 2 vols. (New York, 1827); Theodore Dwight, *A Journal of a Tour in Italy, in the Year 1821* (New York, 1824); Daniel C. Eddy, *Europa: or Scenes and Society in England, France, Italy, and Switzerland*, 15th ed. (Boston, 1860); Wilbur Fisk, *Travels in Europe* (New York, 1838); William M. Gillespie, *Rome: as Seen by a New-Yorker in 1843–4* (New York, 1845); Horace Greeley, *Glances at Europe* (New York, 1851); Grace Greenwood [pseud. of Sara Jane Lippincott], *Haps and Mishaps of a Tour in Europe* (Boston, 1854); John Griscom, *A Year in Europe . . . in 1818 and 1819*, 2 vols. (New York, 1823); Fanny Hall, *Rambles in Europe*, 2 vols. (New York, 1839); Nathaniel Hawthorne, *Passages from the French and Italian Note-Books* (Boston, 1883); Sophia Hawthorne, *Notes in England and Italy* (New York, 1870); Joel Tyler Headley, *Letters from Italy*, rev. ed. (New York, 1848); Washington Irving, *Notes and Journal of Travel in Europe, 1804–1805*, 3 vols. (New York, 1920); James Jackson Jarves, *Italian Sights and Papal Principles Seen Through American Spectacles* (New York, 1856) and *Italian Rambles* (New York, 1883); Isaac Appleton Jewett, *Passages in Foreign Travel*, 2 vols. (Boston, 1838); William Ingraham Kip, *The Christmas Holydays in Rome* (New York, 1846); Charles Edwards Lester, *My Consulship*, 2 vols. (New York, 1853); Theodore Lyman, Jr., *The Political State of Italy* (Boston, 1820); Henry Maney, *Memo-*

ries over the Water (Nashville, 1854); Valentine Mott, *Travels in Europe and the East, in the Years 1834–41* (New York, 1842); Charles Eliot Norton, *Notes of Travel and Study in Italy* (Boston, 1859); William C. Preston, *Reminiscences*, ed. Minnie Clare Yarborough (Chapel Hill, 1933); Joseph Sansom, *Letters from Europe, During a Tour Through Switzerland and Italy, in the Years 1801 and 1802*, 2 vols. (Philadelphia, 1805); Catharine Maria Sedgwick, *Letters from Abroad to Kindred at Home*, 2 vols. (New York, 1841); Benjamin Silliman, *A Visit to Europe in 1851*, 2 vols. (New York, 1854); James Sloan, *Rambles in Italy; in the Years 1816 . . . 17* (Baltimore, 1818); Samuel Topliff, *Topliff's Travels*, ed. Ethel Stanwood Bolton (Boston, 1906); Robert Turnbull, *The Genius of Italy: Being Sketches of Italian Life, Literature, and Religion* (New York, 1849); Nathaniel Parker Willis, *Pencillings by the Way* (New York, 1844); Theodore Witmer, *Wild Oats, Sown Abroad* (Philadelphia, 1853); Thomas G. Young, *A Wall-Street Bear in Europe* (New York, 1855).

A large periodical literature is concerned with the subject of American impressions of Italy. Especially valuable for this study have been the files of the *American Quarterly Review, American Whig Review, Cosmopolitan Art Journal, Crayon, Harbinger, Harper's New Monthly Magazine, Knickerbocker, Literary World, Monthly Anthology, New Englander, North American Review, Port Folio, Southern Literary Messenger, United States Catholic Magazine, United States Magazine and Democratic Review*, and, in the latter part of the century, the *Atlantic Monthly, Lippincott's Monthly Magazine*, and the *Nation*.

Some of the biographies and collections of personal letters and journals stand out as especially important in bringing insights to this subject. See especially Edgar P. Richardson, *Washington Allston* (Chicago, 1948); M. A. DeWolfe Howe, *The Life and Letters of George Bancroft*, 2 vols. (New York, 1908); Louis L. Noble, *The Course of Empire, Voyage of Life, and Other Pictures of Thomas Cole* (New York, 1853); Charlotte Cushman, *Letters and Memories of Her Life*, ed. Emma Stebbins (Boston, 1878); John Durand, *The Life and*

Times of A. B. Durand (New York, 1894); Margaret Fuller, *At Home and Abroad*, ed. Arthur B. Fuller (Boston, 1856); James L. Woodress, Jr., *Howells and Italy* (Durham, N. C., 1952); Robert L. Gale, "Henry James and Italy," *Studi Americani*, III (1957), 189–203; Francis Steegmuller, *The Two Lives of James Jackson Jarves* (New Haven, 1951); Ina Tosi, *Longfellow e l'Italia* (Bologna, 1906); Samuel F. B. Morse, *Letters and Journals*, 2 vols., ed. Edward Lind Morse (Boston, 1914); Charles Eliot Norton, *Letters*, 2 vols., eds. Sara Norton and M. A. DeWolfe Howe (Boston, 1913); Joshua C. Taylor, *William Page: the American Titian* (Chicago, 1957); Francis Parkman, *Journals*, 2 vols., ed. Mason Wade (New York, 1947); Henry James, *William Wetmore Story and His Friends*, 2 vols. (Boston, 1903); George Ticknor, *Life, Letters, and Journals*, 2 vols., eds. Anna Ticknor, George Stillman Hillard, and Anna Eliot Ticknor (Boston, 1909); John Galt, *The Life and Studies of Benjamin West* (Philadelphia, 1816).

Particularly useful for the general backgrounds of American travel in nineteenth-century Italy have been the following works: Diego Angeli, *Le Cronache del "Caffè Greco"* (Milan, 1930); C. P. Brand, *Italy and the English Romantics* (Cambridge, Eng., 1957); John England, *Explanation of the Ceremonies of the Holy Week*, 3d ed. (Rome, 1854); John Chetwode Eustace, *A Classical Tour Through Italy, an. MDCCCII*, 4 vols., 3d ed. (London, 1815); Joseph Forsyth, *Remarks on Antiquities, Arts, and Letters During an Excursion in Italy, in the Years 1802 and 1803* (London, 1813); H. Stuart Hughes, *The United States and Italy* (Cambridge, Mass., 1953); Livio Iannattoni, *Roma e gli Inglesi* (Rome, 1945); Paul Franklin Kirby, *The Grand Tour in Italy (1700–1800)* (New York, 1952); R. S. Lambert, ed., *Grand Tour, A Journey in the Tracks of the Age of Aristocracy* (London, 1935); H. N. Maugham, *The Book of Italian Travel (1580–1900)* (New York, 1903); William Edward Mead, *The Grand Tour in the Eighteenth Century* (Boston, 1914); Samuel Rogers, *Italian Journal*, ed. J. R. Hale (London, 1956); William Wetmore Story, *Roba di Roma*, 6th ed. (London, 1871); Lilian Whiting, *The Florence of Landor* (Boston, 1905).

NOTES

Introduction

1. American consuls were named at Leghorn in 1793, Naples in 1796, Rome in 1797, Genoa in 1799, and Florence in 1819. Regular diplomatic relations were established with the Kingdom of Naples and the Two Sicilies in 1816, the Kingdom of Sardinia in 1840, and the Papal States in 1848. The United States and Tuscany did not maintain regular diplomatic relations.

In 1777, Ralph Izard was named American commissioner to the Tuscan court, but he failed to obtain a sought-for loan or to establish commercial relations, despite the sympathies of the Tuscan grand duke for the newborn republic. In 1779, Filippo Mazzei, friend of Franklin and Jefferson, was sent by the state of Virginia to Tuscany to negotiate a loan and acquire military supplies; he published pamphlets in Florence on the American cause, but also failed to obtain a loan.

2. Antonia Fiva began to give Italian lessons in New York in 1772, and Carlo Bellini was named professor of Italian at William and Mary College in 1779.

3. Howard R. Marraro, *Diplomatic Relations Between the United States and the Kingdom of the Two Sicilies* (New York, 1951), I, 49; Francis B. Loomis, "Americans Abroad," *Lippincott's Monthly Magazine*, LIII (May 1894), 679.

4. Bancroft to John Thornton Kirkland, Rome, Feb. 10, 1822, quoted in M. A. DeWolfe Howe, *The Life and Letters of George Bancroft* (New York, 1908), I, 142.

5. Quoted in Robert E. Spiller, *Fenimore Cooper, Critic of His Times* (New York, 1931), p. 148.

6. Henry Adams, *The Education of Henry Adams* (Boston, 1918), pp. 85–86.

7. Unlike the Americans, who tended to become increasingly sentimental and romantic about Italy by midcentury, English trav-

elers of the 1840's and 1850's, one student of this period has found, tended to be "less sentimental and more realistic. They saw through the romantic veil and laugh[ed] at their parents' naïveness." The Italian tour was no longer so fashionable among the English as it had been thirty years before. C. P. Brand, *Italy and the English Romantics* (Cambridge, England, 1957), p. 24. Throughout the nineteenth century the lag of the United States in taking up various British and Continental cultural movements seems to have been about thirty years.

CHAPTER I: The Discovery of Italy

1. George B. Parks, *The English Traveler to Italy, Vol. I: The Middle Ages (To 1525)* (Rome, 1954), 339.

2. *Ibid.*, I, 246, 254–268.

3. *Ibid.*, I, 400, 299.

4. George Sandys, *Relation of a Journey Begun An: Dom: 1610* (London, 1615).

5. Paul Franklin Kirby, *The Grand Tour in Italy (1700–1800)* (New York, 1952), *passim*.

6. *Boswell's Life of Johnson*, ed. George Birkbeck Hill (New York, 1891), III, 41–42.

7. *Records of the Governor and Company of the Massachusetts Bay in New England* (Boston, 1853–1854), I, 275, as quoted in Samuel Eliot Morison, *The Founding of Harvard College* (Cambridge, Mass., 1935), p. 235.

8. John Galt, *The Life and Studies of Benjamin West, Esq.* (Philadelphia, 1816), pp. 106–186.

9. W. Roberts, "An Early American Artist: Henry Bembridge," *Art in America*, VI (Feb. 1918), 96–101; C. H. Hart, "The Gordon Family: Painted by Henry Benbridge," *Art in America*, VI (June 1918), 191–200.

10. Charles Bulfinch, *Life and Letters*, ed. Ellen Susan Bulfinch (Boston, 1896), p. 42.

11. William Dunlap, *A History of the Rise and Progress of the Arts of Design in the United States*, rev. ed. (Boston, 1918), I, 381; William B. Dinsmoor, "Early American Studies of Mediterranean Archaeology," in American Philosophical Society, *Proceedings*, LXXXVII (July 14, 1942), 73.

12. Dunlap, *The Arts of Design*, I, 168; Rembrandt Peale, *Notes on Italy* (Philadelphia, 1831), p. 202.

13. Dunlap, *The Arts of Design*, I, 28.

14. Ralph Izard, *Correspondence*, ed. Anne I. Deas (New York, 1844), p. 46.

15. Dinsmoor, "Mediterranean Archaeology," p. 75.

16. Martha Babcock Amory, *The Domestic and Artistic Life of John Singleton Copley* (Boston, 1882), *passim*; Galt, *Benjamin West*, p. 180.

17. John Carroll, *Biographical Sketch*, ed. John Carroll Brent (Baltimore, 1843), pp. 268–276.

18. John Thayer, *An Account of the Conversion of the Rev. John Thayer*, new ed. (Hartford, 1832); Percival Merritt, "Bibliographical Notes on 'An Account of the Conversion of the Rev. John Thayer,'" in Colonial Society of Massachusetts, *Transactions*, XXV (Jan. 1923), 129–140.

19. Benjamin Pollard, "Diary of a Tour in Europe, 1736–1737" (Winslow papers, Massachusetts Historical Society); see also Massachusetts Historical Society, *Collections* (Boston, 1899), 6th Series, X, 100 fn.

20. John Morgan, *The Journal of Dr. John Morgan of Philadelphia From the City of Rome to the City of London, 1764* (Philadelphia, 1907) *passim*; Antonio Pace, "Notes on Dr. John Morgan and His Relations with Italian Men and Women of Science," *Bulletin of the History of Medicine*, XVIII (Nov. 1945), 445–453.

21. Thomas Jefferson, "Journal and Expense Accounts, Kept During a Tour Through the Wine Growing Districts of France and Italy" (manuscript collection, Henry E. Huntington Library); also *The Papers of Thomas Jefferson*, ed. Julian P. Boyd, XI, Jan. 1 to Aug. 6, 1787 (Princeton, 1955), *passim*. Though Jefferson's Italian letters and journal contain nothing of importance respecting art, religion, politics, or social institutions, one passage shows a certain succumbing to the Italian scene: "If any person wished to retire from their [*sic*] acquaintance, to live absolutely unknown, and yet in the midst of physical enjoiments, it should be in some of the little villages of this coast, where air, earth and water concur to offer what each has most precious" (*Jefferson*, ed. Boyd, XI, 441–442).

22. Rutledge to Jefferson, Rome, Dec. 31, 1788, as quoted in Edward Dumbauld, *Thomas Jefferson, American Tourist* (Norman, Oklahoma, 1946), p. 144.

23. *Ibid.*, pp. 143–147; see also "The Letters of Thomas Jefferson to William Short," *William and Mary Quarterly*, XII (April 1932), 145–146.

CHAPTER II: The Business of Travel

1. Wilbur Fisk, *Travels in Europe* (New York, 1838), p. 343; Charles Edwards Lester, *My Consulship* (New York, 1853), I, 299–300.

2. Ralph Waldo Emerson, *Letters*, ed. Ralph L. Rusk (New York, 1939), I, 381.

3. Howard R. Marraro, "American Travellers in Rome, 1848–50," *Catholic Historical Review*, XXIX (Jan. 1944), 470–509. About eighty of these Americans are included in the *Dictionary of American Biography*.

4. Nathaniel Hawthorne, *Passages From the French and Italian Note-Books*, Riverside ed. (Boston, 1883), p. 231.

5. William Chauncy Langdon, "Recollections of Rome During the Italian Revolution," *Atlantic Monthly*, LII (Oct. 1883), 505.

6. Bayard Taylor, *Life and Letters*, eds. Marie Hansen-Taylor and Horace E. Scudder (Boston, 1884), II, 490–491.

7. William Mitchell Gillespie, *Rome: as Seen by a New Yorker in 1843–4* (New York, 1845); Judith P. Rives, *Tales and Souvenirs of a Residence in Europe. By a Lady of Virginia* (Philadelphia, 1842); Randal W. MacGavock, *A Tennessean Abroad or, Letters from Europe, Africa, and Asia* (New York, 1854); Samuel S. Cox, *A Buckeye Abroad* (New York, 1852).

8. Marraro, "American Travellers in Rome."

9. Rembrandt Peale, *Notes on Italy* (Philadelphia, 1831), p. 5.

10. Anon., "Review of 'A Year of Consolation,'" *American Whig Review*, VI (July 1847), 108.

11. Rev. John Chetwode Eustace, *A Classical Tour Through Italy in 1802* (London, 1815), I, 1–69. The first edition is called *A Tour Through Italy, exhibiting a View of its Scenery, Antiquities, and Monuments, Particularly as They are Objects of Classical Interest*, 2 vols. (London, 1813).

12. Joseph Forsyth, *Remarks on Antiquities, Arts, and Letters During an Excursion in Italy, in the Years 1802 and 1803* (London, 1813).

13. Mme Germaine de Staël, *Corinne: or, Italy* (New York, 1844); the first English edition, in three volumes, was entitled *Corinna, or Italy* (London, 1807); see also J. Christopher Herold, *Mistress to an Age: A Life of Madame de Staël* (Indianapolis, 1958), chap. xv.

14. George Gordon Byron, *Childe Harold's Pilgrimage*, Canto IV (1818).

15. Sophia Hawthorne, *Notes in England and Italy* (New York, 1870), p. 301.

16. Silas P. Holbrook, *Sketches By a Traveller* (Boston, 1830), p. 159.

17. Journal of Russell Sturgis, as quoted in Julian Sturgis, *From the Books and Papers of Russell Sturgis* (Oxford, 1893), pp. 174–176.

18. John Lothrop Motley, *Correspondence*, ed. George William Curtis (New York, 1889), I, 189.

19. In Tuscany, the basic charge for posting, based on the type of carriage, the number of passengers, and the weight of the luggage, was about fifty cents for each horse and thirty cents for each postilion per post. See William Brockedon, *Road-Book from London to Naples* (London, 1835), p. 99.

20. Daniel C. Taylor, "Journals of Tours Through Europe, 1831–1832" (manuscript collection, New-York Historical Society), II, 35.

21. N. Hawthorne, *French and Italian Note-Books*, pp. 230, 479–480; S. Hawthorne, *Notes in England and Italy*, pp. 546–548; James Fenimore Cooper, *Excursions in Italy* (Paris, 1838), pp. 16–17.

22. Washington Irving, *Notes and Journal of Travel in Europe, 1804–1805* (New York, 1920), I, 83.

23. Cooper, *Excursions in Italy*, p. 143.

24. "The Autobiography of Worthington Whittredge, 1820–1910," ed. John I. H. Baur, *Brooklyn Museum Journal* (1942), p. 38.

25. Herman Melville, *Journal of a Visit to Europe and the Levant*, ed. Howard C. Horsford (Princeton, 1955), p. 206.

26. Henry James, *William Wetmore Story and His Friends* (Boston, 1903), I, 11. Margaret Fuller, whose own financial resources were meager, felt that Italy was cheap enough for the rich, but that otherwise Italy was inexpensive only for those with "iron constitutions to endure bad food, eaten in bad air, damp and dirty lodgings" (*At Home and Abroad*, ed. Arthur B. Fuller [Boston, 1856], p. 375).

27. Fisk, *Travels in Europe*, p. 229.

28. *Ibid.*, p. 383.

29. N. Hawthorne, *French and Italian Note-Books*, pp. 209–210.

30. Cooper, *Excursions in Italy*, p. 6.

31. Benjamin Silliman, *A Visit to Europe in 1851* (New York, 1854), II, 9.

32. James, *Story and His Friends*, I, 242.

33. Orville Horwitz, *Brushwood, Picked Up on the Continent* (Philadelphia, 1855), p. 98.

34. William Berrian, *Travels in France and Italy in 1817 and 1818* (New York, 1821), p. 270.

35. Horace Greeley, *Glances at Europe* (New York, 1851), pp. 195–197.

36. Charles I. White, *Life of Mrs. Eliza Seton*, 2d ed. (Baltimore, 1879), pp. 56–83. Converted to Catholicism after her husband's death, Mrs. Seton in 1809 founded the Sisters of Charity of St.

Joseph in America. She died in 1821. Miracles were attributed to her intercession in 1934 and 1952, and in 1963 Mother Seton was beatified by the Roman Catholic Church, the first American-born person to be thus honored.

37. Irving, *Notes and Journal, 1804–1805*, II, 49–84.

38. George Ticknor, *Life, Letters, and Journals*, eds. George S. Hillard, Anna Ticknor, and Anna Eliot Ticknor (Boston, 1909), II, 46–47; Ticknor to N. Appleton, Castel Franco, Oct. 22, 1836 (Appleton Collection, Massachusetts Historical Society); Charles Chauncy Binney, *The Life of Horace Binney* (Philadelphia, 1903), pp. 176–182.

39. Joseph Green Cogswell, *Life of . . . as Sketched in His Letters*, ed. Anna Eliot Ticknor (Cambridge, Mass., 1874), pp. 9–10.

40. Francis Hovey Stoddard, *The Life and Letters of Charles Butler* (New York, 1903), p. 287.

41. Daniel Varè, *Ghosts of the Spanish Steps* (London, 1955), pp. 73–85.

42. Irving, *Notes and Journal, 1804–1805*, II, 26–34.

43. Louis L. Noble, *The Course of Empire* (New York, 1853), p. 144.

44. M. A. DeWolfe Howe, *The Life and Letters of George Bancroft* (New York, 1908), I, 145–146.

45. Samuel Gridley Howe, *Letters and Journals*, ed. Laura E. Richards (Boston, 1909), II, 153.

46. William C. Preston, *Reminiscences*, ed. Minnie Clare Yarborough (Chapel Hill, 1933), pp. 95–106.

47. Fisk, *Travels in Europe*, p. 150.

48. Ralph Waldo Emerson, *Journals*, eds. Edward Waldo Emerson and Waldo Emerson Forbes (Boston, 1910), III, 69.

49. Henry Wadsworth Longfellow, *Life*, ed. Samuel Longfellow (Boston, 1887), I, 140.

50. John Mitchell, *Notes from Over Sea* (New York, 1845), II, 258.

51. George S. Hillard, "Journal," I, 1847 (Hillard papers, Massachusetts Historical Society).

52. Erastus C. Benedict, *A Run Through Europe* (New York, 1860), p. 287.

53. "It is difficult to live here, — perhaps I ought not to say live, but do more than live." Hiram Powers to Edward Everett, Florence, March 7, 1843 (Everett papers, Massachusetts Historical Society).

54. N. Hawthorne, *French and Italian Note-Books*, p. 432.

CHAPTER III: The Italian Scene

1. Horatio Greenough, *Letters to His Brother, Henry Greenough*, ed. Frances Boott Greenough (Boston, 1887), pp. 83–85.

2. Charles Brooks, "Diary in Europe, 1842" (manuscript collection, Houghton Library, Harvard University).

3. George Ticknor, *Life, Letters, and Journals*, eds. Anna Ticknor, George S. Hillard, and Anna Eliot Ticknor (Boston, 1909), I, 160.

4. Howard R. Marraro, *Diplomatic Relations Between the United States and the Kingdom of the Two Sicilies* (New York, 1951), I, 30–31.

5. Washington Irving, *Notes and Journal of Travel in Europe, 1804–1805* (New York, 1920), I, 109–122.

6. Horatio Greenough to Henry Greenough, Genoa, August 24, 1831, as quoted in Greenough, *Letters to His Brother*, pp. 79–80.

7. James Fenimore Cooper, *Correspondence*, ed. J. F. Cooper (New Haven, 1922), I, 157.

8. John Griscom, *A Year in Europe . . . in 1818 and 1819* (New York, 1823), I, 478–479. Henry Bernard, the American educator, called this book "the single most influential educational work of the nineteenth century." See Russel B. Nye, *The Cultural Life of the Young Nation, 1776–1830* (New York, 1960), p. 166.

9. Ticknor, *Life, Letters, and Journals*, II, 44–45, 96–97.

10. Catharine Maria Sedgwick, *Letters from Abroad to Kindred at Home* (New York, 1841), II, 83.

11. Margaret Fuller, *Memoirs*, eds. Ralph Waldo Emerson *et al.* (Boston, 1859), II, 213–214.

12. George Coggeshall, *Thirty-Six Voyages to Various Parts of the World* (New York, 1858), pp. 72–73.

13. James Russell Lowell, "Leaves from my Journal in Italy and Elsewhere," *Fireside Travels* (Boston, 1864), pp. 317–318.

14. Nathaniel Hawthorne, *Passages From the French and Italian Note-Books* (Boston, 1883), p. 277.

15. Cooper, *Correspondence*, I, 163.

16. James Fenimore Cooper, *Excursions in Italy* (Paris, 1838), pp. 40–45, 85–86.

17. Paul Revere Frothingham, *Edward Everett, Orator and Statesman* (Boston, 1925), p. 171.

18. Ticknor's journal, and Ticknor to W. H. Prescott, Rome, Nov. 24, 1856, as quoted in Ticknor, *Life, Letters, and Journals*, II, 49–51, 54, 339–340.

19. Ellen Lemmi Powers, "Recollections of My Father," *The Vermonter*, XII (March 1907), 73.

20. Thomas Ball, *My Threescore Years and Ten*, 2d ed. (Boston, 1891), p. 172.

21. Nathaniel Hawthorne, "Original Manuscript of French and Italian NoteBooks Including His Diary in Florence" (manuscript collection, Henry E. Huntington Library), p. 28. Quoted by permission of The Huntington Library, San Marino, Calif.

22. Louise Greer, *Browning and America* (Chapel Hill, 1952), especially chap. ii, "Italy: The American Pilgrims."

23. N. Hawthorne, *French and Italian Note-Books*, p. 412.

24. The Anglo-Florentine society of the midcentury has been charmingly described in Giuliana Artom Treves, *Anglo-Fiorentini di Cento Anni Fa* (Florence, 1953), transl. by Sylvia Sprigge as *The Golden Ring: The Anglo-Florentines, 1847–1862* (London, 1956).

25. Ralph Waldo Emerson, *Letters*, ed. Ralph L. Rusk (New York, 1939), I, 381–382; also Ralph Waldo Emerson, *Journals*, eds. Edward Waldo Emerson and Waldo Emerson Forbes (Boston, 1910), III, 115–116.

26. Kate Field, "Elizabeth Barrett Browning," *Atlantic Monthly*, VIII (Sept. 1861), 368–376; "English Authors in Florence," *ibid.*, XIV (Dec. 1864), 660–671; "The Last Days of W. S. Landor," *ibid.*, XVII (April–June 1866), 385–395, 540–551, 684–705.

27. Everett to Gino Capponi, Florence, May 27, 1841, and Boston, Jan. 5, 1834, and March 15, 1837; Horatio Greenough to Capponi, Florence, n.d. (Gino Capponi papers, Biblioteca Nazionale, Florence).

28. Ticknor, *Life, Letters, and Journals*, II, 56, 339.

29. Greenough, *Letters to His Brother*, pp. 132, 134.

30. Joseph Sansom, *Letters from Europe* (Philadelphia, 1805), I, 187.

31. N. Hawthorne, *French and Italian Note-Books*, p. 244.

32. John Farley, *Over Seas in Early Days*, ed. Joseph Pearson Farley (Kansas City, 1907), p. 65.

33. Cooper, *Excursions*, p. 209.

34. George Stillman Hillard, *Six Months in Italy* (Boston, 1853), I, 291–292.

35. Henry James, *William Wetmore Story and His Friends* (Boston, 1903), II, 67–68, 148–149.

36. Ticknor, *Life, Letters, and Journals*, I, 182.

37. Everett to Mrs. Nathan Hale, Rome, Jan. 8, 1819 (Everett papers, Massachusetts Historical Society).

38. From Ticknor's journal, quoted in Ticknor, *Life, Letters, and Journals*, I, 181.

39. M. A. DeWolfe Howe, *The Life and Letters of George Bancroft* (New York, 1908), I, 133–134, 138–139.

40. Emerson to Charles Chauncy Emerson, Rome, April 16, 1833, as quoted in Emerson, *Letters*, I, 373.

41. N. Hawthorne, *French and Italian Note-Books*, p. 506.

42. Sophia Hawthorne, *Notes in England and Italy* (New York, 1870), pp. 541–542.

43. Quoted in Anon., "Society in Italy Fifty Years Ago," *All The Year Round*, LXIV (June 15, 1889), 571.

44. Cooper, *Excursions*, pp. 110–111.

45. James Jackson Jarves, *Italian Sights and Papal Principles Seen Through American Spectacles* (New York, 1856), p. 139.

46. Copley to his mother, Parma, June 25, 1775, as quoted in John Singleton Copley, *Letters and Papers of John Singleton Copley and Henry Pelham, 1739–1776* (Massachusetts Historical Society, *Collections* [Boston, 1914]), LXII, 329.

47. Cogswell to William Hickling Prescott, Leghorn, March 26, 1818 (Prescott collection, Massachusetts Historical Society).

48. Cooper, *Excursions*, p. 180.

49. James Russell Lowell to William Wetmore Story, Catania, Sicily, May 7, 1856, quoted in James, *Story and His Friends*, I, 323.

50. Anon., *Records of Travel* (Boston, 1838), pp. 76–111.

51. See William Berrian, *Travels in France and Italy in 1817 and 1818* (New York, 1821), pp. 275, 277; George W. Erving, "History of the Republic of San Marino," *American Quarterly Review*, VI (Dec. 1829), 455–467.

52. N. Hawthorne, *French and Italian Note-Books*, p. 283.

53. William Cullen Bryant, *Letters from the East* (New York, 1869), p. 238.

54. Benjamin Silliman, *A Visit to Europe in 1851* (New York, 1854), II, 53.

55. Cole to Robert Gilmor, Jan. 29, 1832, as quoted in Louis L. Noble, *The Course of Empire* (New York, 1853), pp. 141–142.

56. Cooper, *Excursions*, p. 102.

57. Fuller, *Memoirs*, II, 214.

58. Samuel F. B. Morse, *Letters and Journals*, ed. Edward Lind Morse (Boston, 1914), I, 400.

CHAPTER IV: The Italian People

1. Christopher Starr Brewster to Henry B. Brewster, Florence, Feb. 29, 1868 (privately owned).

2. James Sloan, *Rambles in Italy; in the Years 1816 . . . 17. By an American* (Baltimore, 1818), pp. 164–165.

3. John Stephano Cogdell, "Account of His Journey to Italy" (Rare book collection, Boston Public Library). By courtesy of the Trustees of the Boston Public Library.

4. Theodore Dwight, *A Journal of a Tour in Italy, in the Year 1821* (New York, 1824), pp. 464–465.

5. Bancroft to his father, Naples, Feb. 19 and March 5, 1822 (Bancroft papers, Massachusetts Historical Society).

6. Catharine Maria Sedgwick, *Letters from Abroad to Kindred at Home* (New York, 1841), II, 175.

7. William Berrian, *Travels in France and Italy in 1817 and 1818* (New York, 1821), p. 369.

8. Nathaniel Hazeltine Carter, *Letters from Europe* (New York, 1827), II, 382–383.

9. Nathaniel Hawthorne, *Passages from the French and Italian Note-Books* (Boston, 1883), pp. 436, 216.

10. Robert Baird, *Sketches of Protestantism in Italy and Present State of the Waldenses* (Boston, 1847), p. 201.

11. Caroline Matilda Kirkland, *Holidays Abroad* (New York, 1849), II, 92.

12. Henry T. Tuckerman, *Italian Sketch Book*, 2d ed. (Boston, 1836), p. 264.

13. Mark Twain, *The Innocents Abroad: or The New Pilgrims' Progress* (New York, 1911), I, 242–243.

14. Henry James, "Florentine Notes," *Italian Hours* (Boston, 1909), pp. 393–394.

15. Wilbur Fisk, *Travels in Europe* (New York, 1838), p. 159n.

16. Washington Irving, *Notes and Journal of Travel in Europe, 1804–1805* (New York, 1920), I, 135.

17. George Ticknor, *Life, Letters, and Journals*, eds. Anna Ticknor, George S. Hillard, and Anna Eliot Ticknor (Boston, 1909), II, pp. 57–58.

18. James Fenimore Cooper, *Excursions in Italy* (Paris, 1838), p. 328.

19. Margaret Fuller, *Memoirs*, eds. Ralph Waldo Emerson *et al.* (Boston, 1859), II, 244, 280–281.

20. Alpheus Hardy, "European Journal" (Hardy papers, Massachusetts Historical Society), p. 89.

21. Octavia Le Vert, *Souvenirs of Travel* (Mobile, 1857), II, 182.

22. Cooper, *Excursions*, pp. 135–137.

23. William N. Bates, "Nicholas Biddle's Journey in Greece, 1806," Numismatic and Antiquarian Society of Philadelphia, *Proceedings (1916–1918)*, XXVIII (Philadelphia, 1919), 170.

24. William Furniss, *The Land of the Caesar and Doge* (New York, 1853), p. 379.

25. O. B. Frothingham, *Memoir of G. E. Ellis* (Cambridge, Mass., 1895), p. 28.

26. Samuel Topliff, *Topliff's Travels* (Boston, 1906), p. 158.

27. James Fenimore Cooper, *Letters and Journals* (Cambridge, Mass., 1960), I, 380.

28. James Jackson Jarves, *Italian Sights and Papal Principles, Seen Through American Spectacles* (New York, 1856), p. 315.

29. *Ibid.*, pp. 127–128.

30. Sophia Hawthorne, *Notes in England and Italy* (New York, 1870), p. 293.

31. George S. Hellman, *Washington Irving, Esquire, Ambassador at Large from the New World to the Old* (New York, 1925), p. 24.

32. William C. Preston, *Reminiscences*, ed. Minnie Clare Yarborough (Chapel Hill, 1933), pp. 71–72.

33. Isaac Appleton Jewett, *Passages in Foreign Travel* (Boston, 1838), II, 231.

34. Anon., "Original Letters; from an American Traveller in Europe, to his Friends in This Country," *Monthly Anthology*, VI (Jan. 1809), 10.

35. Cooper, *Excursions*, p. 21.

36. James Russell Lowell, "Leaves from my Journal in Italy and Elsewhere," *Fireside Travels* (Boston, 1864), p. 251.

37. George Ticknor to Richard H. Dana, Rome, Feb. 22, 1837 (Dana papers, Massachusetts Historical Society).

Chapter V: Social Customs and Institutions

1. John Stephano Cogdell, "Account of His Journey to Italy" (Rare book collection, Boston Public Library). By courtesy of the Trustees of the Boston Public Library.

2. Joel Tyler Headley, *Letters from Italy*, rev. ed. (New York, 1848), p. 53.

3. Howe to Charles Sumner, Jan. 19, 1844, as quoted in Samuel Gridley Howe, *Letters and Journals*, ed. Laura E. Richards (Boston, 1909), II, 148–149.

4. Cranch to his wife, Rome, Jan. 20, 1859, as quoted in Leonora Cranch Scott, *Life and Letters of Christopher Pearse Cranch* (Boston, 1917), p. 238.

5. Grace Greenwood [pseud. of Sara Jane Lippincott], *Haps and Mishaps of a Tour in Europe* (Boston, 1854), pp. 235–236.

6. Catharine Maria Sedgwick, *Letters from Abroad to Kindred at Home* (New York, 1841), II, 41.

7. Samuel F. B. Morse, *Letters and Journals*, ed. Edward Lind Morse (Boston, 1914), I, 374–376.

8. Henry James, "From a Roman Note-Book," *Italian Hours* (Boston, 1909), pp. 285–286.

9. Margaret Fuller, *Memoirs*, eds. Ralph Waldo Emerson *et al.* (Boston, 1859), II, 234.

10. Washington Irving, *Notes and Journal of Travel in Europe, 1804–1805* (New York, 1920), II, 135.

11. Francis Parkman, *Journals*, ed. Mason Wade (New York, 1947), I, 176; Francis Parkman, "A Convent at Rome," *Harper's New Monthly Magazine*, LXXXI (Aug. 1890), 449.

12. Theodore Parker, *Life and Correspondence*, ed. John Weiss (London, 1863), I, 222.

13. William Berrian, *Travels in France and Italy in 1817 and 1818* (New York, 1821), pp. 287–288.

14. Nathaniel Hazeltine Carter, *Letters from Europe* (New York, 1827), II, 55.

15. Benjamin Silliman, *A Visit to Europe in 1851* (New York, 1854), II, 135.

16. James Jackson Jarves, *Art Thoughts* (New York, 1869), pp. 165–166.

17. Howe to the *Common School Journal*, as quoted in Howe, *Letters and Journals*, II, 147.

18. *Ibid.*, II, 143; Wilbur Fisk, *Travels in Europe* (New York, 1838), p. 160.

19. Maria Mitchell, *Life, Letters, and Journals*, ed. Phoebe Mitchell Kendall (Boston, 1896), pp. 150–158.

20. Horace Greeley, *Glances at Europe* (New York, 1851), p. 213.

21. Theodore Lyman, Jr., *The Political State of Italy* (Boston, 1820), p. 289.

22. Two English-language newspapers were established in Florence at midcentury, but both were short-lived. *The Tuscan Athenaeum* was started in 1847 when in the brief flood of progressive ideas, Grand Duke Leopold II announced the abolition of censorship. The review took the liberal side in the new political developments and expressed hopes for a regeneration of Italy, favoring moderation as a general policy for reform. Containing reviews of plays, political and artistic criticism, poetry, as well as advertisements, the newspaper lasted less than three months. *The Anglo-Tuscan Advertiser and Florence Record of Literature, Science and Art* followed in 1848, but lasted less than a month, because of inadequate support.

23. Greenwood, *Haps and Mishaps*, p. 390.

24. Francis Tiffany, *Life of Dorothea Lynde Dix* (Boston, 1890), p. 289.

25. Stephen Grellet, *Memoirs of . . . Life and Gospel Labours*, ed. Benjamin Seebohm (Philadelphia, 1874), II, 53.

26. Octavia Le Vert, *Souvenirs of Travel* (Mobile, 1857), I, 198.

27. Irving, *Notes and Journal, 1804–1805*, III, 17–18.

28. Morse, *Letters and Journals*, I, 368–369.

29. Parkman, *Journals*, I, 142.

CHAPTER VI: The World of Art

1. Benjamin West to Antonio Canova, London, May 5, 1816 (Canova papers, Museo Civico, Bassano del Grappa).

2. John A. Clark, *Glimpses of the Old World* (Philadelphia, 1840), I, 302.

3. Ticknor to Richard H. Dana, Rome, Feb. 22, 1837, as quoted in George Ticknor, *Life, Letters, and Journals*, eds. Anna Ticknor, George S. Hillard, and Anna Eliot Ticknor (Boston, 1909), II, 75–76.

4. Chapman to Thomas Sully, Florence, July 27, 1829 (Chamberlain Collection, Boston Public Library). By courtesy of the Trustees of the Boston Public Library.

5. Charles Edwards Lester, *The Artists of America* (New York, 1846), pp. 188–189.

6. Nathaniel Hawthorne, *Passages from the French and Italian Note-Books* (Boston, 1883), p. 77.

7. Nathaniel Hawthorne, *The Marble Faun*, Everyman ed. (London, 1910), p. 109.

8. Rinehart to Frank B. Mayer, Rome, Dec. 7, 1859, as quoted in Marvin C. Ross and Anna Wells Rutledge, "William H. Rinehart's Letters to Frank B. Mayer, 1856–1870," *Maryland Historical Magazine*, XLIII (June 1948), 127–128.

9. James Fenimore Cooper, *Correspondence*, ed. J. F. Cooper (New Haven, 1922), I, 308.

10. James E. Freeman, *Gatherings from an Artist's Portfolio* (Boston, 1883), II, 110–119.

11. Joel Tyler Headley, *Letters from Italy*, rev. ed. (New York, 1848), p. 168.

12. George Loring Brown, "Account Book" (manuscript collection, Museum of Fine Arts, Boston).

13. N. Hawthorne, *French and Italian Note-Books*, pp. 169–170.

14. Robert W. Gibbs, *A Memoir of James de Veaux of Charleston, S. C.* (Charleston, S. C., 1846), *passim.*

15. Mrs. Adams to her father, Paris, April 20, 1873, as quoted in Mrs. Henry Adams, *Letters, 1865–1883*, ed. Ward Theron (Boston, 1936), pp. 94–95.

16. N. Hawthorne, *French and Italian Note-Books*, p. 125.

17. Washington Irving, *Spanish Papers and Other Miscellanies* (New York, 1866), II, 144–145.

18. N. Hawthorne, *French and Italian Note-Books*, p. 181.

19. William Cullen Bryant, *Letters of a Traveller*, 2nd series (New York, 1859), p. 259.

20. Everett to Antonio Canova, Rome, Nov. 28, 1818 (Canova papers, Museo Civico, Bassano del Grappa).

21. Greenough to Robert Gilmor, Florence, Jan. 13, 1832 (Chamberlain Collection, Boston Public Library). By courtesy of the Trustees of the Boston Public Library.

22. Cabot to Thomas H. Perkins, Naples, Feb. 14, 1833, and undated fragments following (Samuel Cabot papers, Massachusetts Historical Society).

23. Charles Eliot Norton, *Notes of Travel and Study in Italy* (Boston, 1859), p. 179.

24. James Jackson Jarves, *Italian Sights and Papal Principles Seen Through American Spectacles* (New York, 1856), pp. 108–111.

25. Martha Babcock Amory, *The Wedding Journey of Charles and Martha Babcock Amory . . . 1833–1834* (Boston, 1922), I, 180.

26. Oliver Wendell Holmes, *Life and Letters*, ed. John T. Morse, Jr. (Boston, 1896), I, 155–156.

27. Erastus C. Benedict, *A Run Through Europe* (New York, 1860), pp. 138–139.

28. Edith Wharton used the story of Thomas Jefferson Bryan as the basis for her short novel *False Dawn* (New York, 1924); the important collection of Italian primitives that James Jackson Jarves gathered was purchased by Yale.

29. Clark, *Glimpses*, I, 359.

30. Sophia Hawthorne, *Notes in England and Italy* (New York, 1870), p. 355.

31. William Ingraham Kip, *The Christmas Holydays in Rome* (New York, 1846), p. 97.

32. William C. Preston, *Reminiscences*, ed. Minnie Clare Yarborough (Chapel Hill, 1933), p. 81.

33. N. Hawthorne, *French and Italian Note-Books*, p. 364.

34. *Ibid.*, pp. 89–90.

35. Horace Bushnell, *Life and Letters*, ed. Mary Bushnell Cheney (New York, 1880), p. 156; Thomas H. Cabot to T. H. Perkins, Naples, Jan. 17, 1833 (Samuel Cabot papers, Massachusetts Historical Society).

36. Bancroft to Andrews Norton, Naples, March 5, 1822 (Bancroft papers, Massachusetts Historical Society).

37. Cole to William Dunlap, n.p., n.d., as quoted in William Dunlap, *A History of the Rise and Progress of the Arts of Design in the United States*, rev. ed. (Boston, 1918), III, 156.

38. N. Hawthorne, *French and Italian Note-Books*, p. 331.

39. Headley, *Letters from Italy*, p. 203.

40. George S. Hillard, "Journal," I (1947) (Hillard papers, Massachusetts Historical Society).

41. Edward Everett, "Journal," CXXXIII (1818) (Everett papers, Massachusetts Historical Society).

42. S. Hawthorne, *Notes in England and Italy*, pp. 404–405, 450, 456.

43. Theodore B. Witmer, *Wild Oats, Sown Abroad* (Philadelphia, 1853), p. 165.

44. Norton, *Notes of Travel and Study*, pp. 153–154.

45. Anon., *Old Sights with New Eyes*, intro. by Robert Baird (New York, 1854), p. 210. The statue is now generally known as the "Dying Gaul."

46. Headley, *Letters from Italy*, p. 149.

47. Motley to his parents, Rome, Nov. 24, 1834, as quoted in John Lothrop Motley, *Correspondence*, ed. George William Curtis (New York, 1889), I, 43.

48. Preston, *Reminiscences*, p. 80.

49. Anon., "Impressions of Italy," *Southern Literary Messenger*, XXV (Nov. 1857), 365.

50. James Fenimore Cooper, *Excursions in Italy* (Paris, 1838), p. 266; William Ware, *Sketches of European Capitals* (Boston, 1851), p. 70.

51. Headley, *Letters from Italy*, p. 150.

52. N. Hawthorne, *French and Italian Note-Books*, p. 291.

53. Valentine Mott, *Travels in Europe and the East in the Years 1834–1841* (New York, 1842), p. 111.

54. Margaret Fuller, *At Home and Abroad*, ed. Arthur B. Fuller (Boston, 1856), p. 224; Emerson to William Emerson, Rome, April 21, 1833, as quoted in Ralph Waldo Emerson, *Letters*, ed. Ralph L. Rusk (New York, 1939), I, 379.

55. Norton, *Notes of Travel and Study*, pp. 52–53.

56. Cooper, *Correspondence*, I, 304.

57. William Cullen Bryant, *Letters of a Traveller*, 1st series (New York, 1850), p. 440; Fuller, *At Home and Abroad*, p. 230.

58. Headley, *Letters from Italy*, p. 187.

59. Bushnell, *Life and Letters*, p. 152.

60. Grace Greenwood [pseud. of Sara Jane Lippincott], *Haps and Mishaps of a Tour in Europe* (Boston, 1854), p. 278.

61. N. Hawthorne, *French and Italian Note-Books*, p. 171.

62. Matthias Bruen, *Essays, Descriptive and Moral . . . By an American* (Edinburgh, 1823), p. 98.

63. Samuel Topliff, *Topliff's Travels* (Boston, 1906), p. 195.

64. Jarves, *Italian Sights*, p. 189.

65. Norton, *Notes of Travel and Study*, pp. 179–180.

66. Samuel S. Cox, *A Buckeye Abroad* (New York, 1852), p. 123.

67. Cooper, *Correspondence*, I, 169.

CHAPTER VII: Religion in Italian Life

1. Erastus C. Benedict, *A Run Through Europe* (New York, 1860), p. 157.

2. Rinehart to Frank B. Mayer, Rome, July 5, 1859, as quoted in Marvin C. Ross and Anna Wells Rutledge, "William H. Rinehart's Letters to Frank B. Mayer, 1856–1870," *Maryland Historical Magazine*, XLIII (June 1948), 132.

3. Daniel Eddy, *Europa* (Boston, 1852), p. 429.

4. Matthias Bruen, *Essays, Descriptive and Moral . . . By An American* (Edinburgh, 1823), pp. 66–67.

5. James Jackson Jarves, "Holy Week at Rome," *Harper's New Monthly Magazine*, IX (Aug. 1854), 318.

6. Mark Twain, *Innocents Abroad: or the New Pilgrims' Progress* (New York, 1911), I, 329.

7. Nathaniel Hawthorne, *Passages From the French and Italian Note-Books* (Boston, 1883), p. 152.

8. William C. Gannett, *Ezra Stiles Gannett* (Boston, 1875), p. 165.

9. Alpheus Hardy, "Journal of a Tour to the East, 1845–1846," (Hardy papers, Massachusetts Historical Society), I, 77.

10. Orville Dewey, *The Old World and the New* (New York, 1836), II, 165–166.

11. From Grellet's journal, as quoted in Stephen Grellet, *Memoirs of . . . Life and Gospel Labours*, ed. Benjamin Seebohm (Philadelphia, 1874), II, 63, 53–55.

12. James Fenimore Cooper, *Excursions in Italy* (Paris, 1838), pp. 257–258.

13. James Jackson Jarves, *Italian Sights and Papal Principles Seen Through American Spectacles* (New York, 1856), p. 303. On the unfounded pretext in 1867 that the American Protestant Church in Rome had been forced out of the city beyond the walls, Congress refused to advance an appropriation for the American mission in Rome, whereupon relations with the Papal States were terminated. This move, though partly dictated by religious feeling, was also an attempt to clear the way for bringing Rome into a united Italy.

14. Lucia Alexander, "Note Book" (manuscript collection, Boston Athenaeum), pp. 81–82.

15. William Wetmore Story, *Roba di Roma*, 6th ed. (London, 1871), p. 437.

16. Cooper, *Excursions*, p. 282.

17. As quoted in William Ingraham Kip, *The Christmas Holydays in Rome* (New York, 1846), p. 60.

18. Story to James Russell Lowell, Rome, April 28, 1848, as quoted in Henry James, *William Wetmore Story and His Friends* (Boston, 1903), I, 100–101.

19. From Ticknor's journal, as quoted in George Ticknor, *Life, Letters, and Journals*, eds. George S. Hillard, Anna Ticknor, and Anna Eliot Ticknor (Boston, 1909), II, 71–72.

20. Charles Edwards Lester, *My Consulship* (New York, 1853), I, 132–133.

21. Theodore B. Witmer, *Wild Oats, Sown Abroad* (Philadelphia, 1853), pp. 112–113.

22. Jarves, *Italian Sights*, pp. 295–296.

23. William Dean Howells, *Italian Journeys* (New York, 1867), p. 177.

24. Sophia Hawthorne, *Notes in England and Italy* (New York, 1870), p. 480.

25. Grace Greenwood [pseud. of Sara Jane Lippincott], *Haps and Mishaps of a Tour in Europe* (Boston, 1854), p. 189; Orville Horwitz, *Brushwood, Picked up on the Continent* (Philadelphia, 1855), p. 104.

26. Story, *Roba di Roma*, p. 182.

27. Longfellow to his brother, Rome, June 28, 1828 (Longfellow papers, Houghton Library, Harvard University).

28. Clement Moore Butler, *Inner Rome: Political, Religious and Social* (Philadelphia, 1866), p. 279.

29. Edward L. Pierce, *Memoir and Letters of Charles Sumner* (Boston, 1877), II, 106–109.

30. Francis Parkman, "A Convent at Rome," *Harper's New Monthly Magazine*, LXXXI (Aug. 1890), 450; Francis Parkman, *Journals*, ed. Mason Wade (New York, 1947), I, 190–195, 162–163.

31. Theodore Lyman, Jr., *The Political State of Italy* (Boston, 1820), pp. 127–128, 138–139, 142.

32. John England, *Works* (Cleveland, 1908), VI, 222.

33. Fanny Hall, *Rambles in Europe* (New York, 1839), I, 174–175.

34. William C. Preston, *Reminiscences*, ed. Minnie Clare Yarborough (Chapel Hill, 1933), pp. 72–73.

35. Margaret Fuller, *At Home and Abroad*, ed. Arthur B. Fuller (Boston, 1856), p. 299.

36. J. W. De Forest, *European Acquaintance* (New York, 1858), p. 253.

37. Ticknor, *Life, Letters, and Journals*, I, 173–174.

38. Grellet, *Memoirs*, II, 78–80.

39. Jonathan Russell, "Journal of Jonathan Russell in 1818–19," Massachusetts Historical Society, *Proceedings*, LI (June 1918), 450.

40. Samuel F. B. Morse, *Letters and Journals*, ed. Edward Lind Morse (Boston, 1914), I, 380–381; Albert Brisbane, *A Mental Biography* (Boston, 1893), pp. 145–146.

41. Hall, *Rambles*, I, 219–220.

42. Wilbur Fisk, *Travels in Europe* (New York, 1838), p. 322.

43. From Ellis's journal, quoted in O. B. Frothingham, *Memoir of George E. Ellis* (Cambridge, Mass., 1895), p. 27.

44. Hillard to Rogers, Rome, Dec. 29, 1847 (Hillard papers, Massachusetts Historical Society).

45. Lester, *My Consulship*, II, 201–206.

46. From remarks of G. P. A. Healy, as quoted in James E. Freeman, *Gatherings from an Artist's Portfolio* (Boston, 1883), II, 129–130.

47. Dewey, *The Old World*, II, 111.

48. Thomas Appleton, "Account Book" (Rare book collection, Boston Public Library). By courtesy of the Trustees of the Boston Public Library.

49. Emerson to William Emerson, Naples, March 23, 1833, as quoted in Ralph Waldo Emerson, *Letters*, ed. Ralph L. Rusk (New York, 1939), I, 370.

50. William Ware, *Sketches of European Capitals* (Boston, 1851), pp. 229–230, 212–213.

51. Theodore Parker, *Life and Correspondence*, ed. John Weiss (London, 1863), I, 232.

52. George S. Hillard, *Six Months in Italy* (Boston, 1853), I, 332.

53. Henry M. Field, *The Good and the Bad in the Roman Catholic Church* (New York, 1849), p. 17.

54. As quoted in Theodore S. Woolsey, "Theodore Dwight Woolsey — A Biographical Sketch," *Yale Review*, new series, I (July 1912), 636.

55. Cooper, *Excursions*, p. 327.

56. Nathaniel Hawthorne, *The Marble Faun*, Everyman ed. (London, 1910), pp. 89–90.

CHAPTER VIII: Government and the Economy

1. Sumner to George Washington Greene, Naples, July 21, 1840 (miscellaneous papers, Massachusetts Historical Society).

2. Charles Eliot Norton, *Notes of Travel and Study in Europe* (Boston, 1859), p. 72.

3. James Sloan, *Rambles in Italy* (Baltimore, 1818), p. 11.

4. Letter of James Hamilton, Rome, Feb. 27, 1848, as quoted in James A. Hamilton, *Reminiscences* (New York, 1859), p. 361.

5. Thomas G. Young, *A Wall-Street Bear in Europe* (New York, 1855), p. 129.

6. *Ibid.*, p. 130.

7. Orville Horwitz, *Brushwood, Picked Up on the Continent* (Philadelphia, 1855), p. 165.

8. George S. Hillard to Rogers, Rome, Dec. 29, 1847 (Hillard papers, Massachusetts Historical Society).

9. Sloan, *Rambles*, p. 29.

10. Henry James, *William Wetmore Story and His Friends* (Boston, 1903), I, 135–136.

11. Elizabeth Barrett Browning to Mary Russell Mitford, Florence, October 1848, as quoted in James, *Story and His Friends*, I, 119; see also, I, 164–165.

12. Albert Brisbane, *A Mental Biography* (Boston, 1893), p. 281.

13. Harry Nelson Gay, "Garibaldi's Sicilian Campaign," *American Historical Review*, XXVII (Jan. 1922), 234–238.

14. Henry Adams to Charles Adams, Palermo, June 9, 1860, as printed in the Boston *Courier* and quoted in Anon., "Henry Adams and Garibaldi, 1860," *American Historical Review*, XXV (Jan. 1920), 241–255; also Henry Adams, *The Education of Henry Adams* (Boston, 1918), pp. 94–95.

15. Horace Greeley, *Glances at Europe* (New York, 1851), p. 224.

16. William Wetmore Story, *Roba di Roma*, 6th ed. (London, 1871), p. 354.

17. Anne Tuttle Jones Bullard, *Sights and Scenes in Europe* (St. Louis, 1852), p. 174.

18. Nathaniel Hazeltine Carter, *Letters from Europe* (New York, 1827), II, 153.

19. S. I. Fisher, *Observations on the Character and Culture of the European Vine* (Philadelphia, 1834), p. 111.

20. Theodore Dwight, *The Roman Republic of 1849* (New York, 1851), pp. 118–119.

CHAPTER IX: The Meaning of Italy

1. Ticknor to Charles S. Daveis, Rome, Nov. 19, 1817, and to Elisha Ticknor, n.p., Jan. 15, 1818, as quoted in George Ticknor, *Life, Letters, and Journals*, eds. George S. Hillard, Anna Ticknor, and Anna Eliot Ticknor (Boston, 1909), I, 169, 173.

2. Bancroft to John Thornton Kirkland, Rome, Feb. 10, 1822,

as quoted in M. A. DeWolfe Howe, *The Life and Letters of George Bancroft* (New York, 1908), I, 142.

3. Nathaniel Parker Willis, *Pencillings By the Way*, 2d. ed. (New York, 1844), pp. 329–330.

4. From Ephraim Peabody's diary, as quoted in Francis G. Peabody and Robert Peabody, *A New England Romance* (Boston, 1920), p. 151.

5. Fuller to her mother, Rome, Nov. 16, 1848, as quoted in Margaret Fuller, *Memoirs*, eds. Ralph Waldo Emerson *et al.* (Boston, 1859), II, 248.

6. Henry James to William James, Rome, Oct. 30, 1869, as quoted in Henry James, *Letters*, ed. Percy Lubbock (New York, 1920), I, 24.

7. Story to Lowell, Berlin, Jan. 30, 1850, as quoted in Henry James, *William Wetmore Story and His Friends* (Boston, 1903), I, 210.

8. As quoted in Theodore Clarke Smith, *The Life and Letters of James Abram Garfield* (New Haven, 1925), II, 758.

9. James Fenimore Cooper, *Excursions in Italy* (Paris, 1838), p. 325.

10. Bayard Taylor, *Life and Letters*, eds. Marie Hansen-Taylor and Horace E. Scudder (Boston, 1884), I, 54.

11. Charles Eliot Norton, *Letters*, eds. Sara Norton and M. A. DeWolfe Howe (Boston, 1913), I, 404.

12. Walter Savage Landor, "King Carlo-Alberto and Princess Belgioioso," *Imaginary Conversations* (London, 1891), VI, 420.

13. Johann Wolfgang von Goethe, *Travels in Italy* (London, 1883), pp. 136, 114.

14. Fuller, *Memoirs*, I, 266–267.

15. William Ingraham Kip, *The Christmas Holydays in Rome* (New York, 1846), p. 33.

16. George Stillman Hillard, "Journal," I, 1847 (Hillard papers, Massachusetts Historical Society).

17. Catharine Maria Sedgwick, *Letters from Abroad to Kindred at Home* (New York, 1841), II, 22.

18. Henry Maney, *Memories Over the Water* (Nashville, 1854), p. 180.

19. Samuel Topliff, *Topliff's Travels* (Boston, 1906), p. 160.

20. Thomas Cole, as quoted in William Dunlap, *A History of the Rise and Progress of the Arts of Design*, rev. ed. (Boston, 1918), III, 154.

21. As quoted in a letter of T. H. Cabot to T. H. Perkins, Florence, March 11, 1833 (Samuel Cabot papers, Massachusetts Historical Society).

22. John Stephano Cogdell, "An Account of His Journey to Italy" (Rare book collection, Boston Public Library). By courtesy of the Trustees of the Boston Public Library.

23. Ellen Lemmi Powers, "Recollections of My Father," *The Vermonter*, XII (Feb. 1907), 46.

24. Amasa Hewins, *A Boston Portrait-Painter Visits Italy*, ed. Francis H. Allen (Boston, 1931), p. 74; Samuel F. B. Morse, *Letters and Journals*, ed. Edward Lind Morse (Boston, 1914), I, 395.

25. Hillard, "Journal," I (July 19, 1847).

26. William C. Preston, *Reminiscences*, ed. Minnie Clare Yarborough (Chapel Hill, 1933), p. 91.

27. Francis Parkman, *Journals*, ed. Mason Wade (New York, 1947), I, 198.

28. Lowell to Charles Lowell, Rome, Feb. 1, 1852 (Lowell papers, Houghton Library, Harvard University).

29. Livio Iannattoni, *Roma e Gli Inglesi* (Rome, 1945), p. 80.

30. Fuller, *Memoirs*, II, 228–229.

31. Nathaniel Hawthorne, *Passages From the French and Italian Note-Books* (Boston, 1833), pp. 456–457.

32. Margaret Fuller, *At Home and Abroad*, ed. Arthur B. Fuller (Boston, 1856), pp. 250–252.

33. James to his mother, Florence, Oct. 13, 1869, as quoted in Henry James, *Letters*, I, 22.

34. Henry James, *Italian Hours* (Boston, 1909), pp. 502–503.

35. Cooper, *Excursions*, p. 180.

36. Lowell to John Holmes, Rome, n.d., as quoted in Horace Scudder, *James Russell Lowell* (Boston, 1901), I, 342.

37. From Cole's journal of Aug. 24, 1831, as quoted in Everett P. Lesley, "Some Clues to Thomas Cole," *Magazine of Art*, XLII (Feb. 1949), 45; other, slightly revised versions are found in Thomas Cole, "Volterra," *Literary World*, No. 105 (Feb. 3, 1849), 97–98, and in Louis L. Noble, *The Course of Empire* (New York, 1853), pp. 135–136.

38. Taylor to E. C. Stedman, Rome, April 27, 1868, as quoted in Bayard Taylor, *Unpublished Letters*, ed. John R. Schultz (San Marino, Calif., 1937), p. 112.

39. James to Alice James, n.p., n.d., as quoted in F. O. Matthiessen, *The James Family* (New York, 1947), p. 291.

40. James, *Story and His Friends*, II, 209–210.

INDEX